Embracing the Ordinary

Lessons From the Champions of Everyday Life

Michael Foley

SIMON &
SCHUSTER

London · New York · Sydney · Toronto · New Delhi

A CBS COMPANY

First published in Great Britain by Simon & Schuster UK Ltd, 2012
A CBS COMPANY

1 3 5 7 9 10 8 6 4 2

Simon & Schuster UK Ltd
1st Floor
222 Gray's Inn Road
London WC1X 8HB

www.simonandschuster.co.uk

Simon & Schuster Australia, Sydney
Simon & Schuster India, Delhi

A CIP catalogue record for this book is available
from the British Library.

ISBN 978-1-84983-912-9

Typeset in Garamond by M Rules

Printed and bound by CPI Group (UK) Ltd, Croydon, CR0 4YY

For Maria, who embraced the ordinary with exemplary intelligence, spirit and humour.

Contents

PART I

The Significance of the Insignificant

1

All Aboard the Orient Express!

All aboard, ladies and gentlemen, all aboard now for life, the gleaming Orient Express that will bear you smoothly and swiftly away from the dreary familiar and onwards into exotic glamour, adventure and excitement.

Ah but what is this? It turns out that the train is not a sleek express but a rusty old English branch line engine, puffing slowly round the dreary familiar, with lengthy stops at Hankering, Frittering, Fretting, Bickering, North, South, East and West Dithering, Wearing Central, Stillborn Parkway – and up ahead is that dismal terminus, Slavering.

What happened? Where did it go wrong? After much lengthy pondering and questioning there arises the familiar lament of the no-longer young: If only I could go back and start again, knowing what I know now, I would do it all differently.

Like many another of a certain age, I have felt disappointed, disillusioned and trapped, caught up in obligation and weighed down by burdens, rapidly running out of time, hope, opportunity and energy. Consumed by regrets, resentfully blaming others for everything, I too have yearned to go back, begin again, and do everything differently, with the principal difference of course being more frequent, varied and exciting sex. But after a while it came to me that my circumstances were entirely of my own choosing and not the fault of anyone else and that in fact I had had a good life, a privileged life, even a charmed life, certainly a life as mysterious and rich as any other. This brought a new regret. In the course of all the brooding and whining and demanding and blaming, all the lethargy and fantasy and denial and grievance, much of my mysterious, rich and only life had gone by without my noticing it. And with this new regret came a new wish – to go back and begin again but, instead of doing it all differently, doing it all *in exactly the same way*, except this time paying it the full attention it deserved. But after another while I realised that this too was misguided. There is no going back and regret is futile. The crucial thing is to start paying attention *now*.

This commandment to pay attention is as old as the ten commandments handed down to Moses, going back to Buddha in the middle of the first millennium BCE and repeated regularly ever since – but no commandment is easier to preach and harder to practice. There seems to be something intrinsically ungraspable about the present. Nothing is more difficult to understand than the apparently obvious and nothing more difficult to see than what is directly before the eyes. And the present of everyday life is even more elusive. The novelist Georges Perec expressed this problem eloquently: 'To question the habitual. But that's just it, we're habituated to it. We don't question it, it doesn't question us, it doesn't seem to pose a problem, we live it without thinking, as if it carried within it neither questions nor answers, as if it weren't the bearer of any information. This is no longer even conditioning, it's anaesthesia. We sleep through our lives in a dreamless sleep. But where is our life? Where is our body? Where is our space?'[1]

One reason for this sleep is the negative perception of everyday life as so depressingly dull that it is best to close eyes, ears and mind. The key quotidian experiences are anonymity, repetition, banality and an uneventfulness that resists representation and significance, incapable of entering history or of being shaped into a satisfying drama – and all this can make everyday life appear dreary, trivial, meaningless, burdensome and unfulfilling. In the end it comes to seem like an open prison that deprives its wretched inmates of the authentic life elsewhere and forces them to waste away, day by day losing identity and volition, condemned to grow old and die without ever having lived. This is a terrifying prospect and creates an overwhelming need not to attend to the here and now but to escape from it, at least temporarily, by means of entertainment, travel, partying, alcohol, drugs or sex. But escapism does not work. Soon the escapee is back in prison, even more depressed than before, and also very likely out of pocket, hungover, exhausted and afflicted by guilt, shame, dread and a nasty, state-of-the-art STD.

Even when there is a desire to engage with everyday life, its utilitarian bias – heavily reinforced by the demands of employment and family life – imposes a tendency to see, feel and think only what is necessary for immediately useful action. And reinforcing this tendency is the anaesthetising effect of familiarity and habit. Habit is an effective tranquilliser but its side effects include blindness, deafness and atrophy of the brain.

Then there are cultural factors such as the new obsession with celebrity that makes anonymous, mundane life seem worse than death – and the many technological devices that offer distraction from the immediate environment. All these developments exacerbate the perennial problem of the distracted self – the fretting, fussing, nagging, fearful consciousness, relentless self-obsession and constant fantasising and anticipating that make it almost impossible to notice, and engage with, the present.

There is even evidence that not only has Western culture encouraged certain modes of thinking, it has actually influenced brain function.[2] In animals the left brain hemisphere (LH) evolved to provide the narrow attention needed to concentrate on specific tasks such as eating lunch, and the right hemisphere (RH) to provide the wider attention required to scan the environment for predators and so avoid *becoming* lunch. In humans the two hemispheres developed in line with these original functions. LH is highly selective, filtering out everything that is not immediately useful, prioritising the known and expected, categorising and compartmentalising, abstracting experience into dogma and rules, rejecting ambiguity and denying discrepancy. It prefers the inanimate, especially anything mechanical, to living things, likes to control and manipulate, has unshakeable self-belief and becomes angry if contradicted or opposed. RH, on the other hand, is open to all experience, welcomes the unexpected, actively seeks out discrepancies, relishes ambiguity and uncertainty, takes a global rather than a local view, prefers living things and is capable of self-awareness and empathy. Both hemispheres are necessary and frequently cooperate in appropriate ways. In processing language, LH understands syntax and RH understands metaphor (though, significantly, when a metaphor becomes a cliché it is processed by LH[3]); in reasoning, LH uses rational, sequential logic and RH associative problem-solving; in constructing a world view, LH understands the parts and RH the whole, LH sees structure and fixity, RH sees process and flux; in paying attention, LH attends to the familiar and RH to the new. In general, LH enjoys the utilitarian and literal and RH appreciates the imaginative, comical and spiritual.

So Nature, in her infinite wisdom, has decided that it is best if we are always in two minds, one an authoritarian accountant who respects only practicalities and rejects any form of idealism, and the other a guitar-toting hippy who believes that certainty sucks and paradox rocks. We would much prefer to hitchhike to Kathmandu with the hippy and confine the accountant to an office cubicle to work out the trip expenses on a spreadsheet – but, far from being content with a back office role, the accountant wants nothing less than world domination and has largely succeeded in achieving it. The LH aptitude for bureaucracy and technology has come to dominate Western society and is self-reinforcing. Success in a LH world requires LH skills and this encourages further LH development. But the empire of LH is a drearily functional place. It is significant that infants, with their inexhaustible playfulness, curiosity and wonder, have yet to develop left hemisphere functioning and are entirely governed by the right hemisphere – and equally significant that brain damage in the right hemisphere of adults results in apathy, indifference, loss of vitality and the sense of belonging.[4] Only RH can provide the panoptic attention needed to engage fully with the world, and the imagination, humour and spirituality to interpret it with fascination, laughter and awe.

Combine all these factors devaluing the everyday and it is not difficult to see why ordinary life appears dull. Help is needed – but who can provide it? Where shall wisdom be found? The traditional sources of succour are religion, philosophy and the arts – but religion and philosophy have often been part of the problem rather than the solution.

The Christian religions devalue everyday life by seeing it as a vale of suffering to be endured in order to earn a more rewarding existence in the afterlife – and then they reinforce this depreciation by making ordinary days inferior to the holy days of ritual observance. No wonder so many hate Sunday, which believes itself to be superior to the other days because it was chosen by God. The true everyday is Tuesday, the only day entirely untainted by significance. Monday is permeated with the horror of returning to work, Wednesday is the midweek break, Thursday is already charged with the excitement of the weekend and Friday is the beginning of the weekend. Tuesday alone is anonymous and humble, the only true holy day and holiday – and of course I should not even be saying this because it may give Tuesday ideas about itself. I would like to establish a strange cult, whose members are not only forbidden to communicate but even to know each other – The Secret Friends of Tuesday.

The Eastern religions are more helpful. Buddhism, with its rejection of a hereafter and focus on the here and now, provides a discipline for controlling the raging core of desire that is obsessed by past dissatisfactions and future gratifications, absorbed in hankering, vexation and resentment and entirely blind to its surroundings. Once the adept has mastered meditation practice, the seething self quietens down, the surrounding world comes into focus and it is possible to contemplate and marvel at what the Chinese describe as The Ten Thousand Things.

I know from personal experience that meditation is effective. When I was suffering from work-related stress, panic attacks and chest pains and so on, I did a meditation exercise every day. The stress symptoms began to ease and there was an unexpected side-effect – the view that I was looking out upon, the noisy, littered railway line behind my home, an estate agent's nightmare, gradually became a place of wonder. The honking of passing trains was as lyrical as the cries of wild geese flying overhead. The rampant Japanese knotweed that had colonised the embankments was a manifestation of the glory and resourcefulness of nature. And the giant graffiti on the back wall of the community centre opposite began to assume the inscrutable beauty and grace of Chinese ideograms.

So I have been a committed meditator ever since? Of course not. As soon as the stress symptoms went away I gave up the meditating. For a while I believed that this was due to lack of patience and discipline but eventually I realised that there was a deeper reason – I'm much too fond of my self to want to suppress it. My greedy desire is to enjoy both the self and the world, to achieve some harmonious combination of inner and outer attention.

However even without meditation it is possible to mitigate some of the worst obsessions of the self – for instance, the pincer jaws of past and future that crush the life out of the present. And in the contemporary world this obsession with past and future tends to take the corrosive forms of resentment and anxiety, looking backward in anger and forward in fear. Both develop from specific circumstances but quickly become general and, soon after, chronic. So it has never been more important to realise that, if Heaven is the place where there is no regret, hope or fear, then the way to attain the Heaven of the present is to regret only regret, hope only for hopelessness and fear only fearfulness.

This was the message of the early Stoic philosophers, especially Seneca ('You must dispense with these two things; fear of the future and remembering ancient woes'[5]) and Marcus Aurelius ('It is in your power to secure immediately everything you dream of attaining by a roundabout route ... if you will leave all the past behind, commit the future to Providence and direct the present alone'[6]). These two thinkers constantly praised the double rightness of right here and right now. Seneca: 'It is characteristic of a great soul to scorn great things and prefer what is ordinary.'[7] Marcus Aurelius was even more positive: 'Manifestly, no condition of life could be so well adapted for the practice of philosophy as this in which chance finds you today!'[8] But both also stressed the difficulty of apprehending the present, the constant effort required to avoid regretting, anticipating and longing to be somewhere else. Aurelius recommended daily exercises to keep the will strong.

All this wisdom was lost in the Christian devaluation of the here and now and emphasis on the hereafter. The idea of living in and for the moment came to be regarded as self-indulgent hedonism. And when humanist philosophy finally resumed during the Enlightenment it retained this disdain for the everyday as a distraction from, and obstacle to, higher things. More recently, Marx's view of modern life as alienated and debased has been hugely influential. When I got married, bought a flat with my wife and had a daughter, a left-wing acquaintance sneered at my 'bourgeois family unit' and made me feel ashamed to have sunk so low. And bohemian elitists have been even more contemptuous of bourgeois family life and employment – my literary acquaintances regarded marriage and a job as apostasy. Then, in the twentieth century, there was Heidegger's rejection of 'everydayness' as a fallen state of mediocrity and averageness and Sartre's view of everyday life as inauthentic and conformist. (This disdain for the ordinary tempted both thinkers to espouse extremism, of the right and left respectively – Heidegger supported Hitler and Sartre supported Stalin.)

Two exceptions were the nineteenth-century French philosopher Henri Bergson and the nineteenth-century American philosopher William James, who, though they did not directly address the everyday, proposed ways of seeing it differently. Bergson was one of the first modern thinkers to reject Western culture's left hemisphere view of life and the world in terms of structure, permanence, familiarity and predictability[9], a mechanistic universe entirely determined by scientific laws and inhabited by eternal souls subject to eternal truths dictated by an immutable, eternal God worshipped in monumental temples of stone. Instead Bergson insisted that life is process, driven by a force he called the *élan vital*, a boundless energy that 'pushes life along the road of time'[10] and produces constant creative evolution. Life does not merely happen but is *driven* and does not just produce change determined by laws but *invents* in a 'continual elaboration of the absolutely new'.[11] So, far from being entirely determined, life is entirely unpredictable – a process generating difference. 'The same does not remain the same'[12] and the dreary predictability is not in the world but in ourselves.

Once dismissed as crackpot mysticism, Bergson's view has now been adopted by science, which tells us that inanimate matter is subject to the law of entropy, an inexorable increase in disorder driving the arrow of time irreversibly forward, and that all living organisms are subject to the opposite tendency – to learn, adapt, develop and create emergent order out of complexity and chaos. In both cases the result is the same, i.e. never the same.

William James also believed in a continuous unfolding of the unforeseeably new: 'Time keeps budding into new moments, every one of which presents a content which in its individuality never was before and will never be again.'[13] But it is difficult to appreciate this because 'most of us feel as if we lived habitually with a sort of cloud weighing on us', so that, 'compared with what we ought to be, we are only half-awake'.[14] How to waken up and live more fully? For James fullness was experience, and experience is gained not by travel or adventure or love affairs but by paying attention ('what is called our experience is almost entirely determined by our habits of attention'[15]). The catch is that attention is not a simple phenomenon and changing attention habits is not easy. 'The only things which we commonly see are those which we preperceive, and the only things which we preperceive are those which have been labelled for us.'[16] Like Bergson, James understood that the problem is in the preperceiving and not in what is perceived. Heightened attention requires a heightened sense of value and meaning.

In the late twentieth century a number of cultural thinkers tackled the quotidian directly[17] in works such as Henri Lefebvre's *Critique of Everyday Life*[18] and Michel de Certeau's *The Practice of Everyday Life.*[19] Lefebvre's view was that everyday life has been vilified as the worthless residue left behind by meaningful activity, the coffee grounds that must be thrown out when the stimulating potion has been brewed. But if the everyday is everything that is ignored by official forms of knowledge and authority, this very invisibility gives it the potential for strangeness, freedom and even subversion.

De Certeau argued that it is possible to subvert everyday functions and roles not by rejecting them but by appropriating them for personal purposes and he advocated a private, transgressive, inventive act defined as the 'ruse'. However, like most French theorists, De Certeau preferred abstract discourse to practical example, though he would surely have approved of photocopying poems on the company machine, booking holidays on the company computer, using the British Museum as a toilet and the skips of neighbours as convenient dumps (recently I sneaked out at night to dispose of an old ironing board in a skip down the street and felt not only thirty years younger but also as lean, tough, resourceful and clandestine as a Viet Cong tunnel rat).

This concept of the ruse strikes me as terrifically useful, especially if it can be elevated from specific acts to a general principle: a governing attitude, a way of escaping without leaving the prison, transgressing without breaking the rules and transcending while remaining completely immersed. So the philosophy of Rusism is a crafty subversion of everyday life by actually *enjoying* its putative dreariness. Ruse it or lose it.

But how to learn to ruse? One approach is to use the arts to develop a new perception, an imaginative relabelling of the everyday world. It is not what you look at that matters but what you see. Bergson: 'What the artist has seen we shall probably never see again, or at least never see in exactly the same way; but the attempt made to lift the veil compels our imitation.'[20]

And persisting in such imitation eventually develops into an attitude, a disposition, an unconscious attunement that combines openness, alertness, curiosity, amusement and wonder. Such attunement is immediate and effortless in its application but takes time and effort to acquire. It is not so much that we see art[21] as that we see *by means of art*. So the work of art is not the impersonal artefact – the poem, novel, painting, photograph or film – but the personal work of engagement and appropriation. Appreciating art is not passive but active, not reverential but familiar, not a worthy act of self-improvement but an audacious and cunning ruse. To seek out what stimulates and *make use of it* – this is the work of art.

Many artists compel imitation – and we must each find our own. Here are a few who have compelled me. After reading Joyce banal conversation is suddenly comical, fascinating and strange. After reading Proust I realise that contemporary celebrities are the exact equivalent of his aristocrats. After a Mike Leigh film I see and hear Mike Leigh characters on buses, trains and in supermarket queues. After an Edward Hopper exhibition I notice Hopperesque old buildings everywhere. After looking at Robert Doisneau's photographs of Paris I go around London framing shots and wishing that I carried a camera and had the expertise to use it. After reading Elizabeth Bishop's poems delighting in confusion and squalor I yearn to wander in run-down districts and write an ode on the glory of neon reflected in a pool of wino's piss.

And the early stories of Alice Munro make the rural poor fascinatingly complex. Annie Ernaux's early novels perform the same miracle for deprived provincial towns. Even affluent suburbia becomes a source of wonder in the novels of John Updike.

This desire to imitate is transformative. Bit by bit perception develops until it has the singularity, intensity and excitement of the artistic vision that inspired it. What each individual perceives is not *the* world but *a* world. Even physics has long since abandoned any hope of capturing objective reality. All observation is subjective. So the re-enchantment of the world is really a personal re-creation of the world. And such re-creation is always possible, as the poet Rainer Maria Rilke so eloquently explained to a depressed young man: 'If your daily life seems poor do not blame it; blame yourself, tell yourself that you are not poet enough to call forth its riches; for to the creator there is no poverty and no poor indifferent place.'[22] However, this is not a fanciful, poetic notion. In philosophy it goes back to Kant's realisation that individual sensibility is the only access to the world, and it has been reinforced by contemporary neuroscience. The clinical psychiatrist and neurologist Iain McGilchrist: 'Through the direction and nature of our attention, we prove ourselves to be partners in creation, both of the world and of ourselves.'[23]

Not surprisingly, the more work that goes into this re-creation the richer the new world will be. Those who lack the resources of God may need more than six days. And where God's creation remained complete, so that He could rest on the seventh day and snooze with a handkerchief over His face, the human creature wakes up on Sunday with a hangover and, haunted by dread at the prospect of work on Monday, has to begin the creation all over again.

Of course there are also many in permanent dread due to circumstances not of their own making. For the sorely afflicted, beaten down by poverty, serious illness, crushing obligation, or all three and more, exhortations to appreciate the everyday will seem not only inappropriate but insulting. Any strategy for enhanced wellbeing requires a minimum level of wealth, health and freedom.

But if those so triply blessed make an effort to re-create the world daily they may trudge out to the old, decrepit branch line train one morning and discover that, miracle of miracles, it is the

Orient Express after all, though the Orient it is travelling to is not the East of glamour and luxury but the East of enlightenment. First you are the Philosopher King of the morning rush-hour carriage, observing with empathic curiosity despite having to sway in the central crush with no support to hang on to and constant sideswipes from your neighbour's back pack; next you are a God in disguise, strolling through the newly created world, well pleased by the old woman pushing a tartan shopping cart past a pile of tinned tomato boxes outside Way 2 Save; then you are the Zen Master of the photocopy room, able to suppress photocopier rage even when you need copies for a meeting that has just started and there are three people in front of you and the one at the machine is trying to do double-sided and is repeatedly getting it wrong, apparently unaware of the desperate colleagues behind.

The extraordinary is not our homeland but the land of our exile. The extraordinary is Babylon. It is the ordinary that is the only homeland. How could we have been so deluded? How could we have wasted so much time? Let us set out for our homeland immediately.

All aboard the Orient Express!

2

The High Priests of Low Life

Classical Greek and Roman literature abounds in exhortations to seize the day – and classical Oriental literature in loving attention to the commonplace. One of the greatest Oriental champions of the everyday was the eighth-century Chinese poet Po Chü-I, who wrote about the frustrations of working as a civil servant, the joys of raising children, the indignities of ageing and going bald and the consolations of reading poetry and drinking wine in the evening:

> In the morning I work at a Government office-desk;
> In the evening I become a dweller in the Sacred Hills.[24]

In prose there was Sei Shonagon, a Japanese tenth-century lady companion to the Empress, whose *Pillow Book* was a remarkably spirited, personal and candid account of everyday life at court. Uninterested in politics or history, Shonagon instead expressed her annoyance at a fellow companion borrowing her writing materials and returning them *with the brush left in the ink*, her pleasure in noticing that her elegant Chinese mirror had become a little cloudy, and her delight in the commonplace objects, such as writing paper, straw mats and fire tongs, which are never noticed: 'I feel I must be free to mention everything that exists and is used in our world.'[25]

It is heartening, even exhilarating, to know that what survives most vividly from these lost cultures of the distant past is not the rise and fall of empires and dynasties but the mundane details of the daily lives of unimportant people.

In the West, however, after the fall of the Roman Empire, the Church discouraged such celebration of the everyday for the next thousand years. It was not until after the Renaissance that the commonplace infiltrated religious paintings when Caravaggio had the cheek to use as models Roman lowlife with ragged clothes, missing teeth and dirty nails. Not Michelangelo's finger of God but Caravaggio's dirty fingernails of lowlife pointed the way forward for art.

Painters in Holland took the hint and abandoned not only religious subjects but also historical, military and classical themes to concentrate instead on the profane glory of everyday life, and in so doing ushered in the Dutch Golden Age. Suddenly paintings had the audacity to declare that peeling turnips was as inspirational as leading the nation's armies to victory, an impertinent kitchen maid scoffing an oyster was as beautiful and provocative as the goddess Diana and a woman delousing a little girl was as worthy of reverence as a Madonna and Child. The people in these paintings were not heroes, legendary figures or saints but ordinary people engaged in the most mundane activities – preparing food, cleaning and tidying kitchens, attending to children, sewing, writing and reading letters, playing cards or musical instruments, drinking, flirting, propositioning or, a delightful Dutch speciality, staring off into space in enigmatic reverie.

The settings were just as unexceptional, frequently domestic, with loving attention devoted to the crumbling mortar of courtyard walls, the folds in hanging towels, the crooked twigs of standing brooms, the sinuous patterns in tapestry table covers and the geometric patterns of shining floor tiles (though there were often homely things lying about on these floors) – and, always, over all this the play of light, as warm and subtle as the blessing of God, back lighting to surround figures and objects in a golden haze, side lighting to provide a sharp but warm apportioning of light and shade, highlights to glow on glass, pewter, porcelain and fruit. And, whatever the setting, always too a sense of serene immersion in the commonplace. Never has ordinary life seemed so alluring.

There was nothing epic in subject matter or treatment or even in the physical size of the paintings; most are small enough to carry off under an oxter – something which I have often been tempted to do. It might be a bit much to slip away with a top-of-the-range Vermeer – but, surely, at least a de Hooch, a van Hoogstraten, a Metsu or a Maes. It is heartbreaking, though also inspiring, to discover how cheap and plentiful such Dutch works were. According to one estimate, Holland produced over 5 million paintings in this period.[26] And in another astounding break with tradition, paintings were no longer solely icons for the Church or the status symbols of the aristocracy; ordinary people bought them in markets, along with food and drink.

Why did this happen in Holland in the seventeenth century? After decades of war with Spain (the Eighty Years War) the Dutch Republic finally cast off the Spanish monarchy and nobility, Spanish militarism and pomp and the Spanish Catholicism of the Inquisition. The Dutch experienced for the first time the freedom to live as they chose – and even tolerated in their midst Baruch Spinoza, the first openly atheist philosopher in Christendom, who would surely have been burned at the stake in any other Christian country and whose books were banned in the rest of Europe for generations to come. To be free to enjoy ordinary life was a miracle more astounding than any in scripture and therefore more worthy of being celebrated in paint.

Where did it go wrong? Oh, the usual. The Dutch began to take freedom for granted and to interpret their good fortune as evidence of superiority – the bourgeois delusion. They forgot to be grateful – and this ingratitude was punished, as it always is. Dutch painting turned to shit and never recovered.

The eighteenth century in general had little interest in everyday life. There were only isolated individuals such as Chardin in France who ignored the fashion for all things classical and painted – with the same loving attention as the Dutch Masters – kitchen maids and cooking utensils. But all through the eighteenth century Dutch paintings circulated in Europe and inspired a love of the commonplace that in the following century would lead to Degas's laundresses, Cézanne's apples and Van Gogh's chair. These Golden Age paintings even inspired the growing realism of the nineteenth-century novel.[27] George Eliot was explicit about this influence in her first novel *Adam Bede*:

> It is for this rare, precious quality of truthfulness that I delight in many Dutch paintings, which lofty-minded people despise. I find a source of delicious sympathy in these faithful pictures of a monotonous homely existence, which has been the fate of so many more among my fellow-mortals than a life of pomp or of absolute indigence, of tragic suffering or of world-stirring actions. I turn without shrinking, from cloud-borne angels, from prophets, sibyls, and heroic warriors, to an old woman bending over her flower-pot, or eating her solitary dinner, while the noonday light, softened perhaps by a screen of leaves, falls on her mob-cap, and just touches the rim of her spinning-wheel, and her stone jug, and all those cheap common things which are the precious necessaries of life to her.[28]

The nineteenth-century novel has many examples of homely existences among cheap common things but such commonplace detail was generally employed only as background colour. In Chekhov's stories and Flaubert's 'A Simple Heart' the commonplace becomes the main story but even these masters of the mundane were obliged by the censorship of the times to omit anything too sordid, especially about sex.

In the twentieth century many in the Western world finally enjoyed the Dutch experience of an everyday life without either indigence or pomp, and the artists of the century, finally free to celebrate every aspect of this life, did so with gratitude and joy in paintings, novels and poetry. In New York the Ashcan School, including John Sloan, George Bellows and, later, Edward Hopper, painted the urban life around them; in London the Camden Town Group, led by Walter Sickert, did the same. In Paris, Picasso, Braque and Juan Gris reinvented the still life and found exciting new ways to celebrate the everyday pleasures represented by newspapers, wine bottles and platters of fruit. In poetry William Carlos Williams celebrated, with unique zest, the ramshackle neighbourhoods of the urban poor and Robert Frost, with greater sobriety but equal compassion, the lives of the rural poor in monologues such as *The Death of the Hired Man* and *A Servant to Servants* – which is like one of the Golden Age kitchen maids stepping out of a painting to speak. The beginning of the twentieth century was a golden age of all the arts.

There were even two exuberant new art forms, photography and cinema. These were inevitable, given the technological developments, but another new form was a gratuitous and glorious accident: the creation of one particular magazine at one particular time in one particular place. Let us give thanks for the *New Yorker* cartoon, which enriched the satirical drawing with the richness and resonance of the short story. So, yes, it was a great century, despite the later arrival of Hitler, Stalin, Pol Pot and celebrity chefs.

A full celebration of all this would require a huge series of huge volumes. For a single short book it is necessary to be selective and partial. Poetry, painting, film, photography and the cartoon have each had outstanding successes and I hope to give many of these their due. But the most important champions of the everyday were James Joyce and Marcel Proust and these will be my principal exemplars and teachers. Though their work is now almost a century old, no fiction before or since has included more ordinary life, drawn more useful lessons from it, or made it more numinous, funny and strange. No one has examined ordinary life with more intense curiosity than Proust or celebrated it with greater delight than Joyce. And each combines in a single oeuvre the Holy Trinity of Re-Enchantment – the imaginative vision that discovers beauty, the comic vision that relishes absurdity and the spiritual vision that venerates mystery.

The tragedy is that books like Joyce's *Ulysses* and Proust's *À la recherche du temps perdu* are considered forbiddingly remote from everyday life when in fact they are so much closer to it than the various fantasies – the adventure stories, thrillers and romances – preferred by most readers. The philosopher John Dewey: 'The hostility to association of fine art with normal processes of living is a pathetic, even a tragic, commentary on life as it is ordinarily lived. Only because that life is usually so stunted, aborted, slack, or heavy laden, is the idea entertained that there is some inherent antagonism between the process of normal living and creation and enjoyment of works of esthetic art ... The works and the responses they evoke are continuous with the very processes of living as these are carried to unexpected happy fulfillment.'[29] Dewey objected to putting works of art on a pedestal because it 'deeply affects the practice of living, driving away esthetic perceptions that are necessary ingredients of happiness, or reducing them to the level of compensating transient pleasurable excitations'.

One common way of putting works on pedestals is to separate them from the lives of their creators and in particular from anything undignified, petty and sordid. But there should be no distinction between appreciating the artistry and laughing at the human limitations of the artists. After all, it was an ability to understand their own idiocies that made Joyce and Proust great. As Dewey claimed, the 'task is to restore continuity between the refined and intensified forms of experience that are works of art and the everyday events, doings and sufferings that are universally recognised to constitute experience. Mountain peaks do not float unsupported; they do not even just rest upon the earth. They *are* the earth in one of its manifest operations.' So, to maintain contact with the earth and the human, I intend to have lots of fun with the everyday lives of Joyce and Proust.

The two are rarely considered together because they appear to have nothing in common beyond being writers in Paris at the same time. Their works and personalities seem totally different and their social circles were mutually exclusive – Joyce the drunken Irish immigrant and Proust the darling of the aristocratic salons. So, though they lived in the same city, pursued the same vocation and were acutely aware of each other, it was always unlikely that they would meet. Both monomaniacal egotists, they encouraged discipleship in others but could never themselves be disciples and not only avoided contact but resolutely refused even to read each other's work. There was also Proust's extremely reclusive existence at this time and his previous unfortunate experience with Irish writers. After dining with M. and Mme Proust, Oscar Wilde entertained *le tout Paris* with scathing remarks about the bourgeois vulgarity of their furniture. Oscar might have been more sympathetic if he had known that Marcel would subsequently use it to furnish a homosexual brothel. So a

Joyce – Proust encounter was highly improbable. Yet there was indeed such an encounter and it proved to be both exquisitely banal and wonderfully bizarre, as simultaneously ordinary and extraordinary as anything in their simultaneously ordinary and extraordinary works.

And in the lives and works of both men there were a surprising number of parallels and where the two differed their differences were often complementary.

The most important similarity is that both accepted and were fascinated by every aspect of ordinary life, even the most commonplace and squalid. Joyce declared, 'It is my idea of the significance of trivial things that I want to give to the two or three unfortunate wretches who may eventually read me.' Proust spoke of celebrating the 'infinitely insignificant'. They devoted their lives to becoming the most diligent and dedicated servants of the ordinary, and in particular of everything disregarded or denied in distaste. They had a sacred vocation to celebrate the profane. They were the high priests of low life.

Now, almost a century later, when anything goes, it is difficult to grasp the courage this must have required. The most striking feature of the early response to both writers was outrage that literature, supposedly dedicated to the noble and the sublime, should lower itself to mention things like defecation and masturbation. Virginia Woolf, who was developing techniques similar to those of Joyce, nevertheless dismissed him in disgust as 'underbred' and *Ulysses* as 'the book of a self-taught working man'.[30] George Moore, whose fiction also had affinities with Joyce's work, responded with even more virulent snobbery, 'Joyce, Joyce, why he's nobody – from the Dublin docks: no family, no breeding'.[31] Joyce's response to such outrage was to joke that 'if *Ulysses* isn't fit to read life isn't fit to live'.

Nothing disgusted Joyce or Proust. Though they both admired and were influenced by Flaubert, neither adopted Flaubert's ironic contempt. Joyce did use the Flaubertian manner in his early story collection *Dubliners* (the style he described as 'scrupulous meanness') – like many young writers, he wanted to sound like an aged master – but in writing *Ulysses* he became his own man and abandoned austerity, detachment and contempt for exuberance, immersion and relish. The appropriate term for the mature style would be 'scrupulous generosity'.

The other important similarity between Joyce and Proust is that their writings about everyday life were based almost entirely on their own lives. The works were autobiographical and derived their power from the obsessions and neuroses of their authors. They both understood the crucial paradox: if you write for yourself it will be relevant to everyone and if you write for everyone it will be relevant to no one. So the works of Joyce and Proust were inextricably entangled with the lives, and readers of the works will want to understand the lives. In exposing their bizarrely singular natures, these two novelists revealed that psychological peculiarity is universal. No one is as odd as Joyce or Proust – except everyone.

The parallels between the two lives began early. Both men were the eldest sons of adoring, protective, slave mothers who made them supremely confident and supremely demanding. They remained intensely attached to these mothers but were ambivalent about the attachment and astute enough to restrict the appearances of mammy and mamma in their work. And both men had brothers two years younger, whom they exploited, included in the early drafts of autobiographical books and eliminated from the final versions. Both were also reared in Catholicism and rejected it at an early age, though its influence persisted. In their academic careers both did just enough to get by, ignoring the curriculum to read widely, though in later years they read little as they became obsessed by their own vast works. Both revered Tolstoy: Joyce, 'a magnificent writer';

Proust, 'a serene God'. Both were tyrannically demanding with friends and lovers. Both were priggish in their early work and developed a comic vision only in maturity.

They were also endlessly ingenious in evading traditional employment. Joyce took up the study of medicine on three occasions but never attended more than a few lectures. Proust studied law but also quickly gave it up. Joyce endured a few months as a bank clerk ('To continue as I am at present would certainly mean my mental extinction'), while Proust lasted for only two weeks as a solicitor's clerk ('In my most desperate moments, I have never conceived of anything more horrible than a law office'). Obsessed by books, both considered becoming librarians but Joyce was rejected by the National Library of Ireland as 'totally unsuitable' and, while Proust did succeed in getting a job at the Bibliothèque Mazarine and indeed held a librarian's post there for over four years, he managed this without turning up *for even a single day's work*, an achievement surely unique in the annals of employment.

Lacking the support of wealthy parents, Joyce considered and/or tried many ways of making money, including joining an acting troupe, managing a theatre company known as The English Players, touring the south coast of England singing medieval English songs (accompanying himself on a lute specially made for him by Arnold Dolmetsch), founding a newspaper called *The Goblin*, importing skyrockets into Trieste, developing Galway as a major transatlantic port, becoming the Austro-Hungarian Empire's rep for the Dublin Woollen Company and Irish Foxford Tweeds, and turning himself into a joint stock company and selling shares that would be worth a fortune when his genius was finally recognised. It is unfortunate that Proust never knew of this scheme for he was a keen investor in stocks, though Joyce may not have been sufficiently exotic.

Proust put his money into glamorous projects such as

Australian Gold Mines, Malacca Rubber Plantations, Doubowaia Balka and North Caucasian Oilfields and Egyptian Refineries. Given his belief that railway timetables were the most exciting works in print, it is not surprising that he invested heavily in The Tanganyika Railway, United Railways of Havana and the splendidly named SA Chemin de Fer de Rosario à Puerto Belgrano. Few of these investments brought any returns. As he complained in a letter, 'Rubber stocks, oil shares and the rest always wait until the day after I buy for the bottom to drop out of the market.'

Another unlikely parallel is that, despite their reputations as uncompromisingly elitist producers of high art, both Joyce and Proust were also popular-entertainment entrepreneurs. Joyce attempted to establish a cinema in Dublin and failed but Proust succeeded with his homosexual brothel in Paris.

Neither man had any talent for earning money but both were terrifically good at spending it. Joyce received huge sums from wealthy patrons and blew all the money immediately. Proust inherited a fortune from his parents and worked his way through most of it in a few years. Both men were madly extravagant with tips and gifts. As soon as he got his hands on cash, Joyce bought his wife and daughter expensive jewellery and fur coats. Proust showered his friends and lovers with bejewelled watches, diamond-studded cigarette cases, Gallé vases, paintings and even on one occasion an aeroplane.

Both were profoundly neurotic, superstitious, fearful and plagued by health problems, especially of sense organs. Proust endured 110 nasal cauterisations for his asthma but always had difficulty inhaling fresh air. Joyce had twelve eye operations but his sight still deteriorated and he could bear the light of common day only by wearing dark glasses. Both were also adept at making use of their illnesses to elicit sympathy and support and fend off unwelcome intrusions.

There are further striking parallels in their approaches to fiction. Their first works (which did not appear in their lifetimes) were autobiographical novels with priggish, eponymous writer heroes (*Jean Santeuil*, *Stephen Hero*), so both Proust and Joyce became writers by writing about the process of becoming writers. Later, they came to reject priggish solemnity and in their mature works developed an all-embracing comic vision that relished everyday life but had little time for the conventional apparatus of novels. Neither writer had any interest in important events, conflict or dramatic action, neither could be bothered to describe his characters' appearance, and, as for traditional storytelling, neither man would have known a plot if it crapped in his hat.

There are no plots in their huge and hugely original mature works, *Ulysses* and *À la recherche du temps perdu*, novels that disregarded popular and critical taste, violated social taboos, flouted obscenity laws, put enormous demands on readers and were certain to be rejected by traditional publishers. These books were initially published and printed in limited editions at private expense but eventually won such universal acceptance that the names of both writers have become adjectives, casually bandied about by many who have never read a word of their books.

Of course the writers themselves affected seigneurial indifference to critical acclaim and popularity but in fact both were indefatigable and astute self-promoters who would put contemporary publicists to shame. Though madly unpractical in most ways, they were assiduous in seeking celebrity endorsements, shamelessly badgered friends and acquaintances to write favourable reviews (frequently suggesting outlets and even the actual words of praise) and sent the influential opinion-makers copies of these reviews. To make sure of winning the prestigious Goncourt Prize, Proust bribed the judges with expensive gifts and dinners at the Ritz. And both understood the importance of scandal. Joyce was thrilled when *Ulysses* was prosecuted for obscenity and Proust was bitterly disappointed when *À la recherche* failed to attract similar legal attention (his mistake was to put the dirtiest bits at the end of the book where few readers ever penetrated). They also understood the importance of mystery in developing a legend and refused to explain or discuss their books in order to appear more intriguingly enigmatic. But behind their apparently inscrutable fronts, both raged violently in private at unflattering mentions and negative reviews.

Far from being indifferent to slings and arrows, they were touchy and vindictive, quick to take offence at slights – real or imagined – and determined to exact retribution. Proust actually fought a duel and issued challenges for four more. Joyce, a more modern man, preferred litigation as a means of redress; he pursued one libel action through the courts and threatened to undertake many others. And of course both took revenge in their books on anyone who had had the impertinence to cross them. But this sensitivity also made them hyper-responsive to their environments – human, natural and literary. They were expert mimics and parodists and included parody in their works (Proust settled for parodying only the *Goncourt Journals* but Joyce decided to parody all of English literature). And both celebrated the 'epiphany', a mystical but secular experience that they believed to be the supreme exaltation.

They also affected indifference to society but sought and exploited liaisons with the rich and well connected (Proust was fascinated by aristocrats and Joyce supported by wealthy patrons). On the other hand, they were able to escape class restrictions in their private lives. Both fell in love with servants (Proust with a chauffeur and Joyce with a chambermaid). And both lived with uneducated women who never read their books (Proust with Céleste Albaret and Joyce with Nora Barnacle).

On love and sex they revealed the unromantic truth with a realism, depth and candour unknown hitherto and never surpassed since. Both empathised with women and introduced to literature the concepts of fluid gender and the feminine man. Both experienced and understood sexual jealousy and portrayed it in their work and both were involved in and wrote about triangular sex, where one of two sexual partners is using the other as a proxy for a third person. They were also prescient in understanding the importance in modern sexuality of fetishism, voyeurism and sadomasochism, and showed the heroes of their mature books indulging in the sex act most common of all but until then too sordid for literature – masturbation. It is a sign of the great strides taken by twentieth-century fiction that the heroes of its two greatest novels were wankers. (Only a determined and resourceful scholar could establish manuscript precedence – but in the race to masturbate on a printed page Proust definitely came first.) And both men understood that other common activity – bought sex. Both *Ulysses* and *À la recherche* include extensive brothel scenes (since Proust owned a brothel he had no problem with research). Proust is famous for his rhapsodies on hawthorns but his book has only three of these, whereas there are thirteen scenes in brothels, one especially detailed episode running to more than forty pages. Few critics mention the brothels but they are more fun than the hawthorns.

As for the ways in which the two men complement each other, Proust was homosexual and Joyce heterosexual. Both were sadomasochistic, having been brought up in Catholicism – but Joyce was masochistic, being Irish, and Proust sadistic, being French. In their explorations of the human mind, Joyce investigated consciousness and Proust investigated memory. Both had strong but opposite feelings on rodents. Joyce was terrified of rats and fainted at the sight of them. Proust was sexually excited by rats and used them in foreplay.

But the most crucial complementarity is in their methods. Joyce was the supreme presenter and Proust the supreme explainer, Joyce the master of mimesis and Proust the master of analysis. Joyce provided the data and Proust the interpretation. Joyce showed how people talk, Proust showed the motivation behind their talk. Joyce revealed the richness and strangeness of each day and Proust revealed the richness and strangeness of each life. Taken together, with Joyce showing the texture and feel of the moment and Proust its underlying psychology, with Joyce vividly rendering the sunlit surface and Proust perceptively exploring the murky depths, their works provide an incomparable re-enchantment of the ordinary, a fresh revelation of the splendours and mysteries of everyday life and an encouragement not just to 'Pay Attention' but to obey that other equally old and equally binding commandment, 'Know Thyself'. So, most important of all, these apparently remote works of high art are actually crucial contributions to wisdom literature – at their heart is the key question, *How should we live?* And again their responses were complementary. Proust showed how not to do it and Joyce how to do it.

Yet, though committed to everyday life in their works, and living largely uneventful lives themselves, there is also in both Joyce and Proust something wonderfully extreme, excessive, heedless, extravagant and even lunatic. Each combined, in a single writer, a fervent mystic, a deadpan comedian, a sexual deviant, a penetrating psychologist, a master prose stylist, a lyric poet and a fanatical megalomaniac bent on world domination.

Who could fail to love such sweethearts?

PART II

The Holy Trinity of Re-enchantment

3

Losing the Plot: The Imaginative Vision

It used to be the butler who did it with a croquet mallet in the library and we knew it was the butler because all the evidence pointed to the wastrel nephew with gambling debts or the surly chauffeur with a history of violence. Also, it turned out that the butler had his reasons. Now it is more likely to have been an evil genius fiend who does it repeatedly just for kicks and in the process tortures, mutilates, burns and/or rapes the victim, stir fries and eats the internal organs and/or brains and then relaxes by listening to Mozart in a smoking jacket made from the victim's skin.

But of course the perpetrator is always apprehended, after many unexpected and thrilling twists and turns. Once the detective was an amateur sleuth of genius with a dumbass sidekick; now it is a maverick cop with a failed marriage, an alcohol problem and a rebellious relationship with a careerist superior.[32]

The attraction of plot for the professional writer is that it makes a book more readable and therefore more commercial. The desire to know how it all works out propels the reader relentlessly forward. But in a plot-driven novel the denouement is always disappointing. This is not just because the plotlessness of life makes neat conclusions unconvincing – but even more because plot excitement is all about anticipation, and so *any* resolution, no matter how plausible, is bound to feel like a letdown. And the price of readability is the sacrifice of rereadability. Once a plot novel has yielded its secrets, there will be no desire to return to it. Yet, despite the example of Joyce and Proust, who showed that plotless novels can be richly satisfying, plot has successfully recolonised fiction. Novels are now either 'well plotted' or 'poorly plotted' and the idea of a novel with no plot at all is as baffling to critics and readers as it was in the late nineteenth century. Plot is assumed to be an essential feature of novels when in fact it was a nineteenth-century invention – earlier novels by Rabelais, Cervantes and Sterne had no plots.

This resurgence of plot in fiction is only one example of a wider belief in and respect for narrative, which has increasingly replaced rational argument as a means of persuasion in the media, the human sciences, law, marketing and politics.[33] Even the word 'narrative' is now terrifically potent, one of those key terms, like 'synergy', 'empowerment' and 'innovation', that can impart an almost mystical significance. (If I were writing this book as an academic I would call it *Synergies of the Quotidian: narrative and empowerment in contemporary everyday life.*) While I was working on this chapter I wandered, hopeful as always, into a contemporary London art gallery. In Room 1 a gigantic brown cardboard box was suspended from the ceiling over an even larger brown cardboard box on the floor. This did not encourage me to seek imaginative vision in the other rooms. Back in the foyer the curator was saying, with earnest intensity, to a sceptical visitor, 'Room one has a *wonderful narrative*, I'm sure you'll enjoy it.'

Why has narrative become so appealing? Because it replaces cold reason with warm emotion, bewildering complexity with comforting simplicity, horrible messiness with tidy order and alarming randomness with reassuring meaning, direction and purpose. Above all it appeals to the new infantilism: stories are what adults tell children. Stories reduce, sweeten, package and gift-wrap experience. They tend to smooth away all that is ragged, tangled, complicated, paradoxical, inconsistent, inconclusive, insignificant and sordid – in other words everything that is most characteristic of everyday life. In life there are no plots or endings, only the ceaselessly ongoing moment with its manifold sensations, interactions and connections, its tangled network of links to the past and complex implications for the future. Life, as Henri Bergson explained, burgeons and ramifies ceaselessly in space and time and refuses to be parcelled up into neat plots. And, while it may be tempting to shape one's own life into a satisfying narrative, no 'story' can do justice to the muddle of random events and accidents, the shocking wastage and aimless drifting, the destinations arrived at more by inertia than initiative and the choices that must have seemed sensible at the time but are madly inexplicable in retrospect. The novelist Julian Barnes: 'So if, as we approach death and look back on our lives, we "understand our narrative" and stamp a final meaning upon it, I suspect we are doing little more than confabulating: processing strange, incomprehensible, contradictory input into some kind, any kind, of believable story.'[34]

Another factor is that ingenious plots, ripping yarns and colourful fantasies appeal to the left hemisphere of the brain. In the constant struggle to overcome dreariness and boredom the LH solution is escape into novelty, whereas the right hemisphere prefers originality, in the sense of a return to origins, seeing the familiar anew. LH wants new experience and RH a new way of seeing. So originality is not only different from novelty but can even be said to oppose it. The neurologist Iain McGilchrist: 'This is the distinction between fantasy, which presents something novel *in the place of* the too familiar thing, and imagination, which clears away everything between us and the not familiar enough thing so that we see *it* itself, new, as it is.'[35] But fantasy too is an exercise of the imagination, albeit less useful. Coleridge was more subtle when he distinguished between primary and secondary imagination and described the latter as 'fancy'. The products of fancy can be entertaining but provide only temporary relief rather than lasting satisfaction because they bring about no change in perception: 'The primary imagination I hold to be the living power and prime agent of all human perception.'[36]

Both types of imagination evolved to make perception more effective by including 'what if?' scenarios but, where the secondary form disappears over the horizon into fantasy, the primary feeds back into perception to refresh everyday experience. In the case of art, the artwork is produced by the primary imagination of the artist, largely in the right hemisphere, though the left is also required for ordering and shaping, and enriches the perception of the consumer by energising the consumer's RH and opening it up to wider and deeper receptivity. Both meaningful production and meaningful consumption involve effort, most from the producer but much also from the consumer. Receptivity does not mean passivity. Dewey: 'Perception is an act of the going-out of energy in order to receive, not a withholding of energy . . . We must summon energy and pitch it at a responsive key in order to *take* in.' In fact, 'there is an element of passion in all esthetic perception'.[37]

So, for consumer as well as producer, imagination is process, and with an investment of energy only a little more than that required to read thrillers or watch soap operas, the world may be secretly viewed in colour, H-D and 3-D, sharper, brighter, deeper and more engaging, and with the agreeable accompanying thought that the couch potato majority are still viewing in two-dimensional, low-definition black and white.

But what distinguishes the meaningful products of a creative primary imagination? The right hemisphere appreciates holistic awareness, the sense of an encompassing organic unity that is strong but not static, an ongoing process, a fluid interconnectivity of many sharply individual components (LH thinks in terms of classification, RH in terms of individual cases). And what is a successful poem, novel, film, painting or photograph but a multiplicity of convincing details combined into a satisfying whole?

Poets seem to have pondered these matters more deeply than other artists and what Coleridge said of the poet applies equally well to novelists, painters, filmmakers and photographers: 'He diffuses a tone and spirit of unity.'[38] Two centuries later T. S. Eliot said something similar but more specific (and again substitute 'artist' for 'poet'): 'When a poet's mind is perfectly equipped for its work, it is constantly amalgamating disparate experience; the ordinary man's experience is chaotic, irregular, fragmentary. The latter falls in love, or reads Spinoza, and these two experiences have nothing to do with each other, or with the noise of the typewriter or the smell of cooking; in the mind of the poet these experiences are always forming new wholes.'[39]

This sense of wholeness, this 'tone and spirit of unity', may well be the most important gift of art. The price of developing human self-consciousness has been growing alienation from the world, expulsion from the Garden of Eden, and a spirit of unity goes some way to restoring the original oneness, the sense of belonging to and in a rich world, where everything is connected to everything else and nothing is isolated and separate, least of all one's self. This holistic, right hemisphere experience is increasingly important in a narrowly practical left hemisphere world where there seems to be too much of everything and all of it is fragmentary and unconnected. There is no consolation more profound than the experience of solidarity with others and the world.

Another factor is that consciousness itself is a continuous

creation of unity from the chaotic flux of sensory data, thought and memory (see Chapter 8 for more), so that evidence of similar successful creation is reassuring at the deepest level.

A tone and spirit of unity are the crucial requirements – but the details that have been unified must feel convincing. Intellectual work may be general but imaginative work is always specific. And the details will be charged with deeper significance if they are drawn from the creator's own experience. No research, however assiduous, can produce details with the radioactive energy of a unique personal vision, an obsessiveness that is drawn back compulsively, again and again, though without really understanding why, to the same details and themes.

Joyce and Proust meet all these requirements. *Ulysses* is so absolutely, totally and completely plotless that it would make a telephone directory seem a masterpiece of narrative drive – and as the critic Jean-François Revel remarked of *À la recherche*, 'The only story that Proust ever invented is that his book is a novel'.[40] Not only do *Ulysses* and *À la recherche* lack plot, they barely even have structure. Joyce borrowed his structure from Homer's *Odyssey* but his book constantly threatens to break out of this straitjacket – the chapters become longer and longer as the book goes on. Proust began with a plan but very soon the floodwaters swept away the banks.

Rejecting plot and structure, *Ulysses* and *À la recherche* convey the crucial sense of oneness by means of connexity. Much that appears random in these novels turns out to be cunningly linked. (But much is also genuinely random – it is a mistake, encouraged by critics, to imagine that every sentence is significant.) Many of Proust's huge cast are in the course of time revealed to be connected in various ways. In *Ulysses* characters mentioned in conversation or interior monologue turn up later in person – and vice versa – and many have already appeared in Joyce's earlier books. And the characters not only turn up in thoughts and conversations but throughout the day see, meet, do business with, bump into or avoid each other. All this creates richness and density, a sense of complete, and completely convincing, worlds in which everyone is connected to everyone else. In both Joyce and Proust the essential structure is the network, but a network in which both nodes and links are constantly mutating so that it has the unity, vitality and adaptability of a living organism.

These books also resemble living organisms in the unpredictable ways they grew, adapted, mutated, evolved. *Ulysses* began as a short story and *À la recherche* as a short novel and both continued to grow until artificially arrested by a publishing deadline – or, to be more accurate, a printer's deadline. Both books expanded by a third at the proof stage, driving the printers insane. Proust cut up proofs, stuck them into a notebook and inserted between each pair of proof pages written additions on pages pasted together and folded into concertinas up to a metre long. He was still dictating yet more additions on his deathbed. *Ulysses* and *À la recherche* were never finished, merely abandoned.

Of course both books were already too long. It is not so much that *Ulysses* and *À la recherche* are great novels as that they have great novels *in* them. Each could be cut by a third or more without losing anything essential – but who would wish to be without the weaker bits?

As for convincing detail, both books give the impression of containing little or no invention, of being drawn almost entirely from life. The major exception is Leopold Bloom, the hero of *Ulysses*. Bloom is revealed to be an invention by the number of facts about him Joyce feels obliged to include. We know more about Bloom than about any other character in fiction – but if Bloom were authentic he would not require the support of such a compendious fact file. The mistake was to try to create an everyman when there is no such thing. Bloom remains a concept – but a noble concept, an example of how to live.

In Proust there is no problem with authenticity. Many readers of *À la recherche* have commented on the strange feeling, the certainty, that nothing in this huge book, absolutely nothing, has been invented. Characters have been amalgamated (and occasionally had their genders switched), settings have been changed, and events moved around in time – but everything in it, absolutely everything, happened in real life somewhere at some time. This kind of certainty is one of the most mysterious aspects of reading. Proust's *Belle Époque* Paris is utterly remote now – so how can we be sure that every detail is authentic? Yet it is possible to read any novel, no matter how exotic the characters and setting, a tale of Chinese silk workers or Chilean copper miners, and know immediately whether it is the real thing or made up. It must be that life is so wondrously peculiar it defies any attempt to produce a convincing forgery – and this is a wondrously encouraging thought for everyone except professional novelists.

There is also personal obsession in the themes, settings and characters. Proust speculates that Balzac must have experienced rapture when he realised that he could use the same characters in different novels but Proust was unaware that across Paris James Joyce was doing exactly this, including in *Ulysses* many characters from his first two books. A professional novelist would be horrified by such repetition, believing that each novel should be as different as possible from the others, not only with entirely different characters but set in a different time and place (the ideal a different country for every novel), fondly convinced that this displays impressive range and rich imagination, when in fact it reveals only limitation and poverty.

Like the detail, the characters must be convincing, important, *inevitable*, and in Joyce and Proust most of the characters leap off the page. They are instantly recognisable and eternally memorable. Exceptions include the narrator Marcel's idealised mother and grandmother in *À la recherche* and to some extent Leopold and Molly Bloom in *Ulysses* (memorable but not entirely recognisable). Most of the others seem to have walked straight out of Paris and Dublin and into the books.

Even more impressive than making characters convincing is making them understandable, which Joyce and Proust achieved not by sentimentalising or idealising, but by foregoing anger, hatred and disgust to view the characters from a great height, with the detachment and clarity and honesty of God. To judge, condemn and punish encourages vindictiveness. To reveal and understand encourages tolerance.

The ultimate achievement is to create characters who behave entirely atrociously yet are impossible to hate. In *À la recherche* the Baron de Charlus is a monster of arrogance, conceit and snobbery and yet difficult to dislike. Mme Verdurin is even more atrocious, a malevolent, hypocritical, middle-class social climber, yet she too is hard to loathe. And all Proust's major characters are unpredictably complex, constantly behaving in ways that surprise but convince.

Leopold Bloom does not behave badly – but is a wonderfully unprepossessing figure. He has an ignoble job as a salesman of advertising, is an emasculated husband, an ineffectual father, a coward, cuckold, voyeur and wanker. When *Ulysses* first appeared, many readers and critics were unable to accept that such a man could be treated not just with sympathy but presented as the equivalent of a hero in Homer. Bloom's Jewishness is unexceptional now but a Jewish hero was a courageous concept in the early twentieth century when anti-Semitism was common in literature. Proust, though himself Jewish because of his Jewish mother, lacked the nerve to make Marcel a Jew.

Such characterisation encourages empathy, the source of so

much that is noble in human nature – tolerance, compassion, forgiveness, self-sacrifice. In fact morality itself is based on empathy, the realisation, which came to several different cultures almost simultaneously in the axial age, that others are also conscious and therefore we should do unto others as we would wish them to do unto us. Conversely, lack of empathy encourages so much that is ugly – snobbery, bigotry, racism, aggression, cruelty (the psychiatrist Simon Baron-Cohen has argued that evil should be redefined as 'empathy erosion' and extreme evil as 'a zero degree of empathy'[41]).

There are many who would argue that empathy is not an innate feature of human nature, which is fundamentally selfish, but a cultural phenomenon, more of a pious aspiration than an instinct, and that altruism is only a more cunning form of self-interest. This issue is hotly debated but the primatologist Frans de Waal has claimed that there is evidence of disinterested empathy even among animals.[42] Chimpanzees engage in helping, sharing, consoling, grieving and nursing the wounded. There is even evidence of empathy in rats,[43] which might have made them more acceptable to Joyce though less erotically exciting to Proust. The message seems to be that while self-interest is the primary instinct, it may be overridden or mitigated by empathy, which is also innate but more variable and vulnerable. Empathy has to be nurtured, protected and encouraged.

As many child psychologists have shown,[44] the human ability to empathise develops in infancy from strong attachment to parental figures – but narcissism constantly threatens to overwhelm this ability, which constantly needs to be reinforced. And what is empathy but imagination applied to other people? (Not surprisingly, empathy, like imagination, is a right hemisphere function.[45]) And therefore who better to teach empathy than those who have successfully imagined others, in other words fiction writers who have created entirely convincing characters?

So the most important lesson of good fiction is empathy, the key to all successful relationships, personal, professional and social – and in both Joyce and Proust the social interactions of the characters are made more compelling than any plot. In Joyce's story 'Ivy Day in the Committee Room', all that happens is that a few political canvassers hang about in a shabby room making small talk – but their interplay is as intriguingly complex as a summit meeting of great powers. In *À la recherche* over two hundred and fifty pages are devoted to an afternoon tea party but this is as enthralling as an action movie full of car chases and shootouts.

However, to avoid putting Joyce and Proust on pedestals, it is worth remembering that they empathised only with their fictional characters. In real life they manipulated and exploited everyone around them. Joyce was especially ruthless with his younger brother Stanislaus, whom he treated with contempt as a servant in Dublin and, when James moved to Trieste, used as his Dublin agent, publicist, fact checker, loan canvasser and research assistant. Soon, though, James felt the need of a personal assistant closer at hand and summoned his brother. When Stanislaus arrived in Trieste, he was put to work teaching English the next day and obliged to hand over his pay to James. After a few weeks James, to simplify the procedure, collected Stanislaus's pay himself. Later he borrowed a pair of Stanislaus's trousers and never gave them back. In fact he never returned anything. On several occasions he promised to reward his brother's devoted service, for instance by dedicating *Dubliners* to him, but always failed to keep his word. In the end Joyce never dedicated any of his published books to anyone. Only one of his unpublished works bears a dedication and this is *to himself*: 'To My own Soul I dedicate the first true work of my life'.

Proust was even more ruthless, ensuring undivided dedication by actually imprisoning in his apartment his chauffeur-lover, Alfred Agostinelli, his secretary-lover, Henri Rochat, and his servant, Céleste Albaret, who had to be available day and night and was not even allowed out to attend Mass ('Céleste, do you know you are doing something much greater and nobler than going to Mass?'[46]). Every whim of Proust's had to be satisfied immediately. Once Céleste protested that instant service was 'impossible' and Proust responded, 'My dear Céleste, that word does not exist.' When he felt in the mood for a string quartet at midnight, Proust set off in the taxi of Céleste's husband Odilon, rounded up the *Poulet Quartet* from their homes, fortified them with a tureen of mashed potatoes in the taxi and at one a.m. lay back on his bed while they played for him the César Franck quartet in D major. When they had finished, exhausted, Proust revived them with champagne and fried potatoes, cooked and served by Céleste of course, and made them play the quartet again.

At least Proust revealed some of this tyrannous behaviour in the character of Marcel. Joyce was not so frank but in Leopold Bloom created a character who was his opposite in every way – sexually generous rather than possessive, humble rather than arrogant, self-effacing rather than self-promoting, tolerant rather than touchy, compassionate rather than scornful, always willing to help others rather than demanding help for himself. So Joyce, who abhorred didacticism, was actually more didactic than Proust the compulsive explainer. Bloom is not so much a character as a series of lessons in how to live. What saves this from 'the inanity of extolled virtue', as Joyce himself put it, is that the lessons are so quirky, surprising and funny and so embedded in convincing everyday life that the reader is hardly aware of being instructed and edified.

Successful imaginative fiction requires a rare combination of personal vision, intense observation, accurate recall, empathic understanding of character, psychology and social interaction, a sure instinct for the telling detail and, last but not least, a masterly prose style to make all this swing.

Joyce and Proust had all these attributes and have influenced writers ever since. The Jousting tradition of championing the everyday persists and flourishes and should be acknowledged in a Jousting Prize for plotless novels that bring the everyday to imaginative life. The following would all have been worthy winners:

Caught **Henry Green, 1943**

This is set in a London fire station where volunteers and regular firemen await the Blitz, which begins only at the end of the book and is described in a half-apologetic flashback. What fascinated Green was the waiting, the aimless hanging about, and the way that human idiosyncrasy expands to fill the vacuum of uneventfulness. Nature abhors a vacuum and human nature even more so. John Updike described Green as a 'saint of the mundane embracing it with all his being'.[47]

Morte D'Urban **J. F. Powers, 1956**

This novel, and Powers's stories, may well provide the only accurate account of the everyday lives of priests, embroiled not in spiritual crises or theological disputes, but in petty though ferocious power struggles with housekeepers and superiors. The 'hero' of the novel, Father Urban, is an utterly worldly snob but also, in the true Jousting spirit, utterly sympathetic. There is a touch of sensationalism at the end when he gets knocked out by a golf ball.

The Centaur **John Updike, 1962**

John Updike, heavily influenced by both Joyce and Proust, was a major champion of everyday life: 'My only duty was to describe reality as it had come to me – to give the mundane its beautiful due.'[48] Many of Updike's first-person narrators sound like Proust, especially when they are celebrating youth, and Harry 'Rabbit' Angstrom of the Rabbit novels, who sells cars for a living, is a late-twentieth-century everyman, an American Bloom.

The Centaur covers a few winter days in the life of an adolescent boy in Pennsylvania, during which he alternately loves, is embarrassed by, and angry with, his parents ('there was a tantrum rich and bristling within me'), attends school, goes to a luncheonette and a basketball game, is trapped by snow and obliged to spend a night in the home of friends of his parents. His hostess, the wife, is an attractive older woman and the great set-piece drama at the end of the book is his two hours alone in this house with the woman. There is no sex or even any suggestion of sex. Just to be with her in her home is sufficient rapture.

Lives of Girls and Women Alice Munro, 1971

In a female equivalent of *The Centaur*, a fiercely intelligent young girl grows up in rural Canada, loving but embarrassed by her mother who sells encyclopaedias to farmers, disliking her snobbish aunts (portrayed with devastating accuracy) and needing but secretly patronising her worldly friend who wants only marriage and a comfortable home. Though, unlike the Updike boy, Munro's girl has a sexual fling with a born-again lumberyard worker.

Cleaned Out Annie Ernaux, 1974

Similar in many ways to *Lives of Girls and Women*, but even more direct and raw, *Cleaned Out* (*Les Armoires Vides* in the original French) describes an intelligent girl growing up in a *café-épicerie* in a working-class area of a small town in Normandy. One side of the ground floor of the home is the grocery shop where, as flies buzz over the pâté and cheese, the mother is hypocritically sweet to local women who come to gossip about each other, buy tins of corned beef on credit and poke fingers into the camembert to check if it is ripe; on the other side the father runs the café, where local workers get drunk, puke, fight, try to touch up the girl and expose themselves to her en route to the stinking makeshift toilet in the yard. In between café and bar is a tiny kitchen open to both shoppers and drinkers and above is a single room the girl has to share with her parents and their snoring, farts, floods of piss in a chamber pot and furtive but still noisy sex in the dark. As the girl moves through adolescence she increasingly despises her parents and home and yearns for middle-class good taste. It is this brutal candour that makes the novel so compelling.

The Mezzanine **Nicholson Baker, 1988**

This is the Homeric epic of one office worker's lunch hour, in which he is seduced by the beauty of a stapler and a date stamp, endures the trauma of a broken shoe-lace and a recalcitrant straw in his drink carton, and finally, in the two great set pieces at the end of the book, has perilous, testing encounters with a colleague passing on a down escalator as he is ascending, and a boss peeing in the urinal next to him in the corporate toilet.

That They May Face the Rising Sun **John McGahern, 2002**

A sophisticated couple move to a house by a lake in rural Ireland, employ unreliable workmen to carry out improvements, are visited by and visit neighbours and consume countless plates of ham sandwiches. The big set-piece drama, the equivalent of Father Urban being hit by a golf ball, is when one of the workmen is stung by bees.

The Pale King **David Foster Wallace, 2011**

This unfinished and posthumously published epic celebrates not just work but one of the dreariest kinds of work, bureaucracy, and even one of the dreariest branches of bureaucracy, the internal revenue service. And for good measure it is set in a tax centre that is not just in the dreary American Midwest but in Peoria, one of the 'two grimmest, most blighted and depressed old factory cities in Illinois'. No one could accuse Wallace of going for colourful material. His noble ambition, only partly realised, was to engender empathy for those, known as 'wigglers', who spend their working days processing tax forms.

All these books are heroically plotless and uneventful, dedicated only to giving the mundane its beautiful due and succeeding by the power of imaginative personal vision, the miraculous alchemy that gives to the leaden everyday the lustre of gold.[49] All have valuable lessons to teach – and these will be considered in due course.

Good plotless films about everyday life are even rarer than the literary equivalent – but they do exist. Mike Leigh, a cinematic saint of the mundane, has created a unique oeuvre of such films and should receive a Lifetime Achievement Award for Plotless Dedication to the Ordinary.

With all these works, the most important lesson is that, in revealing worlds at once familiar and strange, they reveal our own familiar world as equally strange. Keats: 'The imagination may be compared to Adam's dream – he awoke and found it truth.'[50]

4

Getting the Joke: The Comic Vision

'That's a grand day now, Mrs Foley.' This was Charlie Deery, the laughing milkman, rattling his crate of bottles in a jubilant carillon to spring. I knew his name only from other boys on the street. My mother would never address a tradesman by his first name – and when she did have to speak to such a person it was in a vague, distant, faint tone.

'It is a lovely day indeed.'

Charlie delivered the bottles, retrieved the empties and accepted his money for the week but instead of withdrawing in silent abasement, as would a tradesman who knew his station, gave my mother a solemn look.

'A great day for the race.'

She allowed a silence to express her disapproval of this unnecessary further familiarity and finally spoke in an even more distant tone.

'What race would that be?'

Charlie looked her gravely in the eye.

'The human race.'

At once he turned and walked swiftly to the garden gate, only then turning back to shake with silent laughter.

My mother, unamused, outraged, disgusted, pulled me back

into the hallway – but not before Charlie gave me a collusive wink and yielded to an even more convulsive silent shake.

This may well have been the first joke I understood as a child and more impressive than the corny joke itself was its subversive effect. Without doing anything flagrantly wrong, Charlie had obviously got the better of the encounter. I realised, in some dim, barely conscious way, that humour was the most effective ruse of the underdog.

But Charlie's humour was as broad as his backside. To be honest, I despised the man a little myself.

The next lesson was from an older street boy called Willie Sharkey who was obviously a slag – he had black-rimmed fingernails and long lank greasy hair built up at the front into a quiff and at the back into a DA (duck's arse, a term for the elaborate rear division favoured by Teddy Boys). My mother would have loathed Sharkey even more than she loathed the milkman – but he had a sly, satirical intelligence that attracted me. He was my first Zen Master and, though an older street sophisticate would usually never be seen with a timid mammy's boy, he seemed to accept me as a potential initiate and even enlightened me with a koan.

'What of the fly that spins?' he asked.

I knew only to keep silent.

'One of its legs is both the same.' Sharkey studied me intently.

Still I said nothing. The silence was rich and resonant.

'Ah,' he said, after a while, nodding, as though I had finally spoken. 'But what of the mouse?' This time his look was even more keenly penetrating.

I sensed that he was checking for signs of irritation and tried to remain attentively serene.

Eventually, leaning very close, he said, with a peculiar softness, 'Because the higher the fewer.'

Yet even now, with the joke complete, Sharkey did not laugh

or allow his profound gravity to be disturbed by the slightest hint of a smile. I had my first momentous revelation of sophisticated deadpan comedy. The greatest comedians do not appear to be funny and the greatest jokes are not really jokes at all.

As it turned out, Sharkey was not just imparting enlightenment. He wanted to sell me his unwanted books – lurid Westerns, science fiction novels and, his personal specialism, accounts of Japanese Second World War atrocities. Yet, though we were both avid readers and desperate for comedy, we never thought of seeking humour in books. Comedy was a street thing.

Nor was there anything funny in popular entertainment. I loathed the sentimental simpering of Chaplin, the crude slapstick of the Three Stooges and the frenetic hamming of Danny Kaye. All these were so obviously desperate to be endearingly funny. The urge to make people laugh is often based on an insecurity that craves affection (and this insecurity also explains why so many comedians are shockingly stingy) – but an obvious desire to be loved is always fatal for comedy. Worse still were the raucous television comedies like *I Love Lucy* with shrieking canned laughter every few seconds. (In 1999 *Time* magazine included laugh tracks in a list of *The 100 Worst Ideas of the Century*, along with prohibition, Muzak and spray-on cheese.[51])

The revelation was *Doctor Strangelove*, a movie indeed truly strange. Far from attempting to be lovable or funny, this was austerely black and white and as solemn as a Requiem Mass for a pope. The subject was the destruction of the world in a nuclear holocaust triggered by a deranged American general (a magnificently grim, brooding performance from Sterling Hayden), a disaster that heads of state were unable to prevent, and throughout the unfolding catastrophe no one even smiled, much less laughed. This was the ultimate black movie in the ultimate deadpan style.

The director, Stanley Kubrick, was an obsessive perfectionist who understood the importance of getting every detail right. The interior of the American B-52 bomber was so authentic that the Pentagon launched an inquiry to find out who had leaked such top-secret information. Kubrick also understood that constantly trying for laughs can be self-defeating. The movie has many long scenes containing nothing remotely funny, for instance where the bomber crew read and implement the attack procedures – resetting course, priming weapons, pushing buttons, flicking switches and exchanging technical data in flat, neutral tones. So, when the comedy arrives it is even more effective. The Russian Ambassador, summoned to the war room to discuss the crisis, is spotted taking photos with a concealed camera and gets into a scuffle with an American general. The President, played by the great Peter Sellers, is profoundly shocked. 'Gentlemen!' he cries in righteous outrage, 'You can't fight in here,' – pause to muster appropriate gravitas – 'this is the *War Room*'.

The equivalent revelation in fiction was Flann O'Brien's *The Third Policeman*, an appropriate successor to *Strangelove* because the novel's tone was even blacker, the presentation even more solemn and no nuclear holocaust was needed because all the characters were already dead (though unaware of this). The lesson from this book was that comedy depends on delivery and that oral and written comedy are delivered entirely differently. Jokes that will make an audience howl with laughter usually die on the page and a sentence that is funny in print usually sounds affected when spoken. O'Brien realised that the literary equivalent of a deadpan expression is using formal, fastidious language that appears to be unaware of humour – and he developed the most extreme formality by writing English as though it was a dead language. This formal narrating voice then sets up a comical contrast with the totally informal demotic of the characters.

It became apparent that comedy was a complicated phenomenon – but would it bear investigation? Surely solemn theories about comedy are themselves a bad joke? And if analysis was successful surely it would kill the very laughter it was attempting to understand? Comedians often avoid analysing comedy for the same reason that poets avoid analysing poetry. In fact comedy is like poetry in many ways, mysterious and indefinable, apparently so simple that anyone can do it but actually difficult to do well, requiring an intuitive feel for rhythm and timing – and when it is done well there is nothing better but when it is done badly there is nothing worse. Alas, it is more often done badly. A really good comic performance is as rare as a really good poem.

The problem with the theories is that they assume humour is a well-defined property of situations and/or performances and that it is universally appreciated. The theories aim at a fixed target – but the target is nebulous and constantly moving. Humour overlaps with play, zest, glee and delight and there is both mirth without laughter and laughter without mirth. More confusing still, there is no such thing as the intrinsically funny. Comedy depends on both delivery and reception. Comedy is process. And funniness is not universal but culturally constrained – what one culture finds funny will not be funny in another. Even within a single culture comedy evolves over time and becomes more sophisticated, though the primitive forms continue to coexist with, and are frequently an element in, the highly developed. And comedy is subjective – what has one person rolling on the floor will leave another as stone-faced as a Mount Rushmore head. Finally, the subjective reaction itself evolves – what seemed hysterically funny in youth is often bewilderingly unamusing in adulthood.

None of this has deterred theorists. Among the many who have attempted to define comedy are Plato, Aristotle, Hobbes,

Kant, Schopenhauer, Hegel, Kierkegaard, Baudelaire, Bergson and Freud. And there is no sign that theorists are wearying. New books on comedy are almost as common as new jokes.[52]

The many theories reduce to essentially three[53] – the superiority theory, which claims that laughter is induced by feeling superior to others; the incongruity theory, which claims that we laugh at the revelation of an incongruity between what was expected and what actually happens; and the relief theory, which explains laughter as the pleasurable discharge of energy bound up in repression.

Each of these theories claims to be universal but explains only certain types of comedy. The relief theory, expounded by Freud in *Jokes and Their Relation to the Unconscious*, seems to me the least convincing and the least generally applicable, relevant only to dirty jokes – so the explanation of the explanation is Freud's obsession with sex.

The interesting thing about the other two is that the superiority theory was advanced by earlier thinkers such as Plato, Aristotle and Hobbes (who defined laughter as a 'suddaine Glory arising from suddaine Conception of some Eminency in our selves, by comparison with the Infirmityes of others'[54]), while the incongruity theory was a later development, espoused by Kant, Kierkegaard and Schopenhauer ('Laughter results from nothing but the suddenly perceived incongruity between a concept and the real object ... between what is abstract and what is actually apprehended ... The greater and more unexpected this incongruity in the apprehension ... the more violent will be the laughter'[55]). This suggests that superiority humour itself came first.

All the theorists agree that the violent convulsion is a profound pleasure – laughter is the orgasm of the mind – and that the convulsion requires an element of surprise, something 'suddaine' and unexpected. This is why speed and timing are so important. A response is often funny just by being instantaneous and if offered ten minutes later will not be funny at all. And timing is crucial in setting up deceptive expectations which intensify the final surprise. These ambiguities and complexities mean that interpreting humour is a non-literal, right hemisphere function and enjoying a laugh is a right hemisphere workout.

The earlier superiority theory is more applicable to primitive forms of comedy such as practical jokes and slapstick, which have an element of cruelty and humiliation. Matthew M. Hurley has suggested that humour began as a ruse, a way for the brain to encourage the search for truth and meaning by developing the enjoyable experience of humour as a reward for the inevitable misconceptions, misjudgements, errors and failures.[56] The idea of early man evolving a ruse is appealing but this feat seems to me far too sophisticated for the primitive brain. An alternative hypothesis is that humour began as an expression of superiority, a crow of triumph at a humiliation that endorsed the superior status of the witness. The first laugh may well have been from one of our ancestors who saw a hated rival slip on a dinosaur turd and so become the ingredients of the next turd. We can gain some insight on palaeohumour from our ancestors the chimpanzees who are still around and, apparently, still game for a laugh. The primatologist Roger Fouts trained a female chimpanzee called Washoe to use sign language and when he was carrying her on his shoulders Washoe urinated all over him, snorted and made the funny sign.[57]

The classic definition of superiority humour is itself an old joke: 'Tragedy is when *I* cut my finger. Comedy is when *you* fall into an open sewer and drown.' Such cruel laughter persists in cartoons and slapstick, and in comedy based on caricature and stereotypes – for instance jokes based on the assumption that certain nationalities are stupid. This type of joke goes right back to ancient Greece where the citizens of the town of Abdera were, like the Irish, Polish and Pakistanis today, mocked for their supposedly irredeemable stupidity.

And satire is a sophisticated form of superiority comedy, where the satirist and audience feel morally superior to the satirised. So when watching *Strangelove* we feel satisfyingly superior to the crazies bent on destroying the world.

The later comedy of incongruity is usually more accepting and humane. At the heart of *The Third Policeman* – a masterpiece of comic incongruity – is a great central scene where the first two policemen, Sergeant Pluck and Policeman MacCruiskeen, take the narrator on a trip to eternity, which is up an Irish country lane and deep underground, accessible only by lift. Visitors to eternity do not age and may have anything they wish, so the narrator, whose brain is 'working coldly and quickly', orders fifty cubes of gold, a bottle of whiskey, precious stones to the value of £200,000, some bananas, a fountain pen and writing materials and a serge suit of blue with silk linings. Then he has another cunning thought and orders a weapon capable of exterminating any man or any million men though small enough to carry comfortably in a pocket.

But when he returns to the lift he is told that he may not take his loot out of eternity. For a moment he is stunned and then bursts into 'loud choking sobs'. MacCruiskeen attempts to ease this anguish by offering a bag of creams but, when the narrator tries to take a sweet, three or four come out together, compacted into a sticky mass by the heat of the policeman's pocket. The sergeant, offered one in turn, refuses on the grounds that it would put him in bed 'for a full fortnight roaring out profanity from terrible stoons of indigestion and heartburn', and then goes into a lyrical rhapsody on the merits of Carnival Assorted: 'Now *there* is a sweet for you.'

All the details are sublimely incongruous, especially the consolation of the sticky sweets. For not any incongruous detail is funny. The trick is to make it both absolutely right for the character and absolutely wrong for the situation. It has to be natural, even inevitable, for Peter Sellers to protest that you can't fight in the War Room.

But what makes O'Brien's eternity scene really great is the weeping of the narrator in the lift. At this point the language, hitherto scrupulously sober, concise and flat, suddenly becomes expansive and lyrical so that we are made to feel personally the anguish, realising that we are equally desirous, deluded and absurd.

However, *The Third Policeman*, like *Strangelove*, is a fantasy, a fable whose characters are all lunatics. Much more empathic is the comedy of recognition where there is nothing fantastic about characters, situations or behaviour, no caricature or farce, no exaggeration or invention. In this comedy, everything is convincingly familiar but is gradually revealed as bizarre and absurd. It is often claimed that comedy requires coldness, even heartlessness – but what is necessary is not so much absence of feeling as detachment, the ability to look down on life from the cold empty reaches of infinite space. And the paradox is that this distancing from the familiar has the effect of bringing it closer. The philosopher Simon Critchley: 'Humour views the world awry, bringing us back to the everyday by estranging us from it.'[58] Such detachment encourages understanding and hence empathy. We see not caricatures to despise and condemn but, as though for the first time, people we recognise in the grip of ridiculous delusions and desires. It is like seeing familiar but profoundly unattractive people having their clothes ripped off while remaining blithely unaware of their nakedness and behaving as though still certain of being thought wonderful. *Oh God, cover your shame. No, no, please don't say another word. Don't incriminate yourself any further. Go and hide in a closet.*

This comedy of recognition is painful, literally excruciatingly funny, because we know that these people are not inventions but all too real, and that there but for the grace of God ... Mixed in with laughter is the fear that we may be equally absurd. *Oh dear God, no.* But the pain and fear teach us to see the people around us through the eyes of the comedian and to understand that their absurdity is a consequence of petrifaction and blindness – an inability to see themselves from the outside and adapt accordingly. As Henri Bergson explained in his classic work *Laughter: an Essay on the Meaning of the Comic*,[59] the lesson of this kind of comedy is not an unassailable superiority over the figure of fun but a realisation of how easy it is to become such a figure. The danger is petrifaction itself, rather than any particular form of hardening. Petrifaction is death and adaptability is life. To adapt and learn, the organism must pay close attention to its environment and the comical character is one who 'slackens in the attention that is due to life'.

The spectacle of such recognisable figures of fun is a powerful incentive to stay awake and give life the attention it deserves. Then it becomes clear that our individual habits and social conventions are as arbitrary and ridiculous as the rites and behaviour of a primitive tribe. Simon Critchley: 'The comedian is the anthropologist of our humdrum everyday lives.'[60]

Writer and director Mike Leigh specialises in the agonising comedy of recognition, where winces and groans accompany the laughs. Leigh does not work top-down, from a story and script, but bottom-up, from situation and character. He selects particularly talented actors and, in the lengthy, gruelling development of his films, expects them to *become* the characters in the situation and create the interactions. The key to his success is fanatical attention to detail. Comedy is precision engineering and depends on absolute exactitude. (Bergson: 'Humour delights in concrete terms, technical details, definite facts.'[61]) Few other filmmakers take so much care to get absolutely every tiny detail exactly right. In a Leigh film the spouse does not ask if the partner would like a biscuit, but rather 'a Jaffa Cake or Garibaldi?' And the partner answers, with the eternally peevish dissatisfaction of the human creature, 'Have we no Penguins left?' If the spouse is working class, the biscuit packet itself will be offered – but if middle class, a floral-patterned biscuit tin.

The homes, clothes, hair and body language of the characters are so exactly right that we are groaning and laughing in recognition even before they speak. Exact impersonation is always funny because it reveals that a human being is nearly all mannerisms and habits that can be copied – the character impersonated has largely petrified into an automaton, as Bergson would put it. In Leigh's films we see people we know to be actors in surroundings we know to be sets, but the illusion of everyday life is so perfect that it reveals life to be a performance of bizarre rituals in bizarre costumes and bizarre settings, for instance tea with a biscuit tin of Jaffa Cakes and Garibaldis.

When the Leigh characters speak the comedy is even more painful, because they have no awareness of how their banal babble reveals a desperate need to be admired or liked or found sexually attractive – and they have as little understanding of others as they have of themselves, so that all the interactions, between relatives, social classes and genders, are fraught with incomprehension and difficulty. It is hard to decide which of his characters are more funny, the desperately garrulous or the desperately inarticulate. In a particularly memorable scene from one of Leigh's stage plays, *Smelling a Rat*, a young man and a young woman stand apart, looking away from each other, in painful silence. Eventually the young man, after much tortured concentration, finds something to say:

'Saw Keith Chegwin in W. H. Smith's yesterday.'

The girl does not appear to have heard but, after a time, suddenly replies, 'Oh yeah?', then appears to lose interest – but then once more, unexpectedly, rouses herself:

'What was he doeen then?'

The young man concentrates, with even more desperate intensity, and after a long time, with an expression of puzzlement, answers:

'Noffeen.'

With this kind of comedy the groans that accompany the laughter ensure that as we laugh we unconsciously change, becoming more adaptable, self-aware and alert. We understand that we can never afford to relax. Bergson: 'To remain in touch with things and men, to see nothing but what is existent and think nothing but what is consistent, demands a continuous effort of intellectual tension. This effort is common sense. And to remain sensible is, indeed, to remain at work.'[62]

Such comedy of recognition will rarely announce itself with nudges and winks, much less a laugh track. It may not even have jokes, in the sense of gags and stories with punchlines: such jokes are to comedy what plot is to fiction – an unnecessary contrivance. The problem is that jokes are back-to-front – the set-up has developed out of the punchline rather than the other way round.

So, a jokeless comedy of recognition may itself be difficult to recognise. One of the first US TV comedy series to dispense with a laugh track and gags and rely instead upon credible characters in credible situations was *The Larry Sanders Show* back in the 1990s. When I first watched this, following a tip from a reliable friend, I was mystified. Where was the comedy? It took several episodes for me to realise that the show was meant to be funny, and several more to realise that it was indeed *very* funny. Like dry wine, dry wit is an acquired taste.

In fact the modern meaning of the word 'wit' is evidence of how comedy has evolved. Until a few centuries ago 'wit' meant 'intellect' and the word only gradually assumed its current meaning – clever verbal humour – while losing the old one, though this survives in the compound adjective 'quick-witted' and my mother was not referring to humour when she screeched at me, 'Have ye no wit at all?' In French, the word '*esprit*' has undergone a similar transformation, though it retains its original meaning and now translates as both intellect and wit. So humour, at least in some of its forms, has become steadily more intelligent and sophisticated, and the evolutionary high point so far is probably the *New Yorker* cartoon where the humour is often so rarified that many are unable to see it as humour, much less laugh.

Similarly, the style of realistic comic writing is often a deadpan drollery that is easily missed by those accustomed to broad humour, broadly signalled and meant to be broadly rewarded with belly laughs. But it is a mistake to measure the success of humour only by the volume of the laughter. As the most sophisticated comedy has no jokes, so the most sophisticated amusement has no laughs – or, rather, a wry twisted grin instead of an uproarious guffaw. In his essay on comedy, George Meredith relishes a 'slim feasting smile' that is 'the sunlight of the mind, mental richness rather than noisy enormity'.[63] There is also the ruse of entirely secret amusement where there is no outward manifestation other than an ironic gleam in the eye, very useful in long boring meetings.

A favourite deadpan trick of writers is to begin a sentence seriously, even solemnly, lulling the reader, and then deliver a wicked sting in the tail. Alice Munro, describing a sophisticated newsreader on a small-town radio station: 'Mr Chamberlain had to read commercials too, and he did it with ripe concern, recommending Vick's Nose Drops from Cross's Drugstore, Sunday dinner at the Brunswick Hotel, and Lee Wickert and Sons for dead-livestock removal.'[64]

It is easy to miss such wit because Munro is considered to be a serious writer, which she certainly is, but the best drollery is often embedded in serious works, and indeed in writers believed to be forbiddingly serious – for instance George Eliot, Franz Kafka and William Faulkner. Anyone deterred by reputations for heaviness should try Squire Cass's New Year's Eve party in *Silas Marner*, K's attempt to sneak out of his office unnoticed in *The Trial*, and the bootlegger's funeral in *Sanctuary*, one of the funniest scenes I have ever read in one of the grimmest books I have ever read.

David Foster Wallace has written perceptively about the difficulty of getting contemporary college students to appreciate that Kafka is funny.[65] The problem is that Kafka's humour does not consist of jokes, wisecracks, slapstick or lampoon: 'Kafka's stories are *not* fundamentally jokes'. And there is an even greater problem with the empathy: 'Perhaps most alien of all, Kafka's authority figures are never just hollow buffoons to be ridiculed, but are always absurd and scary and sad all at once.'

There may be similar problems with Joyce and Proust, beginning with the perception that their books are dauntingly difficult and obscure. And don't the two men themselves look dauntingly solemn and austere? But many of the images of the two are from their mature years, by which time they had affected the dignity of great writers and were depressed by personal problems and poor health. Joyce in later life was known as the 'Melancholy Jesus' and, on his increasingly rare appearances during daylight, Proust looked like the man Jesus brought back from the grave – Lazarus. Certainly neither man appeared to be a barrel of laughs.

But in his earlier years, when he was teaching English in Trieste, Joyce finished his lessons with a sing-along at the piano of one of his own comic songs, followed by a contest to see who could best match the high kick of the prima ballerina at Covent Garden. Joyce, thin and loose-jointed, usually won. Finally, he would slide down the banisters with his pupils behind him (a practice taken an extremely dim view of by mothers of young women who usually cancelled the lessons if they happened to see how they ended). And in the evening Joyce would get drunk, entertain his drinking companions with his legendary spider dance, then bring them home and push them round the apartment block in his son's baby chair, shrieking with laughter (on these occasions it was the neighbours who were outraged). As Joyce's biographer Richard Ellmann puts it, 'No one could laugh more wholeheartedly or more infectiously'.

But perhaps Proust could have matched Joyce. In his youth Proust was famous not for his writing but his *fou rire*, a mad laughter so apparently unjustified, excessive and prolonged that his friends often wondered if he really was insane. And it was not Proust who sought society but society that sought him, because he was known to be one of the two funniest people in Paris (the other was Proust's friend, the poet Anna de Noailles). Both Joyce and Proust were hilarious in company but eventually realised that, rather than expending their comic talent on social occasions, it would be wiser to channel it into their work.

A good place to start is Joyce's story 'Grace', a short masterpiece of recognition comedy, where every setting, every character, every line of dialogue and every detail is achingly true to life and also achingly absurd. The theme of the story is religion and the main joke is that all the characters, slackening badly in the attention due to life, fondly believe themselves to be religious while revealing, entirely unconsciously, that they are worldly through and through.

The central character is Tom Kernan, a tea merchant who goes on one of his regular benders, gets blind drunk and falls down stairs in a bar, biting off a piece of his tongue in the fall. A friend takes him home, other friends come to visit and it is decided that the solution is for Kernan to go on a retreat conducted by the sympathetic Father Purdon.

The characters' views on religion are revealed in a long discussion in Tom Kernan's bedroom, where it becomes clear that they admire Catholicism for what they believe to be its intellectual superiority, and they themselves compete to demonstrate such distinction. They praise the Jesuits for being men of discrimination who 'cater to the upper classes' and Pope Leo XIII for being 'a great scholar and a poet' who also keeps track of technology – one of his dazzling Latin odes is on the invention of the photograph.

Several other comic strands are woven into the story – for instance on drinking and drink. Throughout this meeting to redeem Kernan the drunkard, the participants are themselves drinking: 'The light music of whiskey falling into glasses made an agreeable interlude.' In a particularly sly touch, the priest conducting the retreat is identified by one of the characters as having a 'rather red face' and when he mounts the pulpit is described by Joyce as having 'a massive red face'.

Another strand is the comedy of social status. The gentlemen are all lower-middle class but acutely aware of their precise social ranking within this class and bitterly resentful of any failure to acknowledge this properly. And the 'drink' and 'class' strands come together when the manager of the bar and a policeman inspect the scene of Kernan's fall: 'They agreed that the gentleman must have missed his footing.' It's that 'gentleman' that makes the sentence exquisitely droll. Only riff-raff get blind drunk and fall down stairs. A gentleman 'misses his footing'.

Then there is Mrs Kernan, disappointed, embittered, acid-tongued and savagely practical. 'But that she did not wish to seem bloody-minded, she would have told the gentlemen that Mr Kernan's tongue would not suffer by being shortened.' This woman's religion is based not on snobbery but expediency. 'She believed steadily in the Sacred Heart as the most generally useful of all Catholic devotions and approved of the sacraments. Her faith was bounded by her kitchen, but, if she was put to it, she could believe also in the banshee and in the Holy Ghost.'

The ending to 'Grace' is also wickedly strong. Father Purdon informs the congregation that, contrary to the popular misapprehension, Jesus Christ was profoundly sympathetic to businessmen. So he, Father Purdon, conscious of addressing businessmen, intends to speak to them in a business-like way. 'If he might use the metaphor, he said, he was their spiritual accountant.'

Anyone seeking further divine *Grace* should try J. F. Powers's stories and novels about American priests. In these, as in Joyce, there is no exaggeration and the comedy is based on plausible everyday detail. In fact Father Urban, hero of Powers's novel *Morte D'Urban*, is a mid-twentieth-century American version of Father Purdon. Even their names sound similar (a conscious or unconscious homage?), though Urban also suggests urbane. In *Morte D'Urban* this entirely urban and urbane priest falls foul of his superiors and is exiled to service in a dismal retreat house far out in the sticks. Here he is dismayed by the uncouth priest in charge and the predominance of immigrant names in the guest book of retreatants – impossible to raise the tone of such a benighted place. Yet as Father Urban looks out in despair at the desolate landscape surrounding the house, the Holy Spirit descends and inspires him with a vision – *build a golf course.*

So, as Joyce put it in *Finnegans Wake*, 'teems of times and happy returns. The same anew'. Father Purdon rides again in the American Midwest.

Meanwhile, back in high-society *À la recherche*, the best laughs are in the scenes involving Mme Verdurin and her 'faithful', her 'little clan'. This is a middle-class woman with money who has set up her own salon of the 'faithful' in opposition to those of the aristocrats – and the world of the 'little clan' is riddled with superbly comical contradictions. The Verdurins and their circle believe themselves to be indifferent to the aristocratic opposition but are obsessed by it, believe themselves to be deeply cultured but are totally philistine, believe themselves to be hysterically funny but are totally humourless, and believe themselves to be free and easy whereas Mme Verdurin rules over them with the tyrannical vigilance and punitiveness of a Spanish Inquisitor.

The highest comedy is in the Verdurins' view of themselves as carefree, fun-loving gypsies. As M. Verdurin puts it: 'We're all friends here. Liberty Hall, you know.' So the faithful are never actually invited to dinner but expected to turn up as though on a casual impulse, and evening dress is forbidden because that would make the 'good pals' look like the formal 'boring people' of the fashionable salons. But when the faithful threaten to defect, the response is not so free and easy. '"You don't suppose she'll die, your mother," exclaimed Mme Verdurin bitterly, "if you don't have dinner with her on New Year's Day, like people in the *provinces.*"'

And this pretence of being carefree is maintained by 'a feigned but continuous hilarity'. On one occasion the hilarity is so extreme that Mme Verdurin dislocates her jaw. This does not rule out further hilarity but makes the registering of it more cautious. 'Since the accident to her jaw, she had abandoned the effort involved in whole-hearted laughter, and had substituted a kind of symbolical dumb-show which signified, without endangering or fatiguing her in any way, that she was "splitting her sides".'

Proust really loved this appalling woman – and so do his readers. I swoon with pleasure at every appearance of the little clan and, thankfully, they turn up all through *À la recherche*. The most lasting image is of Mme Verdurin presiding, like some grotesque monarch, over her subjects. 'So, stupefied with the gaiety of the "faithful", drunk with good fellowship, scandal and asseveration, Mme Verdurin, perched on her high seat like a cage-bird whose biscuit has been steeped in mulled wine, would sit aloft and sob with affability.'

The lesson here is that the humour of the little clan, facetiousness, differs from comedy not in degree but in kind. Facetiousness is not a milder form of comedy but its opposite. Facetiousness conceals and comedy reveals; facetiousness upholds and comedy subverts; facetiousness conforms and comedy rebels. Facetiousness is not comedy but pre-comedy, a survival from the origins of laughter (as distinct from comedy) in the tickling and grooming rituals of chimpanzees. The anthropologist Robin Dunbar believes that in human evolution social laughter preceded language development and was 'a form of chorusing, a kind of communal singing without the words'. His theory is that 'this kind of social laughter came on stream, built up out of more conventional chimpanzee-like laughing, to supplement grooming as a bonding mechanism'.[66] The human laughter of superiority came later and developed out of the mirthless social laughter, or perhaps even separately from it. The two ways of laughing, the humorous and the humourless, are even physiologically distinct and use different facial muscles. Mirth at something funny is known as Duchenne laughter, after the French doctor Guillaume Duchenne who first identified the difference in his patients, and the mirthless alternative is non-Duchenne laughter.

Facetiousness, an advanced form of social laughter, is still used as a means of mutual reassurance and bonding by groups of the like-minded such as work forces and religious communities: it would be hard to decide which is more awful – the humour of colleagues or the humour of clerics. Joyce has a great example of priests' humour in *Ulysses* when Father John Conmee S. J. asks a young boy to post a letter for him: 'But mind you don't post yourself into the box, little man.' Proust more than matches this with doctors' humour. The physician Dr Cottard is fond of putting heart and liver patients on a milk diet, recommending in particular broth *au lait*, and adding, as much for the benefit of the accompanying medical students as the patient: 'You'll enjoy that, since Spain is all the rage just now; *olé, olé*!'

Facetiousness also remains the favourite bonding agent of middle-class ladies. I had aunts who presided over social gatherings in exactly the same way as Mme Verdurin, shrieking with feigned insouciance and hilarity, publicly proclaiming their rejection of convention while privately imposing it with ferocious zeal. And in Alice Munro's *Lives of Girls and Women* the narrator has aunts like this, who constantly joke and laugh but are outraged at any breach of propriety. Like Mme Verdurin, these women are envious and spiteful, with a 'nimble malice that danced under their courtesies'. Similarly, in *Ulysses* the relentlessly facetious Buck Mulligan uses the pretence of humour only as a way of 'honeying malice'.

Of course Proust is funny about many things other than the antics of the little clan (the antics in brothels, for instance – see Chapter 12) but the comedy is always based on accurate reporting and given a deadpan delivery in fastidious language (a technique he praises in his fictional author, Bergotte, whose jokes are 'made even more comical by the writer's solemn and magnificent prose'). And Proust was a master of the droll, apparently innocuous sentence. In the following example, note how the initial, rather pompous subordinate clause deceives the reader and sharpens the final sting: 'He had, what may be sufficient to constitute a rare and delicate whole, a fair, silky beard, good features, a nasal voice, bad breath and a glass eye.'

About halfway through *Ulysses* Joyce adds to droll reporting a new comic exuberance which makes banality funny by expressing it in various kinds of incongruous language. The episode in Barney Kiernan's bar introduces the device of bathos, where an elevated passage is suddenly undercut by low-down demotic. Leopold Bloom is under attack from an aggressive Irish nationalist who emphasises his contempt by 'spitting a Red Bank oyster out of him right in the corner'. The man then needs a handkerchief and is offered one embroidered with various Irish scenes.

> The scenes depicted on the emunctory field, showing our ancient duns and raths and cromlechs and grianauns and seats of learning and maledictive stones are as wonderfully beautiful and the pigments as delicate as when the Sligo illuminators gave free rein to their artistic fantasy long long ago in the time of the Barmecides, Glendalough, the lovely lakes of Killarney, the ruins of Clonmacnois, Cong Abbey, Glen Inagh and the Twelve Pins ... all these moving scenes are still there for us today rendered more beautiful still by the waters of sorrow which have passed over them and by the rich incrustations of time.
>
> Shove us over the drink, says I. Which is which?
>
> That's mine, says Joe, as the devil said to the dead policeman.

This trick was used extensively by both Samuel Beckett and Flann O'Brien[67] – but in *Ulysses* Joyce moved on to other forms of linguistic comedy. Bloom's encounter with the young girl, Gerty MacDowell, is in the style of romantic novels; the encounter with medical students in a lying-in hospital represents birth by a succession of English literary styles; the brothel chapter has two whores, Biddy the Clap and Cunty Kate, who converse in the language of highborn ladies in the era of *amour courtois* and, when Bloom brings the drunk Stephen Dedalus home with him, their banal conversation over cocoa is turned into high comedy by being rendered in the pedantic, long-winded question-and-answer of catechism.

These increasingly manic linguistic high jinks anticipate the mad comedy of *Finnegans Wake*. The most well-known passage in the *Wake* is the great lament for mortality at the end of the book. This fully deserves its fame – but is entirely uncharacteristic. Among its many other unique features, the *Wake* is one of the most zestful books in literature. In keeping with its ambition to include all of history, its comedy often returns to the simplest forms, with exchanges on the meaning of history and life between duos who sound like characters in children's books – Mutt and Jute, Chuff and Glug, the Mookse and the Gripes, the Ondt and the Gracehoper – and children's games are celebrated all through the book. So Joyce had a strange back-to-front career, beginning with aged-master austerity and ending in childlike glee. The *Wake* presents as absurd the self-importance of the human creature and, of course, the self-importance of the author himself – a 'semidemented zany' making ink from his own faeces and urine to write 'puffedly offal tosh'. In this final work Joyce moved beyond the comedy of recognition to a kind of cosmic farce, an ultimate philosophical appreciation of absurdity that returns to the origins of comedy in slapstick. As he said to Jacques Mercanton near the end of his life: 'I am only an Irish clown, a great joker at the universe.'

5

Consecrating the Commonplace: The Spiritual Vision

Father O'Flaherty taught Irish, or, to be more precise, spoke Irish with the country boys who already knew the language and insulted, cuffed and punched the contemptible town corner-boys who knew only English. If a cornerboy made an especially grotesque mistake, as often happened, Flah took the soft flesh of the boy's cheek between his finger and thumb, violently shook the boy's head till he gurgled, roared in disgust, 'Are ye goin' to give us yer breakfast, ye slabber?' and slammed the head into the partition (the classroom was part of a prefabricated hut divided by wooden partitions). He seemed to be constantly seething with rage, though now and then his troubled spirit found a kind of peace. On these occasions he remained jovially at the front of the classroom and settled for the milder punishment of six from a leather strap.

'Your tiny hand is frozen,' he would cry, with a demented laugh, opening out the numb, reluctant, curled-up fingers, 'but don't worry . . .' And raising the strap high with a joyous shout, '*Ah'll warm it up for ye.*'

Flah was extreme but his fellow Irish priests, while less violent, were just as unedifying. These apostles of Christ were materialistic instead of spiritual, proud instead of humble, mean instead of generous, contemptuous instead of compassionate, angry instead of loving, intolerant instead of accepting, punitive instead of forgiving – and their religion seemed to me a combination of absurd doctrines and meaningless observances enforced by a vindictive authoritarianism. In fact Irish Catholicism seemed to be obsessed almost exclusively with the imposition and maintenance of authority.[68] The only correspondence with the New Testament was the striking similarity of priests and senior laity to Pharisees.

So, like many another, I rejected all religion because of contempt and disgust for one debased, aberrant version. For decades I was unable to tolerate anything to do with religion or religions. But the need for some sort of meaning, the God-shaped hole, would not go away and led me to dabble in philosophy, though surreptitiously (philosophy is equally anathema to the religious and irreligious Irish – both reject it as pretentious crap). And, like my mother, though much less awesome and scary, God kept turning up uninvited in my writing, albeit as a comic figure. I was constantly poking fun at a being I did not believe existed. This struck me as ludicrous. How could religious feelings and symbols persist without a belief in religion?

As so often, the heart of the problem is a misconception. What has come to be accepted as timeless religion is in fact only a recent development, so that many of those who reject religion are mistaking the new for the eternal. This is not surprising. All believers, religious or secular, like to give the impression that their belief system dates back to the palaeolithic age, whereas in most cases it is a fairly new invention or distortion.

The standard Western view is that religion means belief in a single personalised supreme being who created the universe from nothingness, supervises it constantly and could intervene if need be, and gave humankind sacred books expounding a set of doctrines that the faithful are obliged to accept. But in fact much, perhaps even most, religion is none of these things.

For a start, in pre-modern and Eastern religions the absolute was not *a* being but being itself. As the religious historian Karen Armstrong explains, 'The ultimate reality was not a Supreme Being – an idea that was quite alien to the religious sensibility of antiquity; it was an all-encompassing, wholly transcendent reality that lay beyond neat doctrinal formulations'.[69] The Vedic tradition in India expressed this in the concept of Brahman, being itself, but added crucially that the human psyche, Atman, was part of this transcendent being. Brahman *was* Atman and Atman *was* Brahman. The sacred self could merge with the transcendent reality. In the Chinese Taoist tradition the equivalent of Brahman was Tao, all of reality. For Brahmanism and Taoism, as for Buddhism, there was no question of a single supreme being, a God.

And there was no question of abstract doctrine in the modern sense. Religion was concerned not with ideas but practice, and the most common form of practice was spiritual exercises for achieving distance from everyday life and control of the ego and its raging demands. Only hard-earned detachment and humility made it possible to experience oneness with the transcendent reality.

Even in the original monotheist religion, Judaism, the concepts of God and divine creation that now seem so fundamental were slow to develop. The first chapter of Genesis was added *after* many of the other early biblical narratives, and unequivocal monotheism did not emerge until Second Isaiah. And as Armstrong explains, even the meaning of the word 'belief' was different. Up to the seventeenth century, to believe meant not to accept a creed but to commit to a practice, a way of living. Religion was process.

Most of the aspects of religion that many now find repugnant were late developments in the Judeo-Christian tradition. It was several centuries after Christ before doctrines were formulated. The idea that God created the world out of nothing, now considered fundamental to Christianity, emerged only in the fourth century CE and, as Armstrong puts it, 'Creation *ex nihilo* tore the universe away from God. The physical world could not tell us anything about the divine, because it had not emanated naturally from God'. The doctrine of the Trinity was also developed in the fourth century by Basil, Bishop of Caesarea. In the fifth century, Augustine of Hippo expounded the doctrine of original sin based on an entirely novel interpretation of Genesis claiming that Adam's sin had condemned the entire human race to eternal damnation (Armstrong remarks dryly, 'one of his less positive contributions to Western theology'). And in the twelfth century Anselm of Canterbury decided that God must have become man in order to atone for Adam's sin. In the thirteenth century Thomas Aquinas attempted to prove the existence of God, which no one before had ever thought necessary or possible, and produced the famous five proofs that, even as a boy, I found laughably inadequate. Aquinas's proofs, however, opened the door to all manner of abstruse theology.

But it was not until the nineteenth century that the bible stories were interpreted as literal truth. This was a Protestant idea. Not to be outdone, the Catholic Church responded with the doctrine of papal infallibility – the source of its obsession with authority. These two ideas, intended to bolster the Christian faith, have probably done more to discredit religion than anything since human sacrifice.

But the nineteenth century also produced alternatives to religious extremism. Wordsworth's poetry expounded a pantheistic spirituality remarkably similar to the Brahman/Atman concept, a profound awareness of a transcendent presence in nature that could also dwell in the individual:

> . . . a sense sublime
> Of something far more deeply interfused,
> Whose dwelling is the light of setting suns,
> And the round ocean, and the living air,
> And the blue sky, and in the mind of man:
> A motion and a spirit, that impels
> All thinking things, all objects of all thought,
> And rolls through all things.[70]

In philosophy the American thinker Ralph Waldo Emerson believed in a divinity that was not a person but immanent in the universe. And Emerson's compatriot, William James, insisted (in his classic work *The Varieties of Religious Experience*) that religion is a matter not of institutions and dogmas but of the individual's relation to the divine, which is 'only such a primal reality as the individual feels impelled to respond to solemnly'.[71] For Hegel this primal reality was not God, or indeed a being of any kind, but 'the inner being of the world, that which essentially is'.[72]

At the end of this century came the extraordinary generation of Joyce and Proust that included Einstein in science, Wittgenstein in philosophy, Picasso in art, Bartok in music, Kafka in fiction and Rilke in poetry. None of these believed in orthodox religion but all retained an essentially religious attitude to life. They rejected the idea of a transcendent divinity but retained a transcendent sense of the divine. Even physicists and logicians could be spiritual. Einstein for instance: 'The most beautiful emotion we can experience is the mystical. It is the sower of all true art and science. He to whom this emotion is a stranger . . . is as good as dead. To know that what is impenetrable to us really exists, manifesting itself to us as the highest wisdom and the most radiant beauty, which our dull faculties can comprehend only in their most primitive forms – this knowledge, this feeling is at the centre of all true religiousness. In this sense, and in this sense only, I belong to the ranks of devoutly religious men.'[73]

The scientist sounds like a Vedic sage – and indeed Einstein's friend and fellow physicist Erwin Schrödinger, the discoverer of quantum mechanics, actually embraced the Vedic beliefs, claiming that the most beautiful equation was not '$E = mc^2$' but 'Brahman = Atman'. In fact most of the major physicists of the twentieth century developed mystical views and expressed these in writing.[74]

And the philosopher Ludwig Wittgenstein's *Tractatus Logico-Philosophicus*,[75] a work bristling with the symbols of mathematical logic, suddenly veered off at the end into the mysticism of the unknowable: 'There is indeed much beyond the power of words to express. This *makes itself manifest*; this is the mystical.' For Wittgenstein mysticism was a response to the old question, Why is there something rather than nothing? Or, as he put it, 'Mysticism wonders not *how* the world is but *that* the world is'. He, too, believed in a transcendent but ineffable reality, 'wonderful beyond words', was 'disgusted' by the idea of God as a supreme being and found the language of religion useful in a merely symbolic way. Like the pre-modern religious practitioners, Wittgenstein believed that transcendent reality could be experienced only after a suppression of the ego in humility, a bowing down 'in humble resignation to the dust'.

Similarly, Heidegger rejected a personal God and believed that the ultimate reality was not *a* being but 'being'. And, again like the pre-moderns, he believed that the way to get in touch with 'being' and bring about 'the return of the holy', was through spiritual exercises – meditative thinking practised constantly over a long period.

In this remarkable generation even theologians rejected the concept of God as a supreme being. Paul Tillich, a German professor of theology, denounced this traditional attitude as 'idolatry' and spoke instead of 'the ground of being' and 'the power of being'.[76]

Never *a* being, always 'being' – Brahman.

Rilke too, attracted to Eastern religion, celebrated something like Brahman in these beautiful lines:

> Strength plays such a marvellous game –
> it moves through the things of the world like a servant,
> groping out in roots, tapering in trunks,
> and in the treetops like a rising from the dead.[77]

In *Finnegans Wake* – with its mythopoeic desire to encompass the history of the world, and its characters who merge into each other and with the landscape – Joyce made a mad attempt to capture in a book the transcendent unity: Brahman. And though Joyce vehemently rejected Catholicism, he filled his books with religious images and language and described his literary vocation in religious terms. In *A Portrait of the Artist as a Young Man* Stephen Dedalus wishes to become 'a priest of eternal imagination, transmuting the daily bread of experience into the radiant body of eternal life'. In *Ulysses* Joyce also shows the hankering of the irreligious for religion by having Bloom, who is Jewish, feel the need to go into a Catholic Church during Mass: 'The cold smell of sacred stone called him.' But Bloom makes it clear that he would prefer the more relaxed and tolerant Eastern religions that value enlightenment rather than suffering. 'Buddha their god lying on his side in the museum taking it easy with hand under cheek. Jossticks burning. Not like Ecce Homo. Crown of thorns and cross.' Even so, Bloom can see that the rite of communion answers a deep need. 'There's a big idea behind it, kind of kingdom of God is within you feel.' And, down to earth as always, he can also see the element of hieratic showmanship in the rite. 'The priest was rinsing out the chalice: then he tossed off the dregs smartly. Wine. Makes it more aristocratic than for example if he drank what they are used to Guinness's porter or some temperance beverage Wheatley's Dublin hop bitters or Cantrell and Cochrane's ginger ale (aromatic).'

As for Proust, he wrote in a letter to a friend, 'I have no religion . . . on the other hand a religious preoccupation has never been absent for a single day from my life'. And in another letter, 'Yet the more one is religious the less one dares to move towards certainty', an Eastern attitude reminiscent of Buddha's rejection of metaphysics and doctrine. And the idea of a spirit immanent in all things permeates *À la recherche*.

But this unorthodox spirituality was rejected by the next generation and the second half of the twentieth century brought positivist philosophy that rejected values, reductionist science that rejected mystery and postmodern literature that rejected meaning. All that remained was materialism – but a materialistic world without values, meaning or mystery is a frightening place and fear soon begets anger and anger soon recruits righteousness. So was born fundamentalism, the monstrous progeny of the postmodern years. And fundamentalism cunningly presented itself as a return to authentic tradition when, in each case, Christian, Jewish and Islamic, it was an entirely new development that denied the tradition it claimed to support. The ultra-orthodox were in fact the heretics.

These movements also cunningly substituted 'respect' for 'tolerance' in their demands. Tolerance may indeed be demanded, but respect must be earned. Yet the belligerent demand for respect has often been fearfully granted and the false claim to represent traditional religion has been widely accepted. As a consequence, many repelled by fundamentalism have rejected all religion.

I was one of the rejecters, though always uneasy about using the term atheist, which seemed too pretentious, aggressive and materialistic. But how to retain something unmaterialistic? I was even more uneasy about terms such as spiritual, mystical, sacred, divine.

But everything changes; what is banished returns. The aridity of postmodern culture and the empty distractions of materialism could never be fulfilling, so unorthodox spirituality is back once again.

Many contemporary scientists reject reductionism – the belief that everything can be reduced to elementary particles and fundamental laws – and accept that the cosmos and matter may ultimately be unknowable. This is hardly surprising given the extreme weirdness emerging at both ends of the scale, with cosmologists and particle physicists vying to propose the more bizarre theories. Now cosmologists soberly claim that the universe as we know it is merely a hologram projected from outer space (so we do not really exist at all), and that it is possible to travel to the past or the future via wormholes, the EasyJet of Eternity; while, with equivalent sobriety, particle physicists speculate on a multitude of parallel universes and hidden worlds. Not only is life stranger than fiction but science is stranger than science fiction.

So science, once confident of knowing almost everything, is having to confess that it knows almost nothing. Science, until recently a monster of arrogance, is finally learning humility. Science, master of the universe and ruthless advocate of theological cleansing, may even become once more the servant of religion.

In fact it is now claiming, with a touch of the old arrogance, to be more religious than religion. The cosmologist Paul Davies: 'It may seem bizarre but, in my opinion, science offers a surer path to God than religion.'[78]

The molecular biologist Stuart A. Kaufman sees the God of Being, Brahman, in the phenomenon of emergence, the evolution of self-organisation in nature – a development that obeys the laws of science but exceeds them in the lawlessness of its radical creativity and inherent unpredictability. 'Is it, then, more amazing to think that an Abrahamic transcendent, omnipotent, omniscient God created everything around us, all that we participate in, in six days, or that it all arose with no transcendent Creator God, all on its own? I believe the latter is so stunning, so overwhelming, so worthy of awe, gratitude, and respect, that it is God enough for many of us. God, a fully natural God, is the very creativity in the universe.'[79] This is exactly Bergson's concept of a creative evolution continually inventing the new. God is process.

In fiction there has been David Foster Wallace, one of the most intelligent and gifted of the postmodern writers. His brilliance was recognised and rewarded early but in spite of this things began to go wrong and he experienced what he has described as 'a religious crisis',[80] when 'all my reasons for being alive and the stuff that I thought was important, just truly at a gut level weren't working any more'. This sounds like another example of the God-shaped hole and Wallace's way of filling the hole was revealed in a commencement address to the graduate students of Kenyon College,[81] when the arch-postmodernist made an eloquent plea for the pre-modernist concepts of truth, meaning and empathy.

The crucial thing is 'being conscious and aware enough to *choose* what you pay attention to and to *choose* how you construct meaning from experience'. As an example, Wallace invited his audience to consider 'an average adult day' involving long hours of work followed by a frustrating drive in heavy traffic to an overcrowded supermarket where an exhausted cashier tells you to 'Have a nice day', in a 'voice that is the absolute voice of *death*', and you push bags of groceries in a cart with 'one crazy wheel that pulls maddeningly to the left' out to a squalid, littered parking lot and then endure more heavy traffic before finally getting home to shove a foil carton in the microwave. The usual response, the default setting, is to regard as repulsive and stupid the people talking loudly on mobile phones at the check-out and selfishly trying to jump the traffic queues. But an alternative is to exercise empathy and realise that many of these annoying people may have 'much harder, more tedious or painful lives'. And this realisation may transfigure the dreariness. 'It will actually be within your power to experience a crowded, hot, slow, consumer-hell-type situation as not only meaningful, but sacred, on fire with the same force that lit the stars – compassion, love, the subsurface unity of all things.'

Here, the cool, postmodern ironist also sounds like a Vedic sage celebrating Oneness, which must have required courage, especially in front of an audience of college students. But Wallace eventually realised that the height of sophistication is naïvety, the height of knowingness is innocence and the coolest thing of all is a warm heart.

However it is necessary to add that in 2008 Wallace committed suicide by hanging himself in his garage. With hindsight, it is possible to detect an undercurrent of desperation beneath the brilliant surface of his work. He was trying to convince himself as much as his readers that ordinary life is not only meaningful but sacred. Yet it is just this personal need that makes his best work so compellingly sincere, and the fact that in the end he failed to make his own life worth living does not invalidate the affirmation. Instead it makes this message even more urgent. Any one of us could be engulfed at any moment by some horror, real or imagined, and the vulnerability of the human organism makes it imperative to appreciate the miracle of conscious existence as much and as long as is possible.

So we should rejoice that even in French philosophy, the very citadel of postmodernism, which gave the movement the revered masters who believed they had disposed once and for all of values and meaning, there has arisen an eloquent champion of values and meaning and what would once have seemed an absurd oxymoron – atheist spirituality. Refreshingly tolerant and relaxed, André Comte-Sponville does not make the militant-atheist mistake of trying to counter righteous anger with the opposite righteous anger. He even has a sense of humour (unheard of in a professor of philosophy at the Sorbonne) and begins his book on atheist spirituality with a joke. Two rabbis stay up late discussing God and come to the conclusion that He does not exist. But in the morning one is perplexed to find the other at ritual prayers and, when he questions this, receives the response, 'What does God have to do with it?'[82]

Even more refreshingly, Comte-Sponville admits that he himself would much prefer to believe in God – God is by far the most satisfactory solution to life. But the very fact that God so perfectly fulfils human needs is the most convincing reason for not believing in Him. As Nietzsche put it, 'Faith saves, therefore it lies.'[83] Besides, 'If the absolute is unknowable, what right do we have to believe that it is God?'[84] Kierkegaard understood that there is only one honest theological argument – to accept that belief in God is absurd and then believe in spite of this and make the famous leap of faith. But why leap into the God absurdity rather than another? And such an arbitrary belief scarcely justifies righteousness. I have always accepted the Church's view that atheism is a form of intellectual pride. But Comte-Sponville neatly turns the tables by arguing that the original righteous theism was the arrogant act – belief in God is a sin of pride and atheism is a form of humility.

So atheist spirituality is a terrific ruse that allows us to enjoy the benefits of religion without subscribing to any religion, without having to go to church and listen to sermons or, even more painful, laugh at clerical jokes.

But what is atheist spirituality? What, for that matter, is spirit? 'The spirit is not a substance. Rather, it is a function, a capacity, an act (of thinking, willing, imagining, empathising, making jokes).'[85] In other words, spirit is process. And the key capacity, the essence of spirituality, is to register the sheer improbability of the infinite, eternal universe and the finite human consciousness that briefly inhabits it – a combination simultaneously absurd and sublime. This is where the imaginative, comic and spiritual visions come together. In all three approaches, the essential first stage is a rising above or a stepping outside of everyday life, what the Greeks defined as *ekstasis*, the root of the word ecstasy. All three visions are ways of establishing meaning – life is more interesting, more comical and more mysterious than you think – and the search for meaning is itself a form of transcendence. And the three visions, though distinct, are really one vision – a true Holy Trinity. At the same time the vision is always rooted deep in ordinary life. So it involves being simultaneously inside and outside. This is the transcendence of willing immersion.

I never accepted the old doctrines but I loved the old religious vocabulary – Sacrament, Holy Trinity, Paradise, Heaven, Angel, Satan, God. Jousting could be defined as a religion using these symbolic terms. Its God would be a merry prankster who created the world to amuse himself. So life is the comic novel of God – and what a comic masterpiece it is. There is some justification in the Old Testament for this view of God. The Book of Job has a curious prologue where God happens to bump into Satan. 'And the Lord said unto Satan, Whence comest thou? Then Satan answered the Lord, and said, From going to and fro in the earth, and from walking up and down in it.' It is as though God says, 'Hey, you old Devil you, where have you been hiding yourself?' And Satan replies with a casual wave, 'Oh, you know . . . Here and there. Round and about . . .' They sound like two old politicians, obliged to appear implacable foes in public, but having more in common with each other than with the naïve electorate. Then they get to chatting and decide to torture Job to see how he responds – as a prank, to amuse themselves, just for kicks.

In the religion of Jousting the prophets are of course Joyce and Proust and their books the Holy Scriptures. But Marcel is John the Baptist and Leopold Bloom the Redeemer. *À la recherche* should be read as the confessions of a sinner, the manual on how not to live, and *Ulysses* as the New Testament, the revelation of a new way of life. (This is why Bloom is a concept rather than a character. There are no Messiahs in Dublin.)

The writings of the others in the Jousting tradition are also holy books. As John McGahern pointed out, 'Most good writing, and all great writing, has a spiritual quality that we can recognize but never quite define'.[86]

The Jousting faithful are required to read the holy books daily. As the medieval monks understood, reading is a spiritual exercise (*lectio divina*, they called it), a way of silencing the ego and stepping outside everyday life in order to see it more clearly and experience it more intensely.

This religion also has its own creation myth. When God was obliged to expel Adam and Eve from Paradise, He experienced the problem of the contemporary parent – that it is impossible to get rid of the children unless they are provided with alternative accommodation. For God this would mean the tedious chore of creating a new world. For a time He sighed and groaned at the tiresome bother of it all. Then the simple solution came to Him. Why go to the trouble of creating a new world when all that was necessary was to make Adam and Eve blind to the fact that they were in Paradise, to make them and their descendants eternally dissatisfied and desirous? This had the extra advantage of being not only expedient but funny. So He took away the gift of true vision and gave them instead vexation of spirit. They would never see the marvels surrounding them and always yearn for something else.

Not quite. A refinement suggested itself. He would have to tantalise with a hint. Now and then, but very rarely, one of Adam's descendants would be permitted to see truly and fully – but just for a moment.

Joyce and Proust both had such epiphanic moments of grace when, for no obvious reason, some entirely unexceptional scene is illuminated by radiant beauty, mystery and significance. At these times it seems as though the visible world is only the integument of an invisible spirit, a symbol representing something magical and sublime. Joyce defined the epiphany as 'a sudden spiritual manifestation', the 'revelation of the whatness of a thing', a moment in which 'the soul of the commonest object ... seems to us radiant'. Proust said something similar: '... suddenly a roof, a gleam of sunlight on a stone, the smell of a path would make me stop still, to enjoy the special pleasure that each of them gave me, and also because they appeared to be concealing, beyond what my eyes could see, something which they invited me to come and take but which despite all my efforts I never managed to discover'.

An epiphanic moment could be triggered by a single object but the full epiphany was the revelation of a scene. In *À la recherche* there are several such scenes – for instance when the narrator sees the steeples of a little village from a carriage, sees three trees from another carriage, and when he is overwhelmed by the vision of a hedge of hawthorn near the sea. The epiphany of the steeples is the most fully described – but the most intense pleasure is in the communion with an immanent spirit rather than the sight of the external scene:

> And presently their outlines and their sunlit surfaces, as though they had been a sort of rind, peeled away; something of what they had concealed from me became apparent; a thought came into my mind which had not existed for me a moment earlier, framing itself in words in my head; and the pleasure which the first sight of them had given me was so greatly enhanced that, overpowered by a sort of intoxication, I could no longer think of anything else ...

Proust's epiphanies are experiences of the rural environment. Joyce's epiphanies are urban and often not only feature people but people at their most fatuous. Joyce could find 'a sudden spiritual manifestation' either 'in the vulgarity of speech or of gesture', as in the epiphany based on a scene in his great-aunts' house:

> High up in the old, dark-windowed house: firelight in the narrow room; dusk outside. An old woman bustles about, making tea; she tells of the changes, her odd ways, and what the priest and the doctor said ... I hear her words in the distance. I wander among the coals, among the ways of adventure ... Christ! What is in the doorway? ... A skull – a monkey; a creature drawn hither to the fire, to the voices: a silly creature.
>
> – Is that Mary Ellen? –
>
> – No, Eliza, it's Jim. –
>
> – O ... O, goodnight, Jim –
>
> – D'ye want anything, Eliza? –
>
> – I thought it was Mary Ellen ... I thought you were Mary Ellen, Jim –

Joyce could also be exalted, or, as he put it, in typically religious terminology, 'eucharistic'. The most famous of these epiphanies is the scene near the end of *A Portrait of the Artist as a Young*

Man where Stephen Dedalus sees, standing in the sea, her skirts held up round her waist, a girl with thighs 'soft-hued as ivory', a bosom 'as a bird's, soft and slight' and a face 'touched with the wonder of mortal beauty'. Their eyes meet for a long moment ('Long, long she suffered his gaze') and then: 'Heavenly God! cried Stephen's soul, in an outburst of profane joy.' Even the expression of profanity invokes heaven and God. But, like Proust, Joyce is more excited by the joy than the scene that occasioned it: 'Her image had passed into his soul for ever and no word had broken the holy silence of his ecstasy. Her eyes had called to him and his soul had leaped at the call. To live, to err, to fall, to triumph, to recreate life out of life! A wild angel had appeared to him, the angel of mortal youth and beauty, an envoy from the fair courts of life, to throw open before him in an instant of ecstasy the gates of all the ways of error and glory. On and on and on and on!'

If there exists in literature a more sublime summons to life I would not like to read it or I might die of ecstasy myself.

The epiphanies of Joyce and Proust were mystical experiences, what could be defined as spontaneous mysticism to distinguish it from the willed variety practised by career mystics like the Muslim Sufis, Indian yogis and some Christian saints. But the spontaneous and willed experiences are essentially the same. In *The Varieties of Religious Experience* William James investigated a wide range of mystical states and found that, regardless of the culture and personality of the mystic or the circumstances and cause of the mystical experience, the resulting states had the same features in common. And a century after James the French writer Michel Hulin carried out a similar investigation and found exactly the same features.[87]

Though spiritual exercises may be used to induce the state, there is always a sensation of being possessed and overwhelmed by a superior power, and then the sensation of oneself having superior power – a kind of hyperconsciousness leading to illumination, revelation and insight, a feeling of the opposites and contradictions and multifariousness of the world becoming a sublime unity with which the self ecstatically merges. The self is obliterated in an absolute identification with the world, and past and future are obliterated in an absolute identification with the present, an escape from the tyranny of time into atemporality. It is not so much that time has stopped as that there is no more time, a sense that 'eternity is here'. In fact these experiences take up very little real time, at most half an hour but usually only a few minutes. They are also essentially ineffable, though many have tried to write descriptions. Yet despite their brevity and elusiveness, these experiences have a long-lasting effect, a permanent enrichment (note that 'for ever' in Joyce's epiphany).

Like spirituality, mysticism is usually associated with religion but it is essentially areligious, even antireligious, and orthodox religions have been right to suspect mystics of apostasy. The French Jesuit Henri-Marie Cardinal de Lubac: 'Mysticism eats away at myth, and eventually the mystic can do without it; he tosses it away like an empty shell.'[88] Mysticism is also associated with rejecting the world for the ecstasy of the individual soul – but though it requires detachment and solitude the mystical experience is ultimately a reconciliation of the self with the world.

The secular shortcut to mystical experience is taking drugs. Aldous Huxley has given an eloquent account of the effects of taking mescaline: 'I was seeing what Adam had seen on the morning of his creation – the miracle, moment by moment, of naked existence.'[89] The revelation was of 'a transience that was yet eternal life, a perpetual perishing that was at the same time pure Being, a bundle of minute, unique particulars in which, by some unspeakable and yet self-evident paradox, was to be seen the divine source of all existence'. Huxley's theory was that the brain and sensory system have learned to filter perception, shutting out most of it as irrelevant and admitting only what is familiar and of practical use (in the language of neurology the left hemisphere perception overrides that of the right). So most of the time we have only a greatly diminished awareness. But certain drugs and spiritual exercises reduce the effectiveness of the filter or establish a bypass (i.e. subdue LH or activate RH) and allow consciousness to be flooded by the glory and wonder of pure existence (though Huxley did not advocate habitual drug-taking, warning that long-term side effects outweigh short-term benefits). And other kinds of behaviour, such as long solitary walks or prolonged reading and rumination, can temporarily switch off the filters and permit heightened perception.

Huxley's experience differed in one interesting way from the mystical norm. He was a comic writer with a highly developed sense of the absurd, and the comical and spiritual visions were revealed as the same when he was taken out in Los Angeles under the influence of mescaline and laughed till tears ran down his cheeks at the absurdity of the huge American automobiles. (There was no shortage of absurdity in Los Angeles. Huxley once submitted a movie synopsis to Walt Disney and Walt predictably rejected it because he 'could only understand every third word'.[90])

As Huxley points out, an epiphany is intensely visual and so visual artists may be better able to capture the experience. Indeed, one of the distinguishing characteristics of visual artists is a weaker perception filter that makes them more receptive to their surroundings. Like many before and since, Huxley singles out Vermeer.

Vermeer's paintings are frozen epiphanies, ordinary, mostly domestic scenes somehow charged with mystery and resonance. Vermeer was the first artist to make mystery itself the theme and he invented the hugely influential idea of art as enigma, the image charged with a meaning that simultaneously demands and resists decipherment. How did he do it? One of the things that makes him stand out from his contemporaries is that the people in his paintings are enjoying a rich inner life and this makes them simultaneously worth knowing and impossible to know. Most of these people are women, always more mysterious than men, and they are mostly alone, absorbed and ruminant. Even in company they seem sequestered in thought. In *Woman Writing a Letter, with her Maid*, look at the enigmatic half-smile on the face of the serving girl as she turns away from her mistress to the window. This serene absorption conveys a beguiling sense of atemporality, of moments lifted outside time. Then there is the inscrutable presence of the interiors Vermeer's women inhabit, a resonant depth in which everyday objects, casually but uniquely disposed, relate to each other and the light. All this combines to invest the scenes with epiphanic enchantment – a heightened awareness of reality and unity, a feeling of assumption into eternity, a profound harmony of inner and outer, a loving union of Atman and Brahman.

It is no accident that both Joyce and Proust loved Vermeer (as did John Updike[91]). Joyce and Proust were even obsessed by the same painting, the *View of Delft.* A reproduction of this was the only artwork that Joyce permitted to share wall space with his family portraits. Proust described it as 'the most beautiful painting in the world', made one of his last outings to see it in an exhibition in Paris and in *À la recherche* has a character die for a glimpse of it.

As with writers, many painters have tried to capture the epiphanic experience but few have succeeded, possibly only one or two every hundred years or so. In the seventeenth century there was Vermeer, in the eighteenth Chardin (another favourite of Proust's), in the nineteenth Van Gogh and Vilhelm Hammershøi (very Vermeerish in his preference for domestic interiors with mysterious women) and in the twentieth Edward Hopper (who painted epiphanies of the urban world). A few photographers also have the rare gift of imbuing an ordinary scene with mysterious enchantment. Walker Evans, for instance, was the Vermeer of photography: 'It's as though there's a wonderful secret in a certain place – and I can capture it. Only I can do it at this moment, only this moment and only me.'[92] A twenty-first century contender is the English painter George Shaw who makes ordinary urban scenes mysterious in the manner of Edward Hopper (see Chapter 11).

Like their literary equivalents, artistic epiphanies lead back to life and the world and enable a deeper and richer appreciation of the everyday. They share the purpose of early religion – not to escape the profane world but to sacralise it in order to live in it with awe. As the religious historian Mircea Eliade said of this form of religious experience: 'The sacred reveals absolute reality'; 'the sacred is pre-eminently the *real*'; 'the religious man deeply desires *to be*, to participate in *reality*'. His description of the experience of sacred space is like a definition of an epiphany: 'where the sacred manifests itself in space, *the real unveils itself*, the world comes into existence'.[93]

As Joyce, Hopper, Walker Evans, George Shaw and many others have shown, it is possible even for the modern urban world to unveil itself and come into existence. A character in Foster Wallace's *The Pale King* has a sort of near-epiphany while watching daytime TV and it will be a great day for humanity when someone has a proper full-scale epiphany in a shopping mall and is sufficiently gifted with pen, brush or camera to sacralise malls for the rest of us. Alas, I am not likely to have such an experience. For me the mall will always induce the anguish and alienation of the exiled Psalmist. By the sweaters of Benetton I sat down and wept.

I am probably too old for epiphanies of any kind. Another

common feature, not mentioned by William James or Michel Hulin, is that these spontaneous experiences are largely a phenomenon of youth. Joyce and Proust had all their epiphanies as young men, when they were free of entanglements and obligations and could spend hours every day on solitary walks in the country or city. It is significant that George Shaw obsessively paints the scenes of his youth, though he now lives elsewhere, and that he confesses to being happiest when alone and to being a habitual daydreamer.[94] Like most chronic daydreamers, he is guilty about wasting time – but the daydreaming is surely the wellspring of his art, an opportunity to silence the fretting, practical left hemisphere and to free the visionary, spiritual right hemisphere.

The problem is that life usually requires the utilitarianism of the left hemisphere rather than the spirituality of the right, which falls into disuse and makes all forms of transcendence increasingly difficult. Even a great transcender like Wordsworth experienced this problem:

> ... the hiding places of my power
> Seem open; I approach, and then they close;
> I see by glimpses now; when age comes on,
> May scarcely see at all.[95]

The heart grows heavy and the mind grows dull. There is an overwhelming temptation to restrict activity to comforting habit, and thought to brooding on the past. It is ever more difficult to remain alert, ever more difficult to ascend. The right hemisphere atrophies, so writers lose the gift of imparting imaginative life, comedians cease to be funny and everyone loses the capacity for experiencing epiphanies.

At least there is the enduring memory of epiphanies for those fortunate enough to have experienced them and the vicarious pleasure of sharing the epiphanies of others. We may not be overwhelmed by ecstasy but there are still enormous benefits in becoming more aware and therefore more grateful. Huxley: 'Our goal is to discover that we have always been where we ought to be.'[96]

It is thirty years since my last epiphany. At the time it seemed to come out of the blue but I can see now that the circumstances were entirely propitious. I was on jury service and so taken out of the work routine (and the sense of doing a citizen's duty freed me from guilt at the thought of colleagues burdened with my teaching). And for most of the service period I was not required for a jury but free to sit in the jury room drinking black coffee (my favourite consciousness-expanding drug) and reading long plotless novels (*lectio divina*). There was also a profoundly humbling experience. When a case finally came up, the jury had, incredibly, the exact experience played out in the *12 Angry Men* movie. Most of us were convinced that the defendant was indeed guilty of inflicting grievous bodily harm, but one insisted that, however overwhelming our certainty, the evidence was not conclusive. It was sad though chastening to discover that I was not heroic Henry Fonda but one of the eleven-strong lynch mob. In this case Henry Fonda was a milkman from Finchley.

The court building was off a shabby little high street, torpid and dim on an overcast day in October. But suddenly the street was illuminated, transfigured, a portal to infinite being. Everything became sublime – especially the little caff with its gauchely handwritten menu full of spelling errors, advertising 'egg's, sausage's and tomato's'. Those misplaced apostrophes tore at my heartstrings like orphan children, blessed like the first timid snowdrops of February, sparkled like a dusting of precious stones. I wanted to rush in and embrace the illiterate proprietor. To die of a heart attack from one of his fry-ups would surely be the ideal way to go to Heaven.

Almost as wonderful was a cramped, overcrowded newsagent with, outside, an ancient shackled bubblegum dispenser and a heavy rusting grill over the window, and inside a counter lined with trays of lurid, carcinogenic four-a-penny sweets and shelves packed with magazines bearing photographs of young women with astoundingly hypertrophied breasts. Then a bookmaker's surrounded by a surf of cigarette butts, a fish and chip shop and a heavily graffitied minicab office, VIP RADIO CARS. Behind the soiled windows of VIP were a weary, vexed black woman talking on the phone and several beefy drivers regarding me with jaded hope. *Sorry, my friends, but I have no desire to be transported anywhere else. I want to stay here forever, to cry out in ecstasy like the Psalmist, 'For a day in thy courts is worth more than a thousand elsewhere'.*

At the end of the high street was exactly what I needed now – a dingy estate agent's with, behind a single desk piled high with ring-binder files, a middle-aged woman in a heavy cardigan snuffling disconsolately into a tissue and leaning over a two-bar electric fire to expose the white roots at the parting of her badly dyed hair. I wanted to go in, tell her that I understood her disappointments and difficulties and then help pay to have her roots done by renting a one-bedroom flat above a launderette. This would need no mod cons and have no attractions but a rear view over a railway line and a front view over the high street. In the morning I would thrill to the pungent aromas of a fry-up and in the evening to those of fish and chips cooking in old and much-used animal fat, and all day I would write paean after paean in praise of the ordinary. The Wordsworth of fry-ups! The Whitman of fish and chips!

PART III

What We Say and What We Do

6

The Opera of Everyday Speech

When I began teaching forty years ago the most frightening revelation was not the ignorance of the pupils but the emptiness of the minds of the teachers as revealed in staffroom conversations of relentless and astoundingly absolute banality. How could supposedly educated people, many puffed up with self-importance at the superiority conferred by this education, talk such utter rubbish all day every day? I was a self-important prig myself and closed my ears to avoid contamination. Now I would love to hear again, in glorious uncut detail, one of those long leisurely exchanges on how Sainsbury's has gone to the dogs because the staff have no time for you these days and you can never get toilet rolls or eggs on a Monday. Now I understand that most conversation is not communication but meaningless noise, an aural comfort blanket intended to reassure, console and soothe – and the very meaninglessness of this noise should be a source of delight. With banal conversation the ruse is to enjoy its very banality.

According to the anthropologist Robin Dunbar,[97] idle chatter is a bonding ritual evolved from the mutual grooming of monkey tribes, a more sophisticated 'vocal grooming', 'a kind of grooming at a distance' (and this connection between grooming and chatting may explain why hairdressers are so garrulous). The contact itself is the message and the content is irrelevant. So as much as two thirds of conversation has no practical or intellectual function and is made up of bragging, reminiscence, gossip, whingeing, immensely detailed accounts of personal likes and dislikes, health problems, television viewing and the activities of relatives and, above all, word-by-word accounts of earlier exchanges ('I said to him ... and he said to me' – or, for younger talkers, 'So I goes ... and he's, like ...'). Even complaint, which appears to express dissatisfaction and rejection, is really an affirmation of solidarity. When studying workers in a bank the ethnographer John Weeks noticed that, while complaining was constant and universal, most workers did not expect or seek redress, and those who complained most often were also most likely to defend the bank from external criticism.[98] This applies to many other groups, from families up to inhabitants of towns and citizens of nations. If group members complain about the group it is perfectly acceptable, vocal grooming, but if outsiders attempt the same it is taken as an insult.

So most talk is just monkey grunts, not really meant to be listened to, much less recorded. But this talk, when attended to closely, turns out to be deeply strange. Joyce was one of the first writers to listen to how people really speak – and his great discovery was that the monkey grunts are sublimely absurd, bizarre, hilarious, and occasionally even virtuoso songs.

This fascination with ordinary speech began early. As Joyce says of Stephen Dedalus, 'his mind, which had from the first been only too submissive to the infant sense of wonder, was often hypnotised by the most commonplace conversation'.[99] Many of Joyce's youthful epiphanies were visions of the strangeness of everyday chatter. And in his first published prose book, *Dubliners*, the dialogue is already perfect.

Of course writers before Joyce had used lively dialogue –

Dickens and Twain for instance – but though they believed this to be authentic (Twain boasted of using seven different Southern dialects in *Huckleberry Finn*), it was always heightened for comic effect. Joyce was the first to record with scrupulous accuracy what people actually said – and in many cases this was as funny as anything in Dickens or Twain.

It is also the most economical way of sketching character. Even a tiny snatch of authentic dialogue can be enough to give a complete and instant sense of the speaker. *Ulysses* has the most concise portrait in literature, when a character reveals himself completely in two words: '*Thanky vous*'. This is Lenehan expressing gratitude for a cigarette and it reveals the ingratiating facetiousness of the sponger – but a sponger who, although currently down on his luck, wishes to make it clear that he is educated and familiar with foreign languages, in other words that he is and will always be a gentleman. The two words of joke French suffice – but Joyce, only human after all, cannot resist repeating the trick. Later in the same scene Lenehan says, in acknowledgement of another free cigarette, 'Muchibus thankibus'. This facetiousness makes me cringe with shame at the ignominy of the human race. But I love Lenehan as much as I love Mme Verdurin and her little clan – and Lenehan would make a perfect member of the faithful. I can't help going back to the Lenehanisms – it's like taking the cork out of a bottle of vomit to sniff it again. Another of his specialties is facetious transposition. 'Hush ... I hear feetstoops.' A final sniff of vomit: 'O for a fresh of breath air!'

Joyce catches so many of the oddities of speech. The excruciating euphemisms, for instance the alcoholic O'Madden Burke: 'Tis the hour, methinks, when the winejug, metaphorically speaking, is most grateful in Ye ancient hostelry.' The omissions and unfinished sentences. M'Coy meeting Bloom who is dressed in mourning for a funeral: 'Is there any ... no trouble I hope? I see you're . . .' The wishes blurted out as truths and then requiring confused qualification: 'My missus has just got an engagement. At least it's not settled yet.' The way husbands and wives rarely listen to each other. Bloom asks Molly if she would like the window open a little and she answers with, 'What time is the funeral?' The agonising exchanges where attempts at banter go wrong. In the story 'The Dead', Gabriel Conroy suggests 'gaily' to a servant girl, 'I suppose we'll be going to your wedding one of these fine days with your young man, eh?' But instead of replying in the same tone the girl answers bitterly, 'The men that is now is only all palaver and what they can get out of you.' The strange but meaningful noises that punctuate speech. Bloom, commiserating: 'Dth. Dth.' A scornfully dismissive drinker: 'Prrtwht!' An indifferent barman's smileyawnnod: 'Iiiiichaaaaaaach!' Molly Bloom, half asleep: 'Mn.'

Joyce makes even animals speak. Bloom's cat says good morning: 'Mkgnao!' But when this pleasant salutation does not immediately bring food the cat becomes angry: 'Mrkrgnao!' And when good-hearted Bloom puts down a saucer of milk: 'Gurrhr!'

Even the inanimate is given a voice. Horses' hoofs: 'Imperthn thnthnthn'. A train going by: 'frseeeeeeeefronnnng'. Crackling fireworks: 'Zrads and zrads, zrads, zrads, zrads'.

After *Ulysses* Joyce believed he could voice anyone or anything and in *Finnegans Wake* was ready for the ultimate challenge, the voice of God: 'bababadalgharaghtakamminarronnkonnbronntonnerronntuonnthunntrovarrhounawnskawntoohoohoordenenthurnuk!'

Much of Joyce's human dialogue is intended to reveal character or attitude or belief but in *Ulysses* he starts to enjoy dialogue for its own sake, for the sheer comic glory of it (though he never uses phonetic spelling to signal and exaggerate the comedy – the speech is funny enough on its own):

– I was down there for the Cork park races on Easter Monday, Ned Lambert said. Same old six and eightpence. Stopped with Dick Tivy.
– And how is Dick, the solid man?
– Nothing between himself and heaven, Ned Lambert answered.
– By the holy Paul! Mr Dedalus said in subdued wonder. Dick Tivy bald?

This sounds like Flann O'Brien because O'Brien made such dialogue one of the main features of his own writing, where the comedy is not in revelations of character through speech (O'Brien had little interest in character) but in the magnificent absurdity of the talk itself. O'Brien learned everything from Joyce but was frequently grudging about the master, though he did acknowledge Joyce's 'almost supernatural skill in conveying Dublin dialogue'[100] and singled out as an example a shout by a bystander at Bloom as he leaves a pub in a hurry, 'Eh, mister! Your fly is open, mister.' It was that second 'mister' that was the touch of genius.[101]

But any reader can find examples of Joyce's dialogue that go beyond being merely very good. For instance, 'Everything went off A1, he said. What?' In this line 'went off A1' is terrifically good but the final redundant 'What?' makes it sublime. What is the meaning of 'What?'? Or when a bad-tempered blind man is bumped by a passer-by and shouts, 'You're blinder nor I am, you bitch's bastard!' This time it's the 'nor' instead of 'than'. Or when Bantam Lyons asks to borrow Bloom's newspaper, 'Is that today's? Show us a minute.' That 'us' instead of 'me'.

These snatches of dialogue do not merely ring true, they *sing* true. What Joyce catches is the excessive, redundant element in speech, which is rarely content with communication or contact and frequently aspires not just to performance but virtuoso performance. The poet Robert Frost, who was fascinated by ordinary speech and attempted to emulate it in his poetry, suggested that spoken sentences often have a 'sentence-sound', something more than the mere words, and that these sentence-sounds are as real as the words. 'You may string words together without a sentence-sound to string them on just as you may tie clothes together by the sleeves and stretch them without a clothes line between them, but – it is bad for the clothes.'[102] Sentence-sounds are instantly recognisable ('You must be able to say Oh yes one knows how that goes') but hard to define. Frost falls back on examples – 'Never you say a thing like that to a man', 'I aint a going to hurt you so you needn't be scared', 'The thing for me to do is to get right out of here while I am able'.

The common quality in all these is a cadence, a rhythm, a melody – certainly a musical effect. A sentence-sound is a short song, a combination of rhythm and melody composed to fit into a single modulated outward breath[103] as the earliest pop songs were composed to fit the two-minute recording time. Many ordinary people are virtuoso composers and performers of sentence-sounds and so ordinary conversation is the people's opera, with the cast competing to sing their lines and yearning to burst into arias. It is essential for a writer of dialogue to be able to register these songs, to have an 'ear'. Frost: 'The most original writer only catches them fresh from talk, where they grow spontaneously.' And no one was better at such catching than Joyce. Sing along with the following:

'Only I'm an old man now I'd change his tune for him.'
'How are all in Cork's own town?'
'It ruined many a man the same horses.'
'I knocked against Bantam Lyons in there going to back a bloody horse someone gave him that hasn't an earthly.'
'I seen that particular party last evening.'
'I was told that by a, well, I won't say who.'

'As God is looking down on me this night if ever I laid a hand to them oysters.'
'If he doesn't conduct himself I'll wring his ear for him a yard long.'
'It's as limp as a boy of six's doing his pooly behind a cart.'
'He made a certain suggestion but I thought more of myself as poor as I am.'
'I let him larrup it into me for the fun of it.'
'Christ, wouldn't it make a Siamese cat laugh?'

In fact there is an intriguing theory that the earliest sound communication between humans was a kind of wordless singing known to anthropologists as 'musilanguage'. According to this theory, when social groups became too large for grooming, musilanguage developed as an alternative bonding technique – grooming at a distance. And eventually this singing evolved into language. Of course such a theory is impossible to prove but there is supporting evidence from several sources – the similarities between music and language suggest a connection; there is no culture without music; in all cultures poetry, based on rhythm, developed before prose; newborn babies respond to timbre, inflection, intonation and rhythm long before they can understand language and, in the Amazon jungle, there is a hunter-gatherer tribe, the Pirahã, who communicate entirely by song.[104] The theory is fully expounded in a book that sounds like a history of heavy-metal rock but is actually a serious work of anthropology, *Singing Neanderthals.*[105] There is surely an opportunity here for composers who find it difficult to write lyrics – and the cast of a Neanderthal opera or musical would of course have to be well built, skimpily dressed and indulge in lots of sex and violence.

And in another version of this theory, the American anthropologist Dean Falk has suggested that language developed from mothers singing to their babies in a form of wordless speech known as 'motherese', which comes naturally to mothers in all cultures and has the rhythm, intonation and pitch of song.[106]

So Joyce's finely tuned ear for speech may have been a consequence of his singing talent. He had a fine tenor voice and at one point considered becoming a professional singer. (Nora would often disconcert worshipful Joyce fans by telling them that 'Jim should have stuck to the music instead of bothering with the writing'.) Later in life Joyce became obsessed by the tenor John Sullivan and devoted much time and energy to promoting Sullivan's career. This was remarkable because Joyce rarely praised anyone and promoted only himself. Needless to say, his approach to publicity was original. Though short of money, he would take a prominent, expensive box at the Paris *Opéra* and shout loudly, '*Bravo Sullivan! Merde pour Lauri-Volpi.*' On one occasion he brought a performance of *Guillaume Tell* to a halt by leaning dramatically forward out of his box and ripping off his heavy dark glasses to cry out, 'Thank God for this miracle – after twenty years I can see the light.'

Composer contemporaries of Joyce were also listening to the music of speech. Leoš Janáček sat in cafés transcribing the melodies of the conversation around him directly onto music staff paper, noting that even a simple phrase like 'Good evening' could be sung in many different ways. When a student addressed this phrase to an esteemed professor it was expressed as a high note followed by three at a lower pitch but when the same greeting was offered to a waitress, the high note moved to the end to suggest coy familiarity. With full sentences, getting the exact tune of each would reveal an 'entire being in a photographic instant'[107] – and Janáček went on to compose naturalistic operas based on the melodies of everyday speech. But the lesson is that it is not necessary to go to an opera house – it is cheaper and more convenient to listen to opera in a café.

However, Flann O'Brien may have touched on something when he suggested that Joyce was supernatural with Dublin dialogue. Joyce's dialogue for his English characters was merely adequate. Human speech is so fantastically singular that, outside its specialist area, even the most finely tuned ear can get it wrong. When the Texas writer Terry Southern, another master of dialogue, was visiting Mississippi he attempted to ask directions in the vernacular, 'Whar the school?' only to be corrected, 'Reckon you mean, Whar the school *at*, don't you stranger?'[108]

It is not only national vernaculars that differ. Every region and sometimes even every town and district has its own richly peculiar speech and these are all constantly interacting and evolving. Demotic and the written language of which it is part are perfect examples of emergent phenomena, immensely complex ordered systems that are under no one's control but driven by a ceaseless creative energy, an *élan vital*, and are entirely unpredictable in their development. The language remains the same language but is never the same. And it may be that language is so rich and fluid that even a writer with a sensitive ear is capable of registering only the speech of one particular time and place.

Joyce has several Northern Irish characters but none of these is given distinctively Northern dialogue. If he were writing such characters today he would have to make them use 'wee' at least once in every sentence. 'Wee' is a wonderful adjective because it instantly establishes a warm, conspiratorial intimacy and suggests that between friends even problems are endearingly insignificant – a crucial illusion in a province where irreconcilable neighbours have been murdering each other for centuries. To reinforce this message, everyone at every opportunity cries gaily, 'No problem!' Checking in to a Northern Irish hotel sets the tone:

Receptionist: I'll get you your wee key card in just one wee second.

Guest: Thank you.

Receptionist (with extravagant gaiety): No problem!

Guest accepts key card and turns to leave.

Receptionist (leaning conspiratorially over the desk): And that wee card gets you in free to the wee nightclub downstairs.

Guest (gazing in wonderment at the magical talisman): Ah!

Receptionist (with nearly demented gaiety): NO PROBLEM![109]

This is vocal grooming at its most effective. Bombarded relentlessly with 'wee' and 'no problem', the visitor forgets about the hatreds and murders and goes home believing that the Northern Irish are the friendliest people on earth.

Of course 'No problem!' is universally used because it is the ideal mantra, the most reassuring monkey grunt – but it has suffered from overuse and is now being replaced by 'No worries!' Recently I had a builder in to do some work and in the course of a brief exchange he said 'No worries' eight times. This should have told me that worries were exactly what I should have – but I had to find out the hard way.

The bad news about distinctive demotic is that it can never be properly translated. Translators make heroic efforts to find equivalents – but these are rarely as effective. Sentence-sounds are as impossible to translate as poetry. In *Cleaned Out* much of Annie Ernaux's pungent French working-class dialogue is less vivid in translation, though a flavour of it comes through occasionally, as when the mother snarls in contempt at her unambitious, easy-going husband, 'If *I* wasn't here you'd be eating shit'. Similarly, with Proust, the English reader has to take on faith the French critics who claim that he caught precisely everyone from Parisian aristocrats to illiterate country servants. Sometimes this is apparent even in English, as when a female servant says, 'Madame knows everything; Madame is worse than the X-rays.' And what always comes through is Proust's analysis of the subtleties of body language and tone: 'she pronounced the "X" with an affectation of difficulty and a self-mocking smile that someone so ignorant should employ this learned term'.

There are even further subsets of specialised speech. Within each region, each professional milieu, social class and age group has its own peculiar talk. Mike Leigh, another master of dialogue, specialises in the banality of the Southern English lower-middle class, the people of the suburbs, but is also good on the aggressive, competitive banter of youth. Two unemployed and penniless youths on a council estate:

> 'Where you going then?'
> 'Steak House.'
> '*What* steak house?'
> '*That* one.'
> 'Where?'
> 'Up Jack's arse and round the corner.'

Henry Green is equally good on London firemen and gave one of them this aria:

> The way she died, mate. It was to do with a duck for her supper. Eighty-six years old she was. She couldn't manage to wring this duck's neck. So she got out the old chopper, held the bird down on the block and plonk, the 'ead was gone. Well, this head, it can't 'ave fallen in the basket. When she bent down to pick up the 'ead, she let the carcass fall. And it fell right side up, right side up that bloody carcass fell, on its bloody feet and all. And did it run! Well she must 'ave taken fright. She must 'ave started runnin', with the duck 'ard after. She run out into the garden. The blood from the stump left a trail behind. It followed 'er every turn, that decapitated duck did. Until in the finish she fell down. Dead as mutton she was.

> 'Eart failure. She'd took fright. But credit it or not, that duck landed on her arse as she lay there, stretched out. That's where my first cousin, the nephew, came on 'em both. Cold as a stone, she was, already.[110]

But the fireman's aria is not typical. Green's dialogue is always alive to the relationships between the speakers, the undercurrents of dislike, hostility and competition. The firemen conduct vicious duels in what appears to be the most innocuous affability. When, in the fire station bar, the barman remarks that he no longer smokes much, another fireman says, 'Not like you used to, eh?', a subtle reference to this barman's habit of enjoying the bar merchandise free. The barman strikes back with, 'Is there anything on tonight?' – a reference to the fireman's exemption from the tedious evening tactical exercises, a favouritism achieved by sucking up to the officer in charge.

This kind of coded exchange is common in the workplace where people who despise and loathe each other are obliged to cooperate with a happy smile and can wound only under cover of friendly cheerfulness. Once I went to work in a bottle-green jacket and trousers, which I thought jived tremendously well together, till a woman colleague looked me up and down, cried, 'You're really well coordinated today, Mike,' and turned with a high malicious laugh to the company who all joined in, the bastards. I never wore that jacket and trousers again, not even separately, and vowed to get even at the first opportunity. Unfortunately the woman left for another job soon after.

As Joyce and Flann O'Brien showed, male conversation is often a contest to establish who can impress most with knowledge, usually half-baked and useless. Robin Dunbar confirms the accuracy of this by citing anthropological research revealing that men 'talk about things they claim to know a lot about'.[111] Women, on the other hand, talk about 'relationships' (with husbands, lovers, relatives, friends) and in as much useless detail as men on their specialisms. Here is Alice Munro on a woman talking obsessively about the lover, Art, who has abandoned her: '"You're built the opposite from Art," she told my father. "The trouble with getting his suits fitted was that he was so long in the body, short in the leg. Ransom's in Tupperton was the only place that could fit him."'[112]

Conversations between women and men are different again. If the sexes are unfamiliar with each other, men perform and women applaud, men tell jokes and women laugh. Alice Munro's narrator on the men she and her friend Naomi have just met in a dance hall:

> Bert began to complain that he didn't want to dance any more. He said he had a lame back. The man I was with – whose name, then or later, I learned to be Clive – let out a startling, rattling, machine-gun laugh and feinted with his fist at Bert's belt buckle.
>
> 'Howdja get a lame back, eh, howdja get a lame back?'
>
> 'Well I was just layin' there, officer,' said Bert in a high whiny voice, 'and she come up and sat down on me, what could I do about that?'
>
> 'Don't be filthy,' said Naomi happily.[113]

But once a man and woman are in a relationship the conversation becomes different again and increasingly complex. In an article on dialogue ('the best way for the novelist to communicate with his readers'[114]), Henry Green illustrated both the enormous potential and equally enormous difficulty of dialogue by considering ways of writing an exchange between a husband and wife. This is a good example because exchanges between married couples are highly charged with significance but so heavily coded that they are almost impossible to decipher. Often the situation is exactly the opposite of what it seems:

Husband (approaching a livid face to that of his wife): Well fuck you.

Wife (thrusting her face angrily forward in turn): No . . . fuck *you.*

Husband (moving an even more livid face closer still): Fuck YOU.

Wife (bringing her face almost into contact with his): Fuck **YOU.**

Surely not a difficult scene to interpret? In fact these two have been married for forty years, are more deeply in love than ever, and, after holding their faces in front of each other for another furious moment, suddenly both burst simultaneously into hysterical laughter. This kind of mock-insult exchange is common between lovers because it acknowledges and draws on the electric tension that always thrums between oppositely charged poles. It's terrifically effective as a foreplay technique, though probably not advisable on a first date.

The following exchange, on the other hand, is between a couple heading for acrimonious divorce:

Wife (with great politeness): Would you mind terribly putting the rubbish out?

Husband (with even greater politeness): Of course, darling. Anything you say.

Most couple exchanges lie between these extremes and involve immensely complex and subtle manoeuvring, as one would expect from a pair of chess masters who have been playing against each other every day for a lifetime. Each knows the other through and through and is aware of being as thoroughly known in turn, which makes disguise and deception incredibly difficult. An overt attack is usually forbidden so an urge to wound must find indirect means. Third parties are useful for this. When two couples are out for a relaxing meal at the weekend, one husband will remark to the other husband, 'Women are always fretting about *something*', or one wife will sigh to the other, 'Men never notice *anything*'.

When one partner wants the other to do something a common stratagem is to say 'we should . . .' when the meaning is 'you should . . .', as in, 'We should do something about that garden', which really means, 'It's high time you got your lazy ass out of neutral and tidied up the garden'. A trickier problem is when one partner wants to do something the other is certain to hate, and has to disguise the desire or somehow render it innocuous, while the resisting partner has to obstruct without appearing to and certainly without revealing anger or hatred, for a display of aggressive emotion will mean forfeiting the game (just as in soccer a violent tackle will result in a red card and a sending off). Responding to a question with a question is a useful obstructive stratagem.

In Green's example the couple are at home together at nine-thirty in the evening and the husband wants to go across the street to the pub on his own. Green calculates that, when the husband expresses his wish, the wife can ask how long he might be away in at least 138 ways (Green lists 15 of these), to cover every mood from acquiescence to outrage – and the wife can even be in several of these moods *at the same time.* Green offers suitably ambivalent dialogue for this exchange but then adds that this is inadequate because it does not include the extra complications of tone of voice, expression and body language. Here is his final version:

> At last he looked at the clock, laid the newspaper aside, and getting out of his armchair, wandered to the door: 'I think I'll go over the way now for a drink,' he said, his finger on the handle.

'Will you be long?' she asked, and put her book down.

He seemed to hesitate.

'Why don't you come too?' he suggested.

'I don't think I will. Not tonight. I'm not sure. I may,' and she gave him a small smile.

'Well, which is it to be?' he insisted, and did not smile back.

'I needn't say now, need I? If I feel like it I'll come over later,' she replied, picking up her book again.

Note the parrying of questions with questions and the husband's cunning stratagem of inviting his wife along when in fact he does not want her company. The trick in such cases is to issue the invitation just a little too late and with just not quite enough conviction, so getting credit for generosity while making it difficult for the other to accept. But the wife's profoundly confused and confusing answer is even more cunning, the 'not tonight' indicating that she has no puritanical objection to bars and that 'small smile' the perfect response to the insincere invitation. The husband's touch of petulance and failure to smile back are bad mistakes, giving deserved victory to the wife who has played a blinder, making the husband feel guilty without accusing him or trying to prevent him from going out, and ensuring that he will not enjoy his drink for, although he knows she will not join him, the mere possibility is enough to ruin the experience. And concluding the discussion by picking up a book is a deadly coup de grâce, dismissing the man as a philistine boor.

Such scenes should be studied by husbands and wives as famous chess games are studied by aspiring grandmasters. Not surprisingly though, authentic couple scenes are rare in fiction. Authentic dialogue of any sort is rare and authentic couple dialogue is rarest of all because it is so indirect, evasive and cunning, usually banal and repetitive on the surface but concealing monstrous emotions, tensions, conflicts and pressures. A great example is Hemingway's story 'Hills Like White Elephants', in which a couple waiting for a train at a station engage in endless banal bickering that circles obsessively round an issue (probably abortion) without ever making it specific.

The good news is that, if such authentic fictional scenes are rare, they abound in real life. Virtuoso duels between couples are commonplace – as are all kinds of equally fascinating exchanges. As Green puts it, 'things are going on in life all the time around us'.[115] We are always in the midst of the people's opera.

This is why eavesdropping is one of the great pleasures of everyday life. Appreciate it while you can. I used to love listening in on conversations – but over the years hearing becomes less acute and particularly so for men (who lose crucial hair in the inner ear as they lose it on top). I began to need to incline towards speakers and must have been doing this one evening in a bar because the woman I was listening to (she was giving intimate revelations about her husband to a friend) suddenly turned to me and said, in a tone of affable menace, 'Did you get all that?', and then, dropping the affability to leave only pure menace, '*Or would you like me to repeat it for you?*'

That, sadly, was the end of my eavesdropping career.

7

The Masquerade of Everyday Behaviour

Why are vampires and cupcakes back in fashion? Why is everyone impressed by drugs beginning with or containing the letter 'z'? Why do women love lighting candles? Why do men hate drinking water? Why do art galleries always induce an overwhelming urge to fart? Why are most male cats left-pawed and most female cats right-pawed? And why, oh why, oh why, are there no white dog turds any more? These are profound mysteries but I am convinced that they all have rational explanations. 'Everything has to mean something', as Duke Ellington's trombone player, Joe Nanton, used to say when asked to explain why he was known as Tricky Sam.

I have always loved explanations, possibly as a reaction to growing up in Catholic Ireland where not only were explanations always impatiently and irritably refused as redundant, but the very idea of asking questions was condemned as the sin of Lucifer, intellectual pride.

In this authoritarian, philistine culture my secret consolation was literature – but the twentieth-century literature I was reading also banned explanation. The key axiom of modernist literature was 'present, don't explain'. It is easy to see how this commandment came about as a reaction to Victorian moralising but it limits writing unnecessarily. Why not present *and* explain? There is nothing unnatural or suspect about explaining. In everyday life we do not just participate but also constantly intuit, deduce, associate, extrapolate, classify and hypothesise. Analysis is not a luxury extra for detached intellectuals but the core activity of every living organism. To ban ideas and explanation may have seemed excitingly liberating in the heady early days of modernism but now it looks like an unnecessary restriction, a fashion that became in turn an orthodoxy as stifling as those it replaced.

A common argument against theorising is that theories are reductionist – they reduce living reality to dead abstraction. But this is not even true of scientific theory. The physicist David Bohm: 'A theory is primarily a form of insight, i.e. a way of looking at the world.'[116] So theories have much in common with works of artistic vision – they are not reductions but additions, ways of enriching reality by stimulating attention and speculation.

But theories should remain hypotheses and never petrify into dogma. Certainty, the turning of fluid truth into tablets of law, is another manifestation of hunger for permanence. But no one knows less than those who are certain of knowing everything. And no one is more dangerous than those who are convinced of knowing all the important final truths and so feel entitled, even obliged, to impose their views on others. Preaching and lecturing are usually futile because something in the listener always rebels against coercion. It may be necessary to feign agreement but the secret self is defiantly showing two fingers. Even rational argument in conversation rarely changes anyone's mind. After a lifetime of engaging in long, passionate discussions I have come to the conclusion that it is a waste of time trying to convince anyone of anything.

And lecturing one's self is as futile as lecturing others. This is why New Year resolutions rarely work. It is the left hemisphere nagging the right, which goes, 'yeah yeah yeah', and then carries on with business as usual. The most effective way to change behaviour is for the full brain to understand it thoroughly and profoundly. Then the behaviour changes without any nagging.

This was the crucial insight of Buddha, the first great psychologist. Buddha did not rant about evil or immorality or sin, or attempt to impose virtue by threatening eternal damnation. Instead he talked mildly of 'unskilful behaviour' which would gradually fade away when it was properly understood. Understanding is itself transformation.

So understanding is a ruse, a way of becoming a better person without any penitent self-flagellation or indeed any pain or inconvenience at all. Simply understand and thy soul shall be healed.

For William James theorising was nothing less than the meaning of life: 'The world must not be regarded as a machine whose final purpose is the making real of any outward good, but rather as a contrivance for deepening the theoretic consciousness of what goodness and evil in their intrinsic natures are. Not the doing either of good or of evil is what nature cares for, but the knowing of them. Life is one long eating of the fruit of the tree of *knowledge*.'[117] So the Judeo-Christian myth of the fall of man should really be the myth of his rise. For James, as for Buddha, knowledge is salvation not damnation.

Like Bergson, James was a century ahead of science. Biologists now accept that the essential function of all living organisms is to learn from their environment in order to adapt to it more efficiently. So paying attention and trying to understand are not the luxury extras but the essentials. Life is fundamentally cognitive. Learn or petrify and become a joke, as Bergson warned.

And cunning evolution has provided a reward for theorisers. In a paper with the thrilling title *Explanation as orgasm*,[118] the philosopher and child psychologist Alison Gopnik argues that we have a theory drive analogous to the sex drive and that successful theorising has rewards equivalent to those for the reproductive need, so that understanding can give as much pleasure as a good come. This theory drive is strongest in children who learn to understand the world by developing and testing theories, just as scientists do, and experience intense joy when a theory produces a convincing explanation, the satisfaction of 'aha' resolving the puzzlement of 'hmm'. However, in adolescence the sex drive kicks in and the theory drive dies out. The organism has learned enough to survive in the world and theorising is preserved into adulthood mainly by scientists for professional reasons. But if scientists can keep it up, everyone else can also enjoy the rewards of theorising past its biological time limit. As Gopnik helpfully reminds us, it is possible to have good orgasms even after the menopause. Moreover, scientific and psychological explanations work in the same way and have the same pay-off: 'the aha of understanding why the wiring doesn't work seems quite similar to the aha of understanding why the electrician won't tell you why the wiring doesn't work'.[119] So the message is simple: catch on and shoot off.[120]

But, as Proust showed, psychology is different from science in that its explanations are not so much new discoveries as revelations of truths already known in some deep but hitherto obscure way. The surprise is not in the novelty but in the familiarity. For the fact that everyone already knows everything is something hardly anyone knows.

As Joyce felt a sacred obligation to *present* everything 'not very nice', so Proust felt a similar obligation to *understand* the psychology of the not very nice – the grotesque, the disgusting, the shameful and the painful, all that is usually denied or concealed. Explanations poured out of Proust as melodies poured out of Mozart – and these explanations were nearly all of everyday behaviour. Though indifferent to the physical sciences, his approach was that of the scientist – to study human behaviour empirically and discover its laws. But his great advantage was that he had no preconceived ideas and did not investigate selectively or attempt to make the evidence fit into a scheme. As a result he was constantly surprised – and therefore so are his readers. The rare and intense pleasure of reading Proust is the steady flow of insights that are unexpected but ring true. There are also insights that do not seem true and explanations that are specious, over-complicated and absurdly far-fetched. But Proust was right sufficiently often to make him the greatest literary explainer. After Proust's death Joseph Conrad wrote, 'I don't think there has ever been in the whole of literature such power of analysis, and I feel pretty safe in saying that there will never be another.'[121] And, commenting on Proust's understanding of human psychology, the French critic Jean-François Revel claimed that Proust rather than Freud had earned the right to the title *The Psychopathology of Everyday Life*.[122]

Like Freud, Proust understood the crucial importance of childhood experience and began *À la recherche* by explaining how his own personality had been formed by the relationship with his mother. This is the famous episode of the goodnight kiss, the first example of an intimate episode so shamefully embarrassing that it creates an overpowering urge to shout at Marcel, 'Oh don't tell me that' and 'Please don't tell me any more' – but of course the scene is so compellingly truthful and revealing that there is no choice but to read on in horrified fascination.

Marcel is accustomed to receiving a goodnight kiss from Mamma but when his parents have dinner guests he is sent to bed without the usual lingering intimacy and experiences an anguish so overwhelming that he refuses even to try to sleep and gets out of bed to wait for the dinner party to end. When his parents finally come upstairs he rushes out and flings himself in 'terror and joy' upon Mamma. The terror is at the thought of the paternal reaction but the father unexpectedly relents and tells his wife, 'Go and comfort him.' So Mamma not only goes in to bestow the kiss but decides to spend the night in the boy's bedroom – at which point he bursts into tears. Mamma herself is soon equally overcome by emotion ('Why, my little chick, my little canary, he's going to make Mamma as silly as himself') and decides to read the boy a novel to distract them both.

At this point many readers will have an overpowering urge to burst into that bedroom and drag Mamma away from her little canary.

It would probably be too late. The damage has been done. The boy has realised that emotional bullying is more effective than reasonable behaviour: 'When I had just committed an offence for which I expected to be banished from the household, my parents gave me a far greater concession than I could ever have won as the reward of a good deed.' And later, when Mamma blames the son's behaviour on 'nerves', he makes an even more significant discovery. 'And thus for the first time my unhappiness was regarded no longer as a punishable offence but as an involuntary ailment which had been officially recognised, a nervous condition for which I was in no way responsible.'

The great psychological truth is that the way to sanction bad behaviour is to evade responsibility by blaming the behaviour on something outside personal control. Marcel is now free to indulge himself. All his subsequent relationships will follow this pattern of demanding submissive, unconditional love. And he will deliberately push every relationship too far because no love will ever be absolute and no submission ever complete.

In all the Jousters who have written about childhood – Annie Ernaux, Alice Munro, John Updike and John McGahern – the mother is the dominant figure, disappointed and frustrated by marriage, and transferring powerful, unfulfilled ambition to the child. The mother gives the child the confidence and will to succeed – but the child must eventually escape, which is especially difficult for sons.

Proust, Joyce, Updike and McGahern all understood the effects of attachment to a mother who has been disappointed in her husband and focuses all her love on the first-born son. The Joyce and Proust fathers conformed to national stereotype in their marital neglect – Doctor Proust went to courtesans and John Joyce went to the pub. The Updike and McGahern husbands were not neglectful but were despised by their wives. For Joyce and McGahern the death of the mother provided escape, though even after death the mother's influence can be stifling. In *Ulysses* Stephen Dedalus sees his mother's ghost with 'glazing eyes, staring out of death, to shake and bend my soul ... to strike me down', and cries out, 'No mother. Let me be and let me live.' Proust lived with his mother till he was thirty-four and right up to her death phoned her several times a day, a dependence that made him hate as well as adore Mamma. Before sex he would work himself up by insulting her and spitting on her photograph (Proust's foreplay techniques were as original as his literary works).

The central Proustian insight is that nothing in human psychology is simple and that no behaviour is more deceptive than that which seems obvious. Everyone not only wears a mask but has a range of masks for different occasions, a wardrobe of masks. Life is a masked ball to which each participant brings a giant box of masks and whips out a different one for every encounter.

And understanding people is further complicated by the fact that all knowledge of others is relative, entirely dependent on the observer (in this Proust was at one with modern physics). There can be no detached, God-like understanding because the observer always influences the behaviour of the observed.

Another problem is that the observed is a moving target – people change continually but in subtle ways that are difficult to detect and even more difficult to describe. One of the sternest challenges for a novelist is to show character as process, always changing in unpredictable ways while paradoxically remaining essentially the same. In minor writers the characters are always in character but in Proust everyone is consistently inconsistent and one of his greatest achievements was to make these inconsistencies entirely convincing.

So social life is a complex interplay between what people actually are, what they imagine themselves to be, what they attempt to appear to be to others and what others actually see. Only rarely do any of these views coincide. People are also constantly changing but are mostly unaware of this, too immersed in the interplay to notice anything beyond their own performances – so the possibilities for misunderstanding and conflict are almost infinite. But for the attentive observer the fascination is also infinite.

The lesson is that empathy has limits and people are ultimately unknowable. Alice Munro's narrator agrees: 'People's lives ... were dull, simple, amazing, and unfathomable – deep caves paved with kitchen linoleum.'[123] We can never know others and how we appear to them is equally unknowable. The impression that anyone can form of us in a nanosecond we ourselves can never grasp even after a lifetime of trying.[124] Yet this is a cause for rejoicing rather than despair. The ultimate unknowability of others is a consequence of their freedom and any claim to know another completely is an imperialism of knowledge, an attempt to dominate and control.

If people wish to appear in a certain way it is often because they are exactly the opposite. Scratch a sentimental person and you will find a cruel person (so, on second thoughts, don't). In *À la recherche* one of the main characters, Charles Swann, thinks to himself that 'as often as not one has only to take the opposite view to the reputation created by the world in order to judge a person accurately'. In a delightful irony, Swann himself, a sensitive, intelligent man, is also deceived by the opinion of the world. When he is entranced by hearing for the first time the Vinteuil sonata, a piece of music he believes to be a masterpiece, he desperately wants to meet the composer and remembers that he has met a shabby old man named Vinteuil in a small country town. Over dinner Swann remarks that if 'the silly old fool' were related to 'the genius' he would undergo any torture, beginning with the old fool's company, to secure an introduction. In fact 'the silly old fool' *is* 'the genius'.

There are revelations like this all through *À la recherche*. The obsequious servant turns out to be a tyrant, the provincial gentleman who derides the aristocracy is revealed as a snob, the young rebel who rants against society becomes the most smug of social conformists, the cultured couple who give musical *soirées* every evening are philistines with no interest in music whatever and the extravagantly masculine man is really an effete homosexual. In fact almost everyone in *À la recherche* turns out to be homosexual, except Marcel, so Proust verified his own theory by wearing a mask in his book.

In particular, anyone who appears to be good is most likely a hypocrite. The genuinely good, a rare breed, never appear so. 'Whenever in the course of my life I have come across, in convents for instance, truly saintly embodiments of practical charity, they have generally had the cheerful, practical, brusque and unemotioned air of a busy surgeon, the sort of face in which one can discern no commiseration, no tenderness at the sight of suffering humanity, no fear of hurting it, the impassive, unsympathetic, sublime face of true goodness.'

All the characters constantly practice concealment and deception. One of the few exceptions is the narrator's grandmother, who is portrayed as a paragon of simplicity and candour and only proves Proust's point by being the least convincing character in the book. Everyone else dissembles and lies. In *À la recherche*, as in life, lying is as universal, constant, casual and unconscious as breathing.[125] Henry Green once expressed this with admirable simplicity: 'People are such liars'[126] (and Green's novel *Party Going* portrays, with equally pitiless accuracy, an English version of Proust's wealthy socialites). Proust's version of this truth is 'Lying is essential to humanity', and he provides not just endless examples but also analyses the psychology and mechanics of lying. Swann's lover, Odette, is a habitual liar who often gives the game away by being too nice to Swann after a lie. Marcel's lover, Albertine, is also a brazen liar, entirely without scruples or guilt, who gives no evidence of mendacity but is often exposed by failing to remember her own lies and subsequently contradicting herself.

The lesson is that people lie all the time and liars are not shifty misfits but charming, popular people like Odettte and Albertine. Also, each liar is different so there is no single, reliable way of detecting lies, which is an intuitive, holistic right hemisphere ability to combine previous experience with present context, language, intonation, expression and gesture in order to flash the red light: LIE! The only effective lie detector is a well-trained, active and alert RH.

Proust also shows that the most effective way to deceive others is to deceive oneself first. 'One lies all one's life long, notably to lovers, and above all to that stranger whose contempt would cause the most pain – oneself.' So *À la recherche* can be read as a diagnostic manual of the many forms of self-deception. One of the most common is convincing ourselves that we do not want, in fact hate and would refuse if offered, the things we secretly crave but cannot have. This is a common way of denying envy. Mme Verdurin, the middle-class hostess, craves the prestige of the aristocratic salons but constantly and viciously dismisses those who frequent them as 'bores'.

Proust also understood the central social force – convention. The problem with conventional people is that they do not believe in conventions. What others understand as arbitrary social customs sanctioned by usage, the conventional revere as divine laws graven on tablets of stone. So social life is governed by absolute commandments and any who sin against these are cast out into eternal darkness. In *Lives of Girls and Women* the narrator's conventional friend, Naomi, is violently contemptuous and dismissive of an unconventional woman: '"A joke, she was just a *joke*!" like someone dispensing, in the face of fumbling heresies, self-evident handsome dogmas.'

It is easy to dismiss Proust's examples as the irrelevant idiocy of a vanished age – but rereading *À la recherche* always suggests uncomfortable contemporary and personal comparisons. Our age believes itself to be wonderfully enlightened and tolerant but is just as dominated by conventions and taboos. And the stratagems of social envy are just the same. For me, literary reputation is the equivalent of a reputation for brilliance in the salons and for much of my life my response to having no reputation was to dismiss most famous writers as careerist phonies and, even using the same term as Mme Verdurin, 'bores'. According to this romantic-outsider theory of literature, all the authentic writers are unrecognised and ignored. This was a wonderfully comforting theory – and the only problem with it was an ongoing severe shortage of unacknowledged geniuses.

If our unedifying behaviour is too obvious to ignore, and self-deception becomes impossible, the next recourse is self-justification. When Swann is shocked to discover himself surreptitiously opening a letter from Odette to another man, he justifies this by telling himself that *not* opening the letter would in fact be 'behaving shoddily' because the opening would rid him of a possibly slanderous suspicion. Ingenious! Even better is Marcel's justification of sadism. *Impossible*, you cry? Not a bit of it. Sexual sadists, Marcel informs us, are 'creatures so purely sentimental, so naturally virtuous' that in order to indulge in the wickedness of sensual pleasure they must impersonate the wicked to 'gain the momentary illusion of having escaped beyond the control of their own gentle and scrupulous natures into the inhuman world of pleasure'. So a sexual sadist is really a sentimental sweetheart. Not even the subtlest of Jesuits could match such casuistry, probably the most outrageous example of self-justification I have ever heard. 'Gentle and scrupulous'!

Proust's *Belle Époque* world has receded into remoteness but the truths he learned from it are increasingly relevant to an age in which we have never been less able to appreciate the present, never been more tormented by desire, more inclined to live in anticipation or, protected from most painful afflictions and dangers, more swaddled in the stultifying comfort of habit.[127] Proust's dissatisfaction and disillusionment are our own – and Marcel's life is an illustration of the despair described so eloquently by Schopenhauer: 'Though we live all our lives in expectation of better things, we often at the same time long regretfully for what is past. The present, on the other hand, is regarded as something quite temporary and serving only as the road to our goal. That is why most people discover when they look back on their lives that they have been the entire time living *ad interim*, and are surprised to see that that which they let go by so unregarded and unenjoyed was precisely that in expectation of which they had lived.'[128]

Marcel never seems to realise that the solution to his problem is to stop living in expectation and begin living in the present. He should have founded his own version of AA – Anticipators Anonymous. 'Hi, I'm Marcel and I'm a pathological anticipator. I really need to live in the present – and that's why I look forward so much to my AA meetings.'

It is impossible to reduce to a single theme a work as rich in insight as *À la recherche* but the most likely candidate for central theme would be the persistence, insatiability and perversity of desire and the inevitability of disappointment in desire realised. 'Desire makes all things flourish; possession withers them.' If we can't have it we want it but as soon as we succeed in having it we no longer want it. Conversely, if we can have it we don't want it but if someone else has it we now desperately want it. Every time I lend someone a book that has been on my shelves for years, unnoticed and unloved, I am overwhelmed by a passionate desire to read that very book. And a few years ago, when a senior post was created in work and I was well placed to fill it, I thought about applying but decided that it was not worth the extra responsibility and stress. Then a colleague who was also an old friend, a sensitive and considerate woman, told me she was interested but concerned that if she applied it would damage our friendship. With the seigneurial detachment of a wise old Master, I waved away the possibility of such pettiness and gave her my blessing. 'Apply, my child.' So she did, and was successful – but as soon as she started in the new post I was consumed by outrage and fury: *the bitch has stolen my job.*

The central development in *À la recherche* is the progression from fantasy and anticipation to disillusionment. Marcel begins by feverishly looking forward and ends by bitterly looking back. Like a contemporary adolescent, he is seduced from an early age by glamour, especially the glamour of exotic places and famous people. He fantasises first about Balbec (a fictional version of the Normandy resort of Cabourg), then about Florence and, finally and most obsessively, about Venice. And, again as it is nowadays, the idea of travel itself is alluring, irrespective of destination. But reality can never match the fantasy. When

Marcel finally gets to the places he has dreamed of, they are all disappointing.

As for the glamour of the famous, Marcel's equivalent of contemporary celebrities was aristocrats. Like a contemporary fan obsessed by a movie star, he stalks the Duchesse de Guermantes, spying on her, lurking outside her home and hanging about on the exclusive streets she frequents. Later, he gains access to the salons, gets to know the Duchesse and is dazzled. Only at the end of the novel is her utter worthlessness revealed.

Social life, if seen clearly, is a maelstrom of complexities, misapprehensions, malice, deceit, envy, scheming and shrieking facetiousness. No wonder Proust spent his last ten years in bed. His characters could also afford to live in seclusion – but none of them can bear to acknowledge that other people are unknowable and that each of us is essentially and irredeemably alone. So they entangle themselves in obligations, rituals, conventions, hierarchies, rivalries and feuds far more complex, time-consuming and exhausting than those imposed by employment. For these people social life is more work than work. Many of them complain about socialising but no one can give it up. They huddle together to keep out the cold and ceaselessly babble to drown out the silence of the void. Even when alone they communicate constantly by writing letters, often several a day, that are delivered by servants, the equivalent of today's obsessive social network messaging.

But when Proust abandoned social life to become a recluse he discovered that other great enemy of attention and appreciation – habit. For over a decade he hardly ever left his apartment and the tiniest details of his days and nights and of the running of the household were determined by rituals prescribed by the master and reverently followed by his faithful servant, Céleste Albaret. From the warming of his clothes in the oven before he rose, to the wrapping of his pyjamas in two hot-water bottles before he slept, every stage and every procedure was exactly the same each day and night.

When Proust woke in the afternoon he rang for Céleste who brought him, in silence, one silver tray with his coffee and croissant and another with his mail which had been disinfected in a formol box (Proust was terrified of germs). Then came the ritual of 'smoking' Legras powder for his asthma. Céleste fetched a packet of powder which Proust poured into a saucer and lit with a square of paper, itself lit from a candle which had been lit in the kitchen to prevent any noxious fumes reaching the bedroom (matches with their sulphurous emissions were of course out of the question). Proust inhaled for anything from half an hour to several hours, often lighting more and more packets of powder, by which time the room would be full of white smoke. When he had had enough he signalled silently that it was time to light the wood fire (coal was also out of the question) to dispel the Legras smoke. Then he donned Turkish slippers and the beloved fur coat that was always on his bed and moved across the corridor to his dressing room, where there awaited a bath with water heated to exactly 50°C, and, on the dressing table, a pile of twenty to twenty-five clean towels. After washing Proust dabbed himself dry, using a fresh towel for each dab (applying a towel more than once would have chapped his sensitive skin). Then he was ready for the vest, pants and shirt warmed to the right temperature in the kitchen oven.

The day continued like this – and it would be difficult to imagine a more completely regulated existence, a more entirely selfish pampering or a more successful exclusion of the world, cut off even from sight by heavy curtains that were never opened. (Proust's father, a doctor who specialised in containing cholera epidemics, recommended houses 'flooded with light and air which are the two most powerful tonics and antiseptics we know' and the extermination of rats as 'the first principle of anti-plague prophylaxis'; his son went as far as is humanly possible in excluding light and air, found rats erotically exciting and used them for foreplay.) Proust himself understood that all this was comical. 'The regularity of a habit is usually in direct proportion to its absurdity.'

And he understood equally well the consequences of a life in thrall to Habit (always written with a capital H): 'If Habit is second nature, it keeps us in ignorance of the first, and is free of its cruelties and enchantments.' The price of protection against the cruelties is the loss of the enchantments.

The hunger for habit is as strong as, and perhaps even stronger than, the hunger for love. We can survive without love but not without habit. 'Of all the human plants, Habit requires the least fostering, and is the first to appear on the seeming desolation of the most barren rock.' In whatever circumstances we find ourselves we immediately try to make their strangeness fit our preconceived ideas and to tame their terrifying uncertainty by establishing routine. The reaction is as immediate and instinctive as raising an arm against a blow and may well have the same source in primitive fear of the unknown environment and involuntary self-defence mechanisms. If extreme reactions like fight or flight are not required, the next necessity is find a favourite spot and a favourite seat.

As with so many undesirable characteristics (anger and hatred for instance), habit is a response to fear of process and time and so is encouraged by the fearfulness of ill health or age. The sense of increasing vulnerability is countered by the reassurance of one's own armchair in one's own living room. The most obvious consequence of habit is a diminishment of attention and a dulling of perception. We become incapable of seeing and considering anything beyond the habitual. But life always takes its revenge. Those who show no interest soon become of no interest.

Proust shows an even more dangerous consequence. Force of habit is so powerful that it can override moral, ethical and intellectual judgement. Swann abhors snobbery and has the same regard for low-income families who ask him to parties in cramped apartments as for the Princesse de Parme who gives the most lavish parties in Paris. But because 'his long inurement to luxury and high society had given him a need as well as a contempt', he can no longer tolerate the spectacle of 'beds converted into cloakrooms, with a mass of hats and greatcoats sprawling over their counterpanes'. Aren't we all familiar with this experience, fondly believing ourselves good egalitarian democrats, but disgusted and outraged by bad taste or even just lack of space? I remember visiting a couple whom I knew to be profoundly generous and kind, people who deserved admiration and respect – and yet I was revolted and outraged by being given milky tea and a marshmallow instead of black coffee and carrot cake.

Proust's answer to the problem of habit is art – but not the art of his socialite dilettantes for whom a thing of beauty is a ploy forever. Art is not about artefacts and artiness. Art is humility, engagement, exploration, discovery, cognition, experience and, above all, renewal. Art is the waters of the Jordan where we come to be cleansed and reborn.

As frequent as Proust's laments at the stultifications of Habit are his rhapsodies at the liberating powers of literature, painting and music, which bestow on us the miracle of renewal thanks to a vision of a re-enchanted world (and as well as celebrating these arts, *À la recherche* includes portraits of a writer, Bergotte, a painter, Elstir, and a composer, Vinteuil). Painting and literature permit us to see the world with new eyes. 'The original painter or the original writer proceeds on the lines of the oculist. The course of treatment they give us by their painting or by their prose is not always pleasant. When it is at an end the practitioner says to us:

"Now look!" And, lo and behold, the world around us (which was not created once and for all, but is created afresh as often as an original artist is born) appears to us entirely different from the old world, but perfectly clear.'

Proust suggests that those of us who look upon the world with contempt and boredom, disgusted by commonplace homes and the unprepossessing people who inhabit them, should contemplate Chardin's paintings of modest lives conducted in humble surroundings. If these paintings provide pleasure it is because we have once enjoyed such scenes ourselves but lost this ability over the years and need an artist like Chardin to raise this enjoyment once more into consciousness. Then in a sense we become Chardin, share his vision, see the world through his eyes – and so the world is re-enchanted. 'Everyday life will delight you . . . Into those rooms where you see nothing but the image of the mundanity of others and the reflection of your own ennui, Chardin enters like the light, bestowing on each thing its colour, summoning all these beings, animate or inanimate, out from the everlasting darkness in which they have been interred . . . Like the Sleeping Princess, each one is restored to life, recovers its colours, begins to converse with you, to live, to endure.'

Literature effects a parallel form of recognition. As painting reveals to us what we have seen but not really seen, literature reveals what we know but do not know that we know.

It might seem that music can offer no recognitions like those of painting and literature. Proust argues that, on the contrary, great music reveals something deeper and truer than paintings or books, the underlying feeling that the expression in words or paint is meant to convey but which words and paint inevitably coarsen and betray – in fact something like the exaltation of an epiphany. Literature and artworks communicate something of the feeling but do not 'recompose it as does music, in which the sounds seem to follow the very movement of our being, to reproduce that extreme inner point of our sensations which is the part that gives us that peculiar exhilaration which we experience from time to time and which, when we say, "What a fine day! What glorious sunshine!" we do not in the least communicate to others.'

So resistance to force of habit must itself become a habit. Or, to put it another way, we have to keep taking the medication. Doses of original literature, painting and music are necessary to dissolve the encrustations of habit and open us up to life and the world. Like all great works of art, Proust's truths show us the way back to life. We must live, my friends, live. The truths illuminate and enrich experience but are never a substitute for experience.

> We do not receive wisdom, we must discover it for ourselves, after a journey through the wilderness which no one else can make for us, which no one can spare us, for our wisdom is the point of view from which we come at last to regard the world.

PART IV

The Everyday Self

8

The Miracle of Consciousness and Memory

Sincere, warm, generous, thoughtful and amusing, the man seems entirely simpatico – yet the message flashed up on my radar is 'ASSHOLE – avoid like the plague'. This is hard to believe – but the radar is more often right than wrong. So I accept the threat warning and take immediate evasive action. But once at a safe distance the question arises – how did the radar do it, how could it contradict the apparently obvious evidence with such speed and certainty? It must have isolated, picked up and linked tiny, almost imperceptible signals, grouped these and searched memory for similar groupings, found a near match or matches, made a comparison and arrived at an accurate character judgement. All in a few milliseconds and in the middle of a conversation. A stupendous miracle – but consciousness and memory combine to perform such miracles constantly every day.[129]

How did this come about? How did a lump of matter that looks like a large pickled walnut become capable of generating a self that has thoughts, emotions, moods, beliefs, values and an ongoing, stable, coherent sense of identity? For many this mystery remains unsolved and many believe that it can never be solved. So if on the way to work next Monday morning you feel like creamed shit, it may help to remember that this very ability to feel like creamed shit is miraculous. Existence itself is a miracle and to be aware of existence is an even more profound miracle. The most mind-boggling question is: how does the mind boggle?

Buddha was one of the first to become conscious of consciousness and he frequently compared it to a blazing fire that is constantly mutating, ceaselessly consuming and re-creating itself. At other times, to get across the idea of human capriciousness, he used the analogy of a monkey restlessly swinging through trees, grabbing out at a branch and immediately letting it go for another. Eventually, seeing mutability and transience everywhere, Buddha extended his theory of consciousness to all life and even – anticipating modern physics by two-and-a-half thousand years – to matter itself, expressing this memorably as: 'Everything is on fire.' And around the same time in Greece Heraclitus expressed the same idea in similar language: 'This world order is a living fire.'

In the sixteenth century Montaigne saw consciousness as like the wavering dance on the ceiling of sunlight reflected from a bowl of water. And, like Buddha, he was acutely aware of the restless, fickle nature of the human mind, a phantasmagoria of 'chimeras and fantastic monsters, one after another, without order or purpose'.[130] Astounded by the endless new configurations of shifting sand dunes on a beach, he came, again like Buddha, to see even the physical world as perpetual mutation. Landscape might seem immutable but Montaigne could see mountains bubbling like porridge. Matter was actually a wild dance of energy. Consciousness is process. Life is process. Matter is process. Everything is process.

Unfortunately, Descartes came along to put a stop to all this dancing madness with his mind – body dualism. For Rational René the human mind was 'constituted by God to enjoy perfect certainty about material things when conceiving them mathematically'. And as for the apparatus that supported this mathematical theorem prover: 'I suppose that the body is nothing but a statue or a machine.'[131]

This mechanistic paradigm of mind and body ruled for three hundred years,[132] until Bergson argued that mind and body form a single unified organism and consciousness is not an eternal soul but a 'confused perception' of 'confused multiplicity', a constantly changing flux where thoughts, memories, feelings and sensations overlap, interpenetrate and intermingle to form a strange 'solidarity'.[133] The essential features are heterogeneity and mutation and each state of the heterogeneous and mutating consciousness is unique. The crucial lesson is that for mind as well as matter 'the same does not remain the same',[134] a restatement of the ancient Heraclitean idea that no one steps in the same river twice, later to be restated again by Joyce as 'the same anew'.

The crucial error of the mechanistic paradigm, a typical production of the brain's left hemisphere, is that it interprets everything as structure whereas everything is process. According to Bergson, Western culture preferred to think in terms of space rather than time because space seemed reassuringly inert.[135] And the view of time was also essentially spatial (and hence structural) because it quantified time in units extending forward and backward in a dimension like the three dimensions of space. But lived, experienced time is not like this. It is qualitative rather than quantitative and, rather than being measured out in fixed units, it flows. We do not measure it but *feel* it. Bergson used the term 'duration' to distinguish lived time from abstract time. 'Pure duration is the form taken by the succession of our inner states of consciousness when the self permits itself to live.'[136] And in consciousness 'duration seems to act as a cause', so that time is a force or a form of energy.

Bergson brought back dancing madness by comparing consciousness to a dancer whose movements naturally flow out of each other, always simultaneously inevitable and surprising. Consciousness, like a dancer, creates a unique form of time and – when it is flowing freely, immersed in becoming – a unique sensation of grace: 'Our ideas and sensations flow more rapidly, as though they have less weight. Our movements no longer require the same effort. Finally our perceptions and memories take on an ineffable quality that we might compare to a certain heat or brightness, something so novel that . . . we feel a sense of astonishment simply at being alive.'[137]

So, hey, the trudge to work feeling like creamed shit is really a dance. You are not an automaton but a ballerina. On your points!

Now, a century after Bergson, biology has espoused this view of life. Like physicists and chemists, biologists traditionally thought in terms of structure but are now interpreting life as process. All living things, from the single cell up to the mammal, are complex systems that are dynamic rather than static, creative rather than programmed, unpredictable rather than determined, networked rather than modular, open rather than closed – and these systems maintain their pattern of organisation while constantly changing structure in response to their environments. The structural changes in turn alter future behaviour and this behaviour includes choosing which parts of the environment to respond to, so that the interactions are cognitive. All living systems learn and, as the structure is a record of the changes brought about by previous interactions, all living systems also have a history. And from time to time the system change is so dramatic that it produces an essentially new structure, something qualitatively different from the original. This is known as 'self-organisation' or 'emergence', the scientific terms for Bergson's creative life force.

According to this paradigm, consciousness is an emergent phenomenon, which derives from but cannot be explained by the neurophysiology of the brain. Attempts to locate the cinema showing the continuous movie in the brain are doomed to fail because there is no continuous movie in the first place. As actual cinema movies create the illusion of movement by showing a succession of still images at high speed, so consciousness combines many disparate brain activities to provide the illusion of unified continuous flow. Consciousness is process, as Bergson claimed.

And as consciousness emerges from neuronal activity to confer on the mad flux a necessary illusion of unity and continuity, so the self emerges from consciousness to provide the necessary illusion of order and control.[138] The self is a master of self-deception and its greatest ruse is convincing itself it exists. Here neuroscience is finally catching up with Buddha who understood that the self is illusory. So the ecstasy of losing self in epiphanies may be due to shedding an illusion and experiencing reality more directly.

The most astounding revelation of physics is that at the heart of all that exists there is only some sort of unimaginable dance – and investigation of the self also finds not a dancer but a dance.[139] 'How can we know the dancer from the dance?' wondered W. B. Yeats, [140] and the answer is that such separation is impossible because the dancer *is* the dance.

In both matter and the self there is nothing there. Yet matter is solid and the self is real. Bergson got round this problem by locating the self in memory as a synthesis of all past states of consciousness, in other words as experience and character, and this conditions but does not determine all subsequent action. The essence of consciousness is freedom – we may do as we wish – and the essence of selfhood is agency – we become what we do.

All this helps to explain why it is so difficult to attend to the here and now. It is because there really is no such thing as a here and now. The physical world is a continuous flow and the concept of here and now is a useful but artificial construct of human consciousness. And if, as many anthropologists believe, consciousness evolved as a successful adaptation because of its ability to predict and plan,[141] then its default mode is anticipation. And if, as many also believe, there is an evolved human tendency to see the future as better than the present,[142] then the default mode is further reinforced. So appreciating the present is a struggle against two immensely powerful effects – the gravitational pull of anticipation itself and the delightfully rosy tint of what is anticipated. We should probably all join Anticipators Anonymous. Then there is the gravitational pull of the past, growing stronger with age and the accumulation of memories. The future is rosy, the past is golden and the present is grey.

Another problem is that, as Bergson explained, scientific and philosophical concepts and even language itself can only falsify the consciousness of flux and flow. 'The brutal word, which stores up what is stable, common, and therefore impersonal in human impressions, crushes, or at least covers over, the delicate and fleeting impressions of individual consciousness. To fight back equally well armed, these would have to express themselves by very precise words.'[143]

In other words, the only resistance to the tyranny of words is an even greater fealty to words. No one is more obsessed with language than writers determined to transcend language.

So Montaigne invented the essay form to escape the strait-jacket of concept and logical argument and follow the meanderings and digressions of actual thought – and the philosopher Maurice Merleau-Ponty described Montaigne as a writer who placed 'a consciousness astonished at itself at the core of human existence'.[144] Proust's immensely long sentences with their endless qualifications were one despairing form of well-armed fighting back.[145] Joyce's exclamations, neologisms,[146] compound words and inversions of customary word order had a similar purpose – and *Finnegans Wake* is the most radical attempt to escape the constraints of conventional orderly language. But both Montaigne and Proust attempted to understand consciousness from the outside. Joyce was the first to do it from inside.

Of course it is impossible to represent consciousness by analogy, concept or literary technique. Even the accepted term 'stream of consciousness', first used by William James, is inadequate. What could adequately render the phantasmagorical flux of sights, sounds, smells, contacts, tastes, inner bodily sensations and monitorings, thoughts, emotions, worries, resentments, plans, anticipations, fantasies, memories and associations, all jostling for prominence, overlapping, merging and mutating? According to neuroscientists, nothing can remain at the forefront of consciousness for more than ten seconds. The problem with representing this in language is that sentences are linear and sequential whereas consciousness is massively networked and its multiple operations are simultaneous.

Many fiction writers are acutely aware of this problem. As a character in one of David Foster Wallace's stories, 'Good Old Neon', puts it, 'What goes on inside is just too fast and huge and all interconnected for words to do more than barely sketch the outlines of at most one tiny little part of it at any given instant'.[147] Nevertheless Wallace did attempt to capture in words this huge, fast and interconnected inside. One of the most successful chapters in *The Pale King* renders the inner life of a tax officer on a flight to Peoria – a rich mix of the physical sensations of a turbulent flight, critical observation of fellow passengers, anxious planning for a forthcoming examination, troubling memories of problems and failures and underlying feelings of unworthiness and self-doubt. Wallace uses a variation of Joyce's interior monologue technique, as have many other writers – but none more effectively than the master himself.

Leopold Bloom's fragmented interior monologues convey the most genuine sense of consciousness as an ongoing 'confused perception' of 'confused multiplicity'. This is achieved in a variety of ways. First, Bloom's background mood is established by the tone of his thoughts – bright and optimistic early in the morning, soporific later on, exhausted in the evening. Unconscious associations are revealed by his choice of metaphors – for instance meaty metaphors on his trip to the butcher's. Conscious association leads to speculation, often humorous. Passing the *Irish Times* office prompts thoughts of small ads: 'Wanted live man for spirit counter.' 'Resp girl (R.C.) wishes to hear of post in fruit or pork shop.' Or he makes confused attempts to understand, as when water lilies remind him of a picture of a man floating on the Dead Sea: 'Couldn't sink if you tried to: so thick with salt. Because the weight of the water, no, the weight of the body in the water is equal to the weight of the. Or is it the volume is equal of the weight?' Every modern mind is awash with the flotsam of popular culture and into Bloom's thoughts pop scraps of music hall songs ('Those girls, those girls, those lovely seaside girls'), doggerel, old jokes and advertising slogans ('What is home without Plumtree's Potted Meat? Incomplete'). The flickering capriciousness of the mind is suggested by unfinished sentences (Bloom on the toilet, worrying about intrusions, 'Hope no ape comes knocking just as I'm'). And when Bloom becomes flustered even the words are incomplete, as when he can't remember which pocket holds a letter ('hell did I put? Some pock or oth.'). The non-verbal nature of much mental activity is indicated by the many exclamations (Ffoo! Paff! Kraahraark! Hu! Hhhn. Oot. Ooeeehah. Hoik! Phthook!). Irruptions of memory are represented by actual irruptions of phrases into sentences ('That fellow that turned queen's evidence on the invincibles he used to receive the, Carey was his name, the communion every morning'). And of course there are frequent interruptions and reminders from the body, the funniest when Bloom's farting interrupts his attempt to read a piece of nationalist rhetoric.

And the individuality of different consciousnesses is represented not just by different content but different rhythm. Stephen Dedalus's interior monologue has the proud, austere rhythm of grand-manner poetry, Leopold Bloom's thoughts are a lively staccato and Molly Bloom's move like an oceanic swell. (But all these monologues are essentially even-tempered and good-humoured. Annie Ernaux used the technique to show a different type of consciousness, the emotional turmoil of the adolescent, a constantly conflicted and inconsistent raging maelstrom of shame, hate, contempt, fear, envy, desire and despair.)

However, Joyce grants interior monologues to only a few of his characters. The likes of Simon Dedalus, Buck Mulligan and Blazes Boylan are given no interior life because they are all public men whose sense of self is entirely based on the impression they make on others. Bergson identified this social self as one of the main obstacles to authentic experience. 'As the self lends itself much better to the demands of social life in general and language in particular, this is preferred, and little by little one loses sight of the fundamental self.'[148] So there is a constant temptation to develop a shallow, conventional persona and this will eventually kill off the deeper, passionate self. This vulnerable deep thing requires protection and nurturing. The authentic self must be a secret self.

Bloom nurtures such a secret self by making no effort to compete with the Dublin characters. He does not seek recognition. He is not a performer. So he is thoughtful without being an intellectual, knowledgeable without being an expert, imaginative without being an artist, religious without being a believer and humorous without being a wit. He understands the triviality of Dublin talk which he dismisses as the 'usual blarney'. And he never cares what others may think of him. Only the immature and narcissistic Stephen Dedalus worries about the impression he has made. 'Speaking about me. What did he say? What did he say? What did he say about me? Don't ask.'

But of course the price Bloom pays is that he is disliked and scornfully dismissed by most of his fellow Dubliners, especially the Simon Dedalus coterie of wits.

It is just as well that Bloom makes no effort to be one of the gang for the gang will always detect a secret self and resent its owner for not fully surrendering to the group. Proust illustrates this with the failure of Swann's desperate efforts to belong to the Verdurin 'little clan' (undertaken only to be close to Odette). No matter how agreeable Swann tries to be, the 'faithful' are resentfully aware that he is not, and will never be, one of them. 'The fact was that they had very quickly sensed in him a locked door, a reserved, impenetrable chamber ... in a word, for all that he never deviated from his affability or revolted against their dogmas, an impermeability to those dogmas, a resistance to complete conversion, the like of which they had never come across in anyone before.'

The crucial process in developing a secret self is attention. It is not surprising that the brain area responsible for voluntary action, the pre-frontal cortex, also coordinates the act of attention. Experience, as William James explained, is what we choose to attend to. Attention creates experience and experience creates the self: 'Our acts of voluntary attention, brief and fitful as they are, are nevertheless momentous and critical, determining us, as they do, to higher or lower destinies.'[149] But for James, attention was not so much a physical as a metaphysical activity: 'belief and attention are the same fact'.[150] Attention is not just observing but needs to be preceded by a motivating vision – and accompanied by enriching analysis.

James also distinguished between two types of attention, a narrow, closely focussed beam that leaves everything around it in darkness and a wider awareness for which 'we may suppose the margin to be brighter and to be filled with something like meteoric showers of images, which strike into it at random, displacing the focal ideas'.[151] Learning to direct a beam is difficult but enjoying a meteor shower even more so because adult life requires the utilitarian beam and rejects the meteor shower as distraction. Infants enjoy a panoptic consciousness of the world but as they grow up develop inhibitory mechanisms that prune what appear to be redundant neural connections. The philosopher and child psychologist Alison Gopnik: 'The attentional spotlight in adults seems more like an attentional lantern for babies. Instead of experiencing a single aspect of their world and shutting down everything else they seem to be vividly experiencing everything at once.'[152] Far from being barely conscious, as was once thought, infants 'are more conscious than we are'. And Gopnik supports this claim with much evidence, including the surprising fact that babies need higher doses of anaesthetics than adults to knock them out. (Though perhaps this should not be surprising – as Georges Perec pointed out, most adults are at least half-anaesthetised already.)

Like William James, Bergson believed that attention is not merely a reaction to the external environment but is motivated 'from within' by 'a certain *attitude* adopted by the intelligence'.[153] And like James he believed that facilitating such an attitude is the crucial task of philosophy, indeed philosophy itself. 'Is philosophy's role not to bring about a fuller perception of reality by a certain reorientation of our attention? This would involve directing attention away from the practical interests of the world, and returning it to what, in practical terms, has no function. This conversion of attention would be philosophy itself.'[154] And Bergson, too, made a clear distinction between the spotlight and the lantern, what many neuroscientists would now describe as left hemisphere and right hemisphere attention.

For Bergson, attention is a dynamic feedback loop of perception and memory. Perception provides the sensory data, then memory supplements this with similar images from the past and the combination becomes a new memory. This loop runs continuously, with memory 'fortifying and enriching perception which, in turn, becomes more and more developed, attracting a growing number of complementary memories'. So improving attention involves widening the range of memories invoked. The more varied and deeper the memories, the richer the perception and the more meaning it can give to the world. In utilitarian, spotlight, left hemisphere attention the accompanying memories are few, relevant only to what is spotlit, and become swiftly, almost instantaneously, merged with perception. But in lantern, right hemisphere attention the accompanying memories are unrelated to action, and so are more numerous, varied, free-floating and long-lived. Bergson does not explain how to stimulate such memories but an effective method is to use the arts. One of the pleasures of reading, looking at paintings or listening to music is that these activities can induce a unique form of hyper-alert reverie that is unconnected with the art but could not be enjoyed without it, a free-associating RH workout creating, stirring and linking memories – and this encourages a similarly enriched response to reality.

RH attention constantly requires such reinforcement because it is always being curtailed by functional LH selectivity. In a remarkable feat of intuition Joyce seems to have sensed the eternal conflict between brain hemispheres and in *Finnegans Wake* personified them not just as rival brothers but *twins* who 'shared the twin chamber'. Shem (RH) is a writer – imaginative, funny and spiritual but also disorderly, irresponsible and self-doubting.

Shaun (LH) is orderly, solemn and self-righteous, 'wisechairman-looking', determined to undermine Shem and impose on the world the 'phullupsuppy' he knows to be correct. Even more remarkably, Joyce understood that Shem and Shaun must cooperate to become a complete person and united them at the end of *Finnegans Wake.*

The problem is Shaun's constant need to suppress Shem, which means that attention to what we find useful tends to harden into attention to what we are used to. We see only what we expect to see. The right hemisphere ceases to engage and the smug left becomes increasingly lazy, noticing hardly anything and filling in most of the scene based on expectation.

Recent research has demonstrated how shockingly limited attention can be. In the famous 'invisible gorilla' experiment[155] people were asked to watch a basketball clip and count the number of passes made by the team in white. During the play a gorilla wanders onto and off the court – but many viewers failed to notice it. In another case[156] an experimenter stopped passers-by to ask for directions – but during the conversation a long wooden door was carried rudely between the two and the original experimenter substituted for another. Incredibly, half of those giving directions failed to notice the change.

Needless to say, the subjects of these experiments were shocked to discover the extent of their inattention. Cunningly deceptive consciousness creates the illusion of a complete and accurate mental representation of reality.

Hearing is similarly limited. Listening to others talk, we believe we hear and understand complete sentences but actually construct meaning from a few words and the context. This is not usually apparent but becomes obvious when trying to understand someone speaking in a foreign language. So it is difficult to write authentic dialogue because, although we are ceaselessly assailed by talk, we rarely hear exactly what anyone says.

The shameful revelation is that in the course of an average day we see hardly anything, hear hardly anything and understand almost nothing at all. But by making an enormous effort we can at least be conscious of this. The height of awareness is becoming aware of being aware of hardly anything.

The other enemy of attention is the innate tendency to anticipate a rosier future. One of Bloom's exemplary talents is an ability to live entirely in the present and to give it his undivided attention. The only time he anticipates is when he looks forward to a bath. Instead he sees, hears, analyses, speculates and associates. Buddha would surely have described Bloom as enlightened, an adept of mindfulness.

Marcel, on the other hand, is profoundly unenlightened, always complaining about the 'incurable imperfection in the very essence of the present moment' and anxiously looking forward to something more satisfying. But those who constantly look forward are doomed to be constantly looking back. Marcel is obsessed by the past because he is obsessed by the future, which constantly slips by unappreciated into the past – and when moments of the past are recaptured by involuntary memory they are vividly experienced as though for the first time because, in a sense, this *is* the first time. These memories have the overwhelming intensity and exaltation of epiphanies. And Proust illustrates Bergson's theory of the interplay between memory and perception by explaining how involuntary memories can make the present vividly real for once. Two similar experiences, one current and the other a recollection triggered by some sensory equivalent, a sound, smell or touch, suddenly and unexpectedly merge to produce an overwhelming awareness of 'existence' and permit 'my being to secure, to isolate, to immobilize – for a moment brief as a flash of lightning – what it normally never apprehends: a fragment of time in the pure state'.

In fact Proust had read Bergson and even been a pageboy at Bergson's wedding to a cousin of Proust's, Louise Neuberger. Yet, despite the family connection, Bergson's Jewishness and the many correspondences of intellectual interest, the two men did not have deep conversations on art, comedy, memory or time. Instead, when they met, Bergson complained about being distracted by noise and Proust recommended Quiès ear plugs. Neither one of the greatest theorists of comedy nor one of its greatest practitioners saw anything funny in this conversation, which is itself a great joke.

An involuntary memory is involuntary at both ends. It has not been created by conscious memorising and may not be retrieved by conscious recall. Conscious memory is thin, restricted to a few bare facts – but involuntary memory delivers a complete experience, all the visual details of a past scene complete with associated sounds and smells, the accompanying emotions and even a return of the self that had the experience. It is not a recalling but a reliving of the past. For a moment, the past supplants the present – and this is always a surprise because the memory was created unconsciously, for reasons that are unclear. So we can remember completely only what we have completely forgotten. And such memories may be triggered only by an accidental repetition of some of the original sensory data. Surprise is of course a factor in the magic but the main enchantment is the complete retrieval of a past moment. Yet the original experience was usually insignificant. Only loss has made it priceless. Can only loss confer enchantment? Proust claimed that it is impossible to apply imagination to what is present – but his youthful epiphanies show that this is not true.

In *À la recherche* Proust describes many involuntary memories, most triggered by smell or taste – for instance the famous episode of the madeleine dipped in tea that brings back his childhood. Other triggering smells include those of lilac, hawthorn, burning twigs, petrol and the musty odour of a public toilet. One of Proust's insights was that taste and smell are uniquely evocative: 'taste and smell alone, more fragile but enduring, more unsubstantial but more persistent ... bear unflinchingly, in the tiny and almost impalpable drop of their essence, the vast structure of recollection'. And neuroscience has confirmed this by discovering that smell and taste are the only senses connected directly to the hippocampus, the location in the brain of long-term memory. All the other senses are first processed elsewhere in the brain and this indirect connection to memory makes them less efficient at recall.

Proust was fortunate in having such an acute sense of smell – and *À la recherche* is as full of odours and scents as is *Ulysses* of noises and music. Not surprisingly for a man who spent so much of his life in bed, Proust was especially sensitive to the smells of stuffy bedrooms, especially 'the central, glutinous, insipid, indigestible and fruity smell of the flowered bedspread'.

Bloom, too, has an involuntary memory triggered by smell that takes him back to his childhood. When he is cutting his toenails last thing at night he sniffs the clippings and becomes once more 'Master Bloom, pupil of Mrs Ellis's juvenile school'. So a proper Jousting day should begin with sniffing a stuffy bedroom in the morning and finish with sniffing toenail clippings at night. To sustain the high in between, nip into public toilets and inhale the heady scent.

But of course such a day is not possible. An involuntary memory experience cannot be repeated. The madeleine works its magic once only. And in fact every retrieval alters a memory and takes it further from the original experience. The more often an experience is remembered the less accurate the memory. This is because memories are not complete experiences, recorded faithfully on date- and time-stamped storage devices and shelved in a brain basement awaiting retrieval, like cans of film in a BBC library. Only a few core details are actually recorded so that remembering is a process of filling in the gaps and linking everything together to provide the illusion of a complete experience. Naturally the brain would like the memory to fit its current view of things and performs the filling-in accordingly. So it is not only dictators who alter the past. Everyone does it. Even the past is not fixed. Even the past is process. Memory is as capricious, deceptive and unpredictable as consciousness itself. And, again like consciousness, memory is creative – it likes to invent satisfactory memories. Mark Twain, lamenting the fading of memory in age, remarked: 'When I was younger I could remember anything whether it had happened or not.'[157]

At least we remember with vivid accuracy traumatic events. Those of a certain age recall exactly where they were when they heard that John F. Kennedy had been shot. We all remember exactly where we were on 9/11. Except that we don't. The day after the US space shuttle *Challenger* exploded, the psychologist Ulric Neisser recorded in detail people's memories of the disaster and three years later recorded their memories once more.[158] Fewer than 7 per cent of the later reports matched the earlier ones, 50 per cent were different on two thirds of the facts and 25 per cent were different on every major detail. A similar experiment on 9/11 memories produced much the same result. William Hirst, one of the neuroscientists who worked on the 9/11 research, has suggested that frequently retrieving memories makes them more convincing.[159] So memory perpetrates an incredible double con – the more often an experience is remembered the less accurate the memory *but the greater the belief in its accuracy.*

And recent research has revealed yet another trick. Memory interferes with chronology, moving shameful episodes further back in time and bringing forward good deeds.[160] So, just like a contemporary politician, memory creates a good-news narrative: yes, you've been an asshole but, hey, you're improving.

No, memory is worse than a politician – more like a corrupt cop, systematically contaminating crime scenes by destroying, distorting and planting evidence and altering the dates on the evidence bags.

But many of its workings remain mysterious. Why do I have vivid memories of the most random inconsequential things but no recollection at all of the decisive moments that changed my life? The answer could be that memories are created by the body in a sensory process but retrieved by the mind in a cerebral process, and what is of great concern to the mind may be of little concern to the body and vice versa. This would also help to explain why, as Proust realised, the senses are better at retrieval than the conscious mind.

So memory is not a passive storage capacity but an active participant in, and potential enricher of, the here and now. Its characteristic movement is not from present into past but from past into present; where the former movement is only occasional the latter is constant. Memory, like consciousness and selfhood, is continuous process.

The idea that *everything* is process was developed into a full philosophy by Alfred North Whitehead early in the twentieth century[161] and further developed by many subsequent thinkers (appropriately, process philosophy is itself an ongoing process, and at the end of the twentieth century offered an alternative to postmodern materialism and relativism). Faced with the perennial question, 'What's it all about, Alfie?', Whitehead's answer was 'process', a 'philosophy of the organism' that defines reality as a vast mega-process endlessly creating novelty (God for those who like religious terminology) and made up of a multitude of interconnecting and interdependent mini-processes (including the human organism), themselves made up of micro-processes (like consciousness, memory and selfhood) and so on all the way down to the brief but hectic fizz of elementary particles, which are not really particles but merely short-lived vibrations.

This rejection of substance and causality is difficult to accept – surely somewhere there has to be some sort of *stuff* and it must be subject to cause and effect? And equally difficult, especially for the young, is the idea that everything is constantly evolving. When young it is impossible to imagine growing old and even more impossible to imagine that the old were once young. The world is a given, as fixed and unchangeable as your opinions about it – inconceivable to think that you could end up preferring Schubert to The Troggs. Then, as the years go by and everything does change, inexorably and relentlessly, there is an overwhelming urge to reject the new or even to deny its existence. For the message of process is that nothing endures. Everything is on fire and each flame may flare uniquely and brilliantly but will also soon gutter and go out. Even the sun will eventually die.

But there is also the message that it is more fun to flare than to petrify. Process philosophy is frightening but also exhilarating, exhausting but also energising, an irrevocable sentence of death but also a potential summons to life. And processism offers a remarkable unity of unities, an ultimate 'many in one'[162] that combines East and West, pre- and postmodern, religion and science, psychology and the arts, or, more specifically: the thought of Buddha, Heraclitus, Montaigne, James, Dewey and Bergson; the physics of entropy and quantum mechanics; the biology of evolution, organism and emergence; the psychology of consciousness and selfhood; the spirituality of pantheism; the comicality of petrifaction and the creativity of Proust and Joyce (*À la recherche* is a meditation on process and *Ulysses* and *Finnegans Wake* are demonstrations of it; the *Wake*, with its shape-shiftings, mergings and mutations, is the ultimate process book). Better still, the philosophy has what Whitehead wanted above all – 'relevance to the ordinary stubborn facts of daily life'.[163] It extends the central aesthetic principle of creativity to all of life, rejects determinism in favour of free will (every individual is responsible for self-creation) and reinforces the commandment to attend to the here and now because there are no final states of being, only the ongoing process of becoming – unpredictable experience created anew in each moment. Surf the process, develop or petrify, learn or die.

9

The Madness of Status and Snobbery

My left hand seemed to be coming off and when I suggested this possibility in a piercing scream none of the horrified onlookers denied it. I had just fallen off a high wall, smashing my wrist, and the boys I had been playing with, apparently blasé toughs equally impervious to surprise and fear, were abruptly both shocked and profoundly afraid. One of them helped me up and across the street to my front door and then they all fled, knowing that my parents would blame them for the accident.

My mother did not deny that the hand seemed determined to detach itself but, instead of screaming for a neighbour to drive me to hospital (my father was at late Mass, a typically disgusting form of male laziness), sat me on a kitchen chair and disappeared upstairs, returning with the Vyella shirt and short-trousered Sunday suit I had been commanded to take off an hour earlier in order to be granted permission to go out to play with the street boys. I could scarcely believe that this was happening but my mother, despite the hand about to come off and my howls of pain and rage, actually removed the cheap shirt and khaki shorts and thrust me into the good shirt and suit. Only then was I fit to be seen by a doctor.

It was this incident that revealed to me the full craziness of snobbery, an imperative so absolute that it overrode everything else, even intense protective love for a first-born son. My mother would rather have my hand come off than be shown up as common.

For a long time it seemed to me that such snobbery was a phenomenon of a particular social group – the lower-middle class, with its desperate craving for respectability. The simple solution was to avoid these lunatics. So, much to my mother's disgust, I befriended only working-class boys and, to her disgust and outrage, went out with and eventually married a working-class girl. The working class seemed socially homogenous, uncontaminated by fantasies of distinction and superiority – until I discovered that my beloved's neighbours regarded her family as appalling snobs because her father had built their home and owned it, whereas the neighbours lived in rented council properties. And my pure-in-heart beloved admitted, rather sheepishly, that she would not be seen dead with anyone from the council houses and dated only middle-class boys.

Hence a revelation – if there was snobbery between working-class next-door neighbours then it was obvious that there were fine distinctions all the way through the social scale, and that social scales were universal and always minutely calibrated.

And social rank is only one way of feeling superior. The most common sources of distinction are wealth, status, fame, religion, race, beauty and culture – the seven deadly wins – and there are shifting distinctions among these ways of seeking distinction. Celebrity and money are now more important than class, and good looks outweigh everything else. But there are legions of alternative strategies – as varied and numerous as the individuals who employ them – and new strategies are constantly being invented. When some forms of superiority become socially unacceptable, race for instance, others take their place. Few in polite society would now jeer openly at black people but it is perfectly acceptable to jeer at the white working class, the 'chavs'. Recently the travel company Activities Abroad advertised 'chav-free' holidays and the London fitness chain Gymbox even suggested using 'chavs' as punch bags: 'Why hone your skills on punch bags and planks of wood when you can deck some chavs?'[164] Imagine the furore if these advertisements had used 'black', 'Paki' or 'Paddy' instead of 'chav'. It seems to be always the irresponsible working class that attracts attention, whether from politicians, writers or filmmakers – the class romanticised in 1960s kitchen-sink dramas as spirited rebels and demonised nowadays as feckless 'chavs'.

Not that any of those demonised are likely to be bothered. An ironic consequence of the egalitarian society is that it has made everyone equal only in their right to feel superior. So the disadvantaged have developed an alternative street culture that sneers back at the mainstream. If you can't be superior in one way, find another. In the Northern Ireland where I grew up Catholics were socially inferior to Protestants so the Catholic solution was to become superior through education, to be twice as smart as smug Prods.

It is usually wiser to cultivate an alternative superiority than to try to play the superior at their own game – even if you do it well you will be despised as a sycophant. There are many ways of being Irish in England but I have never adopted the strategy of trying to sound English. Instead I depend on knowledge, especially cultural knowledge (when a reviewer described me as 'erudite' I almost died of ecstasy). But I am very shaky on classical music, so it was an agonising experience when my daughter was learning the violin and I had to take her to recitals in upper-class homes. Not only socially disadvantaged ('I see you haven't lost your accent') but deprived of cultural superiority as well ('You haven't been to the Benjamin Britten?'), I felt like a medieval serf with his tongue cut out.

Annie Ernaux and Alice Munro are both terrifically good on the ploys of the disadvantaged. In fact the ceaseless struggle for superiority is the main theme of Ernaux's *Cleaned Out.* First the young girl feels superior in her local area because her parents' *café-épicerie* puts them a cut above workers. Then at school she is made to feel inferior by the daughters of opticians and accountants but discovers her intelligence and takes an exultant revenge in academic success, expressing an intellectual contempt as cruel as the social contempt of the snobs ('Fuck you, you bunch of morons'). Later still, just like my own beloved, she rejects factory and farm workers to chase middle-class boys, only to feel inferior once again when the pursuit is successful, but coming to despise them when they fail exams ('I began to think I was superior').

Like many before and since, myself included, both the Ernaux and Munro narrators come to the conclusion that knowledge is the most effective form of superiority. Ernaux: 'I found the solution, that the most cunning way of staying on top is by knowing things that the others didn't know.' Munro: 'Knowledge is the most effective form of superiority for the powerless – because it is secret.' (And as the Ernaux narrator discovers, the realm of knowledge is itself riven by rival superiorities – the arts students despise the science geeks who despise them right back as dilettantes and posers. Then, within the arts and sciences . . .)

And even women without knowledge can feel superior. In Munro's *Lives of Girls and Women* the narrator says of her aunts: 'They respected men's work beyond anything; they also laughed at it. This was strange; they could believe absolutely in its importance and at the same time convey their judgement that it was, from one point of view, frivolous, non-essential.' My own mother and aunts were exactly like this. Even as they exhorted me to pass examinations and not be distracted by 'getting an eye for the girls', they believed that their own sex was profoundly superior and that they were its superior representatives, the guardians of the only true knowledge, whereas I, with my textbooks and maths equations and science experiments, was only a performing monkey, an *idiot savant*, a joke.

Munro is also perceptive on the battles for superiority within the female sex, as hidden but as constant and ferocious as those within the working class. Her narrator's mother is also a snob who writes outraged letters to newspapers signed Princess Ida, and instructs her daughter to say that she does not live on the low-status Flats Road but '*at the end* of the Flats Road'. However the mother is a naïve snob and no match for the 'nimble malice' of the aunts who defeat her with 'tiny razor cuts, bewilderingly, in the middle of kindness'. There is an exquisite moment when the mother offers to teach one of the aunts to read music: 'Aunt Elspeth refused, with a delicate, unnatural laugh, as if somebody had offered to teach her to play pool.'

The superiority of the aunts is an example of the audacious strategy of free-standing distinction – feeling superior for no reason other than the strength of the conviction itself. In many such cases signs of distinction are scornfully rejected as redundant – so the superiority is demonstrated by a refusal to demonstrate it (Munro's aunts dismiss all displays of distinction with the contemptuous remark, 'Don't they think they're somebody'). This kind of unsupported snobbery is often created in families. A parent, usually the father, decides that he and his children are infinitely superior to everyone else and establishes all relationships on this basis – and usually the wife and children are happy to accept this belief. John McGahern's novel *Amongst Women* shows just such a family, the Morans, whose father is totally convinced of his infinite worth and transmits this conviction to his children. The novel shows how successful this can be. Almost everyone defers to the Morans. The alarming lesson is that the world will largely accept a self-estimate. It will believe whatever you wish if you present it with sufficient consistency and assurance.

It seems to be necessary to feel superior in some, and preferably many, ways to some, and preferably many, others, and this necessity affects every aspect of everyday life – where we live, how we furnish and decorate our homes, what we wear and how we groom, what we work at and how we get there, what and where we eat, where and how we holiday and, of course, all cultural preferences and social interactions (Bergson wrote that the purpose of social life is to foster 'an admiration of ourselves based on the admiration we think we are inspiring in others'[165]). Being aware of all this is little help. When one of Alice Munro's heroines gets divorced and leaves the conventional family home, she vows not to waste time and money on improving shabby rented accommodation but is unable to prevent herself from trying to make her apartment look arty.

In fact one of Munro's main themes is the universal and irreconcilable conflict between the rival superiorities of the freedom-loving, independent liberal who rejects convention, and the community-loving, traditional conservative who upholds convention. The liberal despises the conservative as repressed, circumscribed and fearful – a peasant, and the conservative despises the liberal as self-indulgent, irresponsible and pretentious – an idiot.

The French sociologist Pierre Bourdieu has argued that personal taste is always used to signal social class,[166] and this was probably true until recently – but now taste has become an entirely independent form of distinction and this makes it more complex and volatile. Taste likes to pretend to be natural, absolute and innate but is always artificial, relative and learned. Good taste defines itself in opposition to bad taste, so when bad taste tries to move upmarket good taste is obliged to reposition. When peasants trudged along country roads the sophisticated enjoyed driving past, but when the peasants acquired cars the sophisticated took up walking. The positions have changed but the mutual contempt is the same. The walkers despise as vulgarians the peasants roaring by in their ramshackle, mud-stained jalopies and the peasants despise as idiots the walkers in their special boots, shorts, sunhats and dinky rucksacks packed with organic fruit, bottled water, insect repellent and wet wipes. This is the wonderful irony of distinction. We find ridiculous and contemptible the efforts of others to look superior (that dickhead in his sports car) but fondly believe that our own stratagems are terrifically effective (being seen on the train reading Proust is *so classy*).

Put any two people together and each will seek ways of feeling superior to the other. If a ship went down in the Pacific and a single sailor managed to swim to a desert island, would he be pleased to see, ten minutes later, another sailor emerging from the surf? Quite possibly – but only if the new arrival accepted that the first man was now a landed aristocrat while he himself was an illegal immigrant.

Is this need to feel superior innate? It certainly has the strength of a primitive drive. A snobbish reaction is as instinctive, immediate and powerful as the fight-or-flight reflex. I have hated middle-class snobbery since I was a boy but remain a middle-class snob. For instance I register 'council estate person' in less than a nanosecond and feel instant superiority and disdain. It takes a great effort to suppress this reaction and not let it show or influence behaviour. Snobbery management is as difficult and necessary as anger management.

And as difficult as suppressing existing snobbery is resisting new opportunities. When a book of mine had a modest and entirely unexpected success I believed I was much too mature for this to affect me in any way. But as soon as someone told me about the Amazon sales charts I was unable to resist checking my position every day. Hey, I'm beating seven colours of skitter out of Alain de Botton! And soon after this I began to feel that my offhand friends should be showing a little more respect – and that the success should have been more complete. Why hasn't the book been translated into at least eleven languages and done as an audio book and a graphic novel? Why isn't there a bidding war over the next book? Come to think of it, why bother with a next book? Why not trade on my new reputation for irreverence by outsourcing? How about a range of fiery stir-fry sauces called *A Wok on the Wild Side*? An edgy, risk-taking men's fragrance called *Heist*? A softer but subtle and foxy women's fragrance called *Ruse*?

There is further support for the innate theory from the anthropological evidence that status hierarchies are universal in primitive cultures. The anthropologist Nick Long argues that 'the ethic to be egalitarian only seems to arise after exposure to hierarchy, and a realisation of its discontents'.[167] In other words, hierarchy and superiority are natural and egalitarianism is artificial. *The Gift*, by the great anthropologist Marcel Mauss (Mighty Mauss), describes a particularly ingenious strategy used by many different peoples – humiliation by generosity. A member of the community who has become prosperous, for instance by successful hunting or trading, demonstrates superiority to others by constantly showering them with valuable gifts. When I first read this I had an eerie feeling of recognition. I remembered visiting, as a student, an affluent self-made brother-in-law who, in spite of my protestations about not wanting to drink during the day, swept me off to his club where, in spite of further protests, he insisted on buying me round after round. To counter my superior education, he humiliated me with generosity by displaying his superior wealth.

What makes the gift strategy so cunning is that, better even than concealing the snobbery, it disguises it as magnanimity.

And for those too stingy or too busy to offer gifts, there is the equivalent, but free and simple, option of disguising superiority as benevolence in a special kind of smile. The psychologist Paula Niedenthal, an expert on the complexities of the smiley face, has identified a 'power smile' often delivered with a raised chin to reinforce the mental looking-down. '"You're an idiot, I'm better than you" – that's what we mean by a dominant smile.'[168] We are all familiar with this, and probably both from receiving and bestowing. As royalty, celebrities and the rich have always known, a smile is the most subtle and satisfying way of shitting on the inferior.

The human animal is certainly superior at feeling superior. Every town is the centre of the universe, every religion is the one true faith, every group is the ideal community and every individual is superior to everyone else.

The need to feel superior must be absolutely fundamental – and Hannah Arendt has argued that it is an inevitable consequence of consciousness itself, which 'confirms beyond doubt the reality of sensations and of reasoning'.[169] It may be possible to be more specific and assign this need to the brain's left hemisphere. There is a cluster of feelings that overlap and reinforce each other – certainty, superiority, self-importance, self-righteousness and, when these are denied, anger – and the first and last, certainty and anger, have been identified with the left hemisphere (anger is unique among emotions in this respect).[170] So, in the absence of evidence, it seems reasonable to propose that superiority is also a LH phenomenon. And this lack of evidence is itself evidence. Everything has to mean something, as Tricky Sam Nanton said, and there must be a reason for the curious scarcity of psychological or neurological research into snobbery, a human trait so universal and pernicious that it ought to be of consuming interest. But if there are experiments and studies I am not aware of them (Pierre Bourdieu's *Distinction* is a rare exception and this is a work of sociology). It may be that the conviction of superiority is so fundamental and implicit – like awareness of having two hands and feet – that it is difficult to acknowledge, much less consider or challenge. Certainly few snobs are ever aware of their snobbery (so my confession is a good reason for feeling superior to other snobs) and many would be as outraged at an accusation of feeling superior as at a denial of their own superiority.

Indeed the strategies for denying demonstrations of superiority may well be as diverse and ingenious as those for implementing such demonstrations. And as overt displays of class, power and hierarchical distinctions have gone out of fashion such denials have become increasingly important. This is why your boss pretends to be one of the guys.

Fiction more than compensates for psychology's lack of interest. All good novelists are acutely aware of the universal madness of status and snobbery – and the novelists of the Jousting tradition have analysed class snobbery at every level. Proust covers aristocrats, the upper-middle class and servants, Joyce the lower-middle class, David Foster Wallace the urban professional class, Henry Green the urban working class, Annie Ernaux the small shopkeeper class and John McGahern and Alice Munro the rural poor. At the bottom of the scale in rural Canada was a man known as the 'honey dumper' whose job was cleaning out dry toilets (a function performed in contemporary India by women of the 'untouchable' caste). But even the honey dumper found ways of feeling superior, believing that chemical and flush toilets were a terrible mistake and pronouncing 'the *ch* in *chemicals* like the *ch* in *church*' when he informed people: 'Many has got these chemicals in and many has wished they never.'[171]

Superiority, in its multiple manifestations and confrontations, is a major theme of Mike Leigh's films – in *Nuts in May* the moral superiority of the eco-correct countered by the insouciant superiority of the incorrect, in *Four Days in July* the religious superiority of Northern Irish Protestants countered by the 'loveable victim' superiority of Catholics, and all through Leigh's work the boorish superiority of men countered by the icily genteel superiority of women, and the social superiority of the aspirant countered by the mocking superiority of the indolent. Class confrontations are central to many of his films, with the upper and lower protagonists sometimes living next door to each other, as in *Grown-Ups* and *High Hopes*. Leigh is at his best on the lower-middle and working classes (but almost always the responsible working class who actually work, remain married, rear children and care for needy relatives) and his favourite terrain is the fraught interface between these. In *Meantime*, one of his most subtle class studies, a woman who has moved up into the suburban middle class attempts to help the children of her sister who is still in a council flat and with an unemployed husband – but is rejected and humiliated. Is her generous help genuine or a Marcel Mauss attempt to display superiority? Is her rejection justified or motivated by envy and spite? All that is certain is that relations between classes are as complex and difficult as those between genders.

Sometimes different forms of superiority clash within the same individual – as in the Munro and Ernaux narrators, who use their intelligence to escape deprivation but remain conflicted and guilty, secretly ashamed of many aspects of the original background but deeply suspicious of all aspects of the new, and as a result often unsure of how to behave; confused, defensive, touchy, unpredictable. For the Munro character Rose, in *The Beggar Maid*, the vulgarity of her home and the refinement of her university accommodation (with a cultured, older woman who has taken Rose under her wing) have the effect of cancelling each other out. The pretensions of the educated milieu are constantly and savagely undercut by the 'who-do-you-think-you-are?' contempt of the home town (the original Canadian title of *The Beggar Maid* was *Who Do You Think You Are?* – a superior title in every sense). The benefit for the reader is that, in their best work, Munro and Ernaux are acutely aware of the charge of exploiting their impoverished backgrounds to entertain the affluent, and as a result have a fierce hatred of pretension and evasion and a brutal directness and honesty rare in fiction. And the lesson is that while internal conflicts cause endless confusion and even anguish, they may be useful in maintaining checks and balances. The trick is to retain the best of both sides and use each best to curb each worst.

In the endless struggle to keep the many-headed monster of snobbery at bay we need all the help we can get – and *New Yorker* cartoons are another rich resource. For almost a century these have exposed and ridiculed our ceaseless attempts to find ways of appearing superior, often by showing practical women undermining self-important men. For instance the cleaning woman with mop and bucket who remarks to another cleaning woman across a cluttered boardroom, 'The tumult and the shouting dies, the captains and the kings depart'; the secretary who, noting the approach of two grim men in suits and heavy dark spectacles, says to a friend on the phone, 'I'll talk to you later, Stella, it's the return of the Jedi'; the wife who opens the French windows of a new, expensive-looking house to say to the pot-bellied man on the patio gazing solemnly at the moon, 'Philip, *Gunsmoke* is starting.'

À la recherche includes a comprehensive analysis of snobbery – and as a consequence Proust has often been accused of being a snob. He would surely have found it ironic that his merciless savaging of 'society' has been interpreted as admiration.

The exposure of the Duchesse de Guermantes is the most devastating because she is initially presented as glamorous and then, throughout the book, systematically stripped of every vestige of glamour. In the beginning, the young Marcel admires her from a distance, believing in her legendary wit, blithe lack of affectation, deep appreciation of culture and undying loyalty to a circle of brilliant friends. Then, as he is introduced and gets to know her, the wit is revealed to be pitiful inanity and the apparent lack of affectation itself the most extreme affectation. The Duchesse poses as a carefree bohemian who has purely by accident married the wealthiest aristocrat in France, and by having to ask her husband to repeat her witticisms pretends to be unconscious of them. The love of culture and the cult of friendship are just as hypocritical. When the Duchesse's 'greatest friend', Swann, learns that he is dying and goes to inform her, he meets the Duchesse and Duc rushing out to their carriage, already late for a dinner party. To avoid discussing the fatal illness, they pretend that Swann must be joking.

The superiority at the top of the social scale is so absolute that it has no need to demonstrate itself and is often concealed in a charming affectation of modesty and self-effacement. But occasionally it breaks out. One of Proust's great ladies, incensed at being unable to acquire a bigger house than a rival, cunningly turns the tables by inventing a new form of superiority – hiring more servants, forty-five in all. The rival cannot compete because it is necessary to appear superior but even more necessary not to appear to be trying to be superior. The superiority must seem unconscious and effortless.

Moving down a social level, *À la recherche* includes a detailed portrait of a middle-class provincial snob, Legrandin, who yearns for the aristocratic society of the Guermantes and their circle but claims to detest aristocrats, even to be 'a bit of a Jacobin', and constantly issues violent denunciations of snobbery and snobs. Proust explains that Legrandin is entirely sincere in all this.

An even more interesting case study is the career of Bloch. An ambitious young man from the lower end of the upper-middle class, Bloch, who is also Jewish, realises that his Jewishness will make social climbing difficult and becomes instead a passionate enemy of the entire social system. But this kind of rebel does not want to change the system, only his own place within it.[172] The rebelliousness is only a rage for acceptance. When Bloch eventually rises by means of marriage, he becomes as contented and smug as he was despairing and angry. The rebel is the greatest conformist of all.

But the nature of snobbery changes with social level. On the way down through the middle to the serving class the snobbery becomes more idiotic, virulent and naked. (An equivalent phenomenon is that the more limited the social milieu, the more rabid the snobbery – as a character in Updike's *The Centaur* thinks to himself, 'Make Nero look tame, small town aristocrats'.)

Proust is particularly good on the way that servants not only collude with the social order but uphold and then replicate it within their own ranks, often even more vindictively and cruelly than their masters. In *À la recherche* there are several examples of servants hounding fellow servants out of employment. And Marcel's servant, Françoise, is more than happy to procure attractive young serving girls for her master, who orders dairymaids as casually as others order milk. Better still is the lady's maid who believes herself infinitely superior to chambermaids and, on leaving a hotel with her mistress, always defecates in a wardrobe or drawer, 'just to leave a little keepsake with the chambermaid who will have to clean it up'. This is the kind of detail that few Proust scholars mention.

Proust illustrates snobbery from duchesse down to lady's maid – but omits the level he knew nothing of, the lower-middle class of skilled tradesmen, clerks and government officials. In another neat example of the two writers' complementarity, this is the class Joyce came from and wrote about with such acuity. In the lower-middle class social snobbery is at its most intense because these people are closest to the working class and in constant terror of dropping down into it. But close analysis of social class is rare in Irish fiction because Ireland has raised the art of concealing snobbery to the national level by promoting the illusion that there is no such thing as Irish class distinction, that Catholic Ireland is one big, homogenous, genial, generous and easy-going happy family and that snobbery is a vice of English aristocrats, landed gentry and ladies from Tunbridge Wells in lavender twinsets. As the devil's best trick is convincing everyone that he does not exist, so the snob's most effective stratagem is claiming to live in a snobbery-free culture. In fact Irish society is riven with virulent class hatred.

Joyce understood this and his books teem with examples of casual everyday snobbery. One of his crucial insights was that social superiority can endure and flourish even when its social justification has been lost. So the snobbery reflex is not only instant but permanent. Once superior, always superior. In Joyce's Dublin the crucial thing was to become a gentleman and thus be superior forever. A gentleman would always be a gentleman, regardless of how he might come down in the world – the penniless sponger Lenehan could never be associated with Dublin beggars, and the peloothered, falling-down-stairs Tom Kernan of 'Grace' could never be considered a common drunk but, instead, a 'gentleman' who 'missed his footing'.

How did one become a gentleman and thus superior for life? By receiving a proper education, preferably with the Jesuits. A contemporary equivalent is passing the 11-plus examination and going to grammar school. There are many idiots who consider themselves unassailably superior, not just intellectually but in every way, because they managed to pass an examination at the age of ten.

James Joyce understood the gentleman phenomenon because he was a product of it. His father, John Joyce, spent all his money on drink and was incapable of housing, clothing or feeding his family but, however low he sank, he remained always a gentleman – and a gentleman's son must also be a gentleman, so a high priority was to pay for a Jesuit education for James (when he went off to the Jesuit boarding school his tearful mother begged him not to speak to 'the rough boys'). Another priority was to preserve the symbols of social superiority. When the Joyce family was obliged to make one of its frequent moves, often in haste to evade debtors, they piled their belongings on a cart – but John insisted that the sacred family portraits were carried by hand to preserve them from harm. John himself grandly bore along a framed engraving of the coat of arms of the Galway Joyces, crying: 'Head up! Keep our flag flying! An eagle gules volant in a field argent displayed.'

John Joyce was of course not impressed by his son's choice of a literary career. When James first moved to Paris and his mother worried about irrelevancies like his having enough to eat, his father was concerned that James would be a 'fitting representative of *our* family' and exhorted him not to 'do anything unbecoming a gentleman'.

Like everyone, James Joyce was indelibly marked by his upbringing in spite of his strenuous attempts to escape (as Stephen Dedalus acknowledges to himself, 'you have the cursed jesuit strain in you'). Although penniless and in debt in Trieste, as everywhere else, James had the family portraits, now augmented by a portrait of his father, shipped over from Dublin, disposed these stupefyingly dull paintings about the walls of his apartment and, in the Joyce family tradition, took them with him on his many, often hasty, moves around the cities of Europe. The joke is that Joyce, never accused of being snobbish because of his apparently bohemian lifestyle and lower-middle-class fictional characters, may well have been more of a snob than Proust, constantly accused of snobbery because he mixed with, and wrote about, Barons and Duchesses.

Joyce is also good on urban v. rural snobbery. This form of superiority may well also be universal (for instance Annie Ernaux's narrator is constantly contemptuous of 'peasants'), but is particularly common in countries like Ireland where the urban gentry are only recently descended from peasants but do not care to remember the mud on their boots. (As a country becomes more developed the opposite happens – city folk become sentimentally nostalgic for lost rural roots.) Simon Dedalus and his cronies constantly pour scorn on 'country bumpkins', 'thundering big country fellows', 'ignorant bostooms', 'yahoos' – but as always Simon outdoes the others in malevolence, 'Paddy Stink and Micky Mud'. In 'The Dead' even the sensitive Gabriel Conroy is ashamed that his wife Gretta is from the rural West of Ireland. And kindly Bloom has a rare moment of spite at a country woman. 'Country bred chawbacon' is his dismissive description and, noticing the woman's white stockings, 'Hope the rain mucks them up on her.'

Bloom's spiteful thought is not typical; apart from this he never feels superior. It was quite an achievement for Joyce, so supremely arrogant himself, to make his hero self-effacing. But Joyce came to understand that humility is wiser than arrogance. Though 'humility' may not be the best word – it smacks too much of submission to authority. 'Self-unimportance' is better, an awareness of the laughable absurdity of the individual, a nanospeck fleetingly adrift in the cosmos but entirely convinced of being its centre (in the *Wake* Joyce described human existence as 'a farce of dustiny'). Only those with a keen sense of their own absurdity can truly understand the absurdity of others. This is the source of empathy in literature. Writers may at times succumb to intellectual pride but to write well it is necessary to feel an idiot at heart.

The problem with snobbery is not just the damage snobs do to others but the damage they do to themselves. Can a snob have an epiphany? Can a snob even understand anyone else? Feeling superior may seem like an enviable advantage, the key to well-being and a delightful simplification that avoids tiring observation, analysis and empathy, but it is really a grievous limitation because everything inferior is regarded as homogenous and therefore of no interest. The price of superiority is blindness, deafness and ignorance. And possibly also isolation and outrage – because the world frequently declines to defer.

Joyce's story 'A Mother' demonstrates this with cold accuracy. Miss Devlin has learned French and music 'in a high-class convent' and expects appropriate acknowledgement.

> When she came to the age of marriage she was sent out to many houses, where her playing and ivory manners were much admired. She sat amid the chilly circle of her accomplishments, waiting for some suitor to brave it and offer her a brilliant life. But the young men whom she met were ordinary and she gave them no encouragement.

This is a familiar story. I grew up surrounded by aunts who had never married because no one was good enough for them. There was laughably little basis for their superiority – but the shabby-genteel lower-middle class are the most fanatical snobs. These aunts did not even have accomplishments such as Miss Devlin's. They sat and grew old amid the chilly circle of their high opinions of themselves. Alice Munro's aunts suffer a similarly bleak fate.

The problem is that specific superiority quickly becomes general. It is remarkably easy to go from feeling superior in one way to feeling superior in every way. And from there it is another short step to self-righteousness and universal contempt. And contempt tends to generate anger and disgust, and anger and disgust make it difficult to get any pleasure from life.

My worst fault is contempt and my worst fear is disgust. For me, re-enchanting the world is not a luxury but a necessity. This requires unremitting effort because, like any traits acquired in childhood, snobbery and its associated disgust are impossible to eradicate completely. They have become part of the temperament.

When I sat the 11-plus, candidates were not supposed to have seen even sample questions – but my parents cheated, acquired full sets of previous papers and coached me comprehensively and relentlessly. For them, education was the only route to greater social status. Like Socrates, they believed in the examined life, though not in the same way. I remember going to do the exam in winter, with slushy ice on the pavements. I was wearing a 'good' Crombie overcoat and many of the other boys had no overcoats at all – nor any idea of what they were about to do or of its possible consequences on their lives. Not only were they entirely unprepared, most did not even know what an examination was and not one had ever seen an exam paper. Some were so thinly clothed they were cold to their bones and slugs of thick, greenish-yellow mucus crept from their nostrils and rested on their upper lips. I hated the Crombie coat that made me a respectable nice boy – but was also disgusted to the verge of nausea by the mucus. So the lesson from the 11-plus, supposed to be simple and fair, was that life was neither simple nor fair.

10

The Weirdness of Love and Sex

Love is process – or, rather, three processes in one, the two uniquely weird and complex processes of the partners combined in a relationship process that is not just weirdness doubled but weirdness to the power of two, weirdness squared. The true nature of this three-in-one process is as difficult to establish as the true nature of matter and few care to look below the surface, much less investigate in detail the monstrous creatures of the deep. As comforting as the certainties of classical physics, are the reassuring clichés of the human heart. At the beginning of the twentieth century love and sex in literature were still, mostly, treated as high drama, romance and passion, thrillingly tempestuous and conveniently lacking in sordid detail. Then Joyce and Proust, the quantum physicists of the heart, revealed that most everyday love is petty, manipulative and devious and most everyday sex is furtive, squalid and perverse.

These two investigated every stage of relationships, from youthful obsession at a distance, through the turbulence of infatuation and on into the strange world of marriage.

Both writers understood and loved adolescent girls. The equivalent of Proust's band of girls roaming the Balbec seafront in *À la recherche* is Joyce's trio of girls on Sandymount Strand in

Ulysses. Those girls, those girls, those lovely seaside girls. The Balbec scenes capture exactly the extreme contradictions that bewilder, infuriate and intoxicate young men – the imperiousness and timidity, dominance and docility, petulance and exuberance, childish innocence and adult cunning, raging impatience and prostrate inertia, extravagant demands and equally extravagant gifts.

The attraction of this unpredictable plasticity is the energy of process that suggests the exhilarating potential of life. As Proust put it: 'We feel, in the company of young girls, the refreshing sense that is afforded us by the spectacle of forms undergoing an incessant process of change, a play of unstable forces which recalls that perpetual re-creation of the primordial elements of nature which we contemplate when we stand before the sea.' Later the struggle for survival will make the changing faces petrify – but for a brief moment the potential of process illuminates the world.

Of course this is the male view. As Alice Munro and Annie Ernaux reveal, the plasticity that enchants youths is experienced by the young girls themselves as confusion, resentment, uncertainty and doubt – and this volatile mix of emotions is further complicated by class issues.

Proust's seaside girls are upper-middle class, protected and supported by affluence, and so free to be bold, insouciant and careless. They have no sense of the tyranny of time and the fading of allure. They flirt – but entirely for the fun of flirting, not in order to snare a husband. In contrast, Joyce's girls, Gerty, Cissy and Edy, are lower-middle class and acutely aware of their precarious social position, time-bound attractions and limited window of opportunity. Gerty MacDowell is the pretty one, smugly conscious of her superior attractions and determined to put them to good use. (Good looks are an increasingly important form of supremacy – the contemporary world is divided between the attractive and the unattractive as well as between the rich and the poor.)

Joyce wrote the Gerty episode in the style of a cheap novelette to emphasise her sentimental illusions about romance – but there is no contempt or disgust in the portrait. The reader can almost hear Joyce squealing with pleasure as he wrote about Gerty. (There is a similar zest in the chapter about the pair of young barmaids in the Ormond Hotel. These two episodes effervesce with delight.)

Gerty is particularly proud of her undies. 'She had four dinky sets, with awfully pretty stitchery ... and each set slotted with different coloured ribbons, rosepink, pale blue, mauve and peagreen.' And since she does not want a 'prince charming' but 'a manly man with a strong quiet face', she is attracted to Bloom and, also aware that 'Love laughs at locksmiths' and requires 'the great sacrifice', leans back to expose herself:

> ... and there was no one to see only him and her when she revealed all her graceful beautifully shaped legs like that, supply soft and delicately rounded, and she seemed to hear the panting of his heart, his hoarse breathing, because she knew about the passion of men like that, hot-blooded, because Bertha Supple told her once in dead secret and made her swear she'd never about the gentleman lodger that was staying with them out of the Congested Districts Board that had pictures cut out of papers of those skirt-dancers and highkickers and she said he used to do something not very nice that you could imagine sometimes in the bed.

This is the comedy not just of recognition but affectionate empathy. Who said that comedy can't be warm-hearted? And oh that 'Congested Districts Board'! Joyce must have rolled on the floor for ten minutes when he came up with that.

For those who wonder what such young girls may have looked like, there is the work of Joyce's contemporary, John Sloan, one of the American Ashcan School, who painted working-class city girls with as much delight and love as Joyce employed to describe them. *Girls Drying Their Hair*, for instance, shows three girls on a tenement roof in front of a line of washing (Sloan's washing always looks more joyful than any other painter's) and I think of these three as Gerty, Cissy and Edy. I loved this painting when I saw a reproduction of it in an art book and a few years ago the original turned up unexpectedly in a mixed American show at London's Dulwich Picture Gallery. I turned a corner and there it was in all its sublime glory.

At once I went to the gallery director and explained that I was taking this painting home because Sloan had painted it expressly for me. The Director accepted this but pointed out that the painting was owned by the Phillips Academy in Massachusetts and added, in compassion at my despair:

'There is a consolation.'

'What could possibly console me?'

'The Gallery shop is selling it as a fridge magnet.'

And this is how it has come to pass that, on the door of my fridge, enchanting me every time I open it for organic blueberries and low-fat yoghurt, Gerty, Cissy and Edy are drying their hair in front of washing that dances like an exuberant chorus line.

For young men the sexual adventure begins with adoring such young girls from afar. In *À la recherche* Marcel worships, across the gardens of the Champs-Élysées, Gilberte Swann (daughter of Swann and Odette whose love story forms an earlier section of the novel). In Joyce's story 'Araby', the narrator lies on the floor of his parlour with the window blind almost fully down to spy rapturously on the girl across the street. This strange, eerie story is like an early episode from *À la recherche.* There is the same exalted language, a similar unnamed narrator of no specified age who feels himself to be different and superior, and the yearning ends in a similar disillusionment: 'I saw myself as a creature driven and derided by vanity; and my eyes burned with anguish and anger.'

Both Joyce and Proust understood the psychology of infatuation, where the beloved is merely a means to the intoxication of being in love. The actual girl in 'Araby' barely exists for the narrator. And with Gilberte, Marcel is too obsessed with arranging his next love high to see the real girl in front of him.

But the beloved who is invisible to the lover is all too visible to everyone else. The two most frequent and perplexed queries about relationships are, What does she see in *him*? and What does he see in *her*? On Molly's relationship with Bloom, one of the Dubliners asks in annoyance, 'What did she marry a coon like that for?' When Swann falls for Odette his sophisticated friends are shocked and appalled. When Marcel shows a friend a photograph of his great love Albertine, the friend is too stunned by Albertine's lack of distinction to say anything.

There are lots of reasons why so many relationships appear inexplicable. We are always attracted by the unknown and we always want what we can't have, so the mysterious and unattainable are always alluring. Bloom notes perceptively the weakness of Irish women for priests and Molly demonstrates this by thinking, 'I'd like to be embraced by one in his vestments and the smell of incense off him like the pope'. Similarly, my aunts, who were violently puritanical about sex and would have been horrified by Molly Bloom, were always cooing, 'Isn't he a lovely wee priest?' – then the simpering giggle that made me want to throw up on their Persian rug – 'Such a *lovely* wee priest'.

Related to the lure of the unknown is the desire for danger and instability in love. Proust: 'Beneath any carnal attraction that goes at all deep, there is the permanent possibility of danger.' As for the stability that most lovers believe they seek: 'What makes us happy is the presence in our hearts of an unstable element which we contrive perpetually to maintain.' And of course the partner who offers danger and instability is likely to be disastrous in the long term. While the suitable partner, the one with similar temperament, intelligence and interests, will be too safe and comfortable to be exciting.

In *Lives of Girls and Women* the intelligent, articulate young girl feels nothing for the intelligent, articulate boy she talks to every day but is irresistibly attracted to a violent, taciturn, born-again Baptist lumberyard worker. And all through Munro's work the intellectual heroines are contemptuous of their intellectual male peers and even, in one of her more disturbing revelations, of all men who behave honourably. In her story 'Differently', Munro describes a conversation between wives that will chill the heart of any devoted husband. 'They looked at each other bleakly, and laughed. Then they announced – they admitted – what weighed on them. It was the innocence of these husbands – the hearty, decent, firm, contented innocence. That is a wearying and finally discouraging thing. It makes intimacy a chore.'[173] Similarly, but with even more naked candour, Annie Ernaux's later books describe women's impatience and contempt for well-meaning men and their intense affairs with selfish, philistine misogynists.

The lesson of these books is that women need security but are attracted only by danger. So for men the ruse is to appear to be a wild, dangerous outlaw while in reality remaining content to hold down a steady job, shop, cook, change nappies and clean the toilet twice a week. It's a challenging ruse, I agree, but these are challenging times.

Another factor is that the lure of the unknown and unattainable is often most strongly exerted by narcissists. Proust and

Freud discovered this at around the same time but independently. Freud: 'It seems very evident that another person's narcissism has a great attraction for those who have renounced part of their own narcissism ... The charm of the child lies to a great extent in his narcissism, his self-contentment and inaccessibility, just as does the charm of certain animals which seem not to concern themselves about us, such as cats.'[174] The narcissist is the most unknowable of all because, although the sense of mystery is strong, there is actually nothing there to know and so the pursuit of the secret is as endless as it is futile.

And narcissists are also attractive by appearing to be lively and frank, full of laughter and fun – but the animation that appears to be love of life is really only love of self, the laughter and fun are expressions not of humour but delight at being so marvellous, and the frankness derives not from a love of truth but an inability to stop talking about one's endlessly fascinating self. The sure sign of the narcissist is continuous, lively chatter, punctuated by frequent, merry laughs – but always exclusively about the self because nothing else holds any interest. Narcissists are incapable of love or, rather, what they love in others is only the love others show for them. This alone would make narcissists impossible to live with – but they also tend to be wilful and impulsive and to dismiss any criticism of their behaviour.

The psychologist Del Paulhus developed a questionnaire that looks as though it tests knowledge of important public figures, but is in fact a test of deception and self-deception because some of the names are fictitious.[175] Not surprisingly, many taking the test attempt to make themselves appear knowledgeable by claiming to have heard of the non-existent people. The interesting discovery is that, while most of these over-claimers withdraw their claims when informed of the truth, narcissists (identified by earlier tests) continue to insist, often aggressively, that they are familiar with the non-existent. This reminded me that I have often seen such reactions. When narcissists are presented with irrefutable proof of being wrong, they do not recant and apologise but scowl angrily at the evidence as though it is some kind of trickery.

The lesson is simple – learn to recognise a narcissist and when you do so, run a mile.

À la recherche has a terrifying example in Odette de Crecy. All Swann's passionate and eloquent attempts to change her behaviour go unheeded. Or, rather, Odette sees such pleas only as evidence of Swann's growing love for her and this growing love makes heeding him even more pointless. So the attempts to change her are not only futile but counterproductive. (Another equally terrifying narcissist is Rosamund Vincy in George Eliot's *Middlemarch* – her ensnaring and ruin of the high-minded Lydgate is agony to read.)

In Joyce's short story 'Two Gallants', Corley is a narcissist who, despite being physically and temperamentally unattractive, has great success in seducing women. This man, Joyce tells us: 'Spoke without listening to the speech of his companions. His conversation was mainly about himself: what he had said to such a person and what such a person had said to him, and what he had said to settle the matter.' The story concerns Corley's plan to extract money from his latest conquest, a servant girl he describes with contempt as a 'slavey'. The other 'gallant' is Lenehan, the sponger who hopes to share in the proceeds.

The fictional villains who frighten us and teach us caution should not be the violent criminals and murderers most of us are unlikely ever to meet, but the characters such as Odette, Rosamund and Corley, whose like we often have to deal with, and whose strong wills and manipulative charms are so hard to resist.

Another factor is that unsatisfying relationships persist because the desire to penetrate the unknowability of the other quickly develops into jealousy and possessiveness. Swann marries

Odette only to have control over her and, later, Marcel imprisons Albertine in his apartment – as in real life Proust imprisoned in turn his lovers Alfred Agostinelli and Henri Rochat.

Proust was insanely jealous and possessive, and subjected to exhaustive, detailed and astoundingly candid analysis 'the revolving searchlights of jealousy' and the overwhelming urge to possess completely ('The possession of what we love is an even greater joy than love itself'). This urge to possess is another manifestation of the fear of process and change and the hunger for certainty and permanence.

Swann is madly jealous, spies on Odette and soon finds damning evidence of infidelity. But, in a typical piece of Proustian psychological acuity, Swann actually *enjoys* having his worst suspicions confirmed. Contemporary psychology has demonstrated the ability of negative emotions, such as anger, to colonise the mind – but Proust was there first: 'Then his jealousy rejoiced at the discovery, as though that jealousy had an independent existence, fiercely egotistical, gluttonous of everything that would feed its vitality, even at the expense of Swann himself.' But Swann's behaviour is mild compared to the craziness of Marcel. When Albertine has been locked away for a long period, she naturally begs to be allowed out, if only briefly, on parole. Marcel thinks that a Sunday theatre matinée could not be too dangerous and grudgingly allows Albertine to go. Then he reads in a newspaper that the lead actress is a woman he suspects of being a lesbian and is immediately convinced that she will attempt to seduce Albertine by *signalling to her from the stage during the play*, which would certainly be an amazing and possibly unique dual performance. So he sends his trusty servant Françoise to snatch Albertine from the clutches of the lesbian and bring her back safely to prison.

Joyce, too, was an intensely jealous man – but he did not give his jealousy to Bloom. When Poldy returns home to Molly he considers how to respond to her infidelity earlier in the day.

'What retribution, if any?' The answer: 'Assassination, never, as two wrongs did not make one right. Duel by combat, no. Divorce, not now.' There will be no accusations, no recriminations, no revenge. Indeed, although aware in advance of the infidelity, Bloom has thought of Molly only with tenderness. He has brought her breakfast in bed, bought her a bar of soap and a pornographic novel, an unlikely gift from a cuckold, yet Bloom is also proud of Molly's attractiveness and sexual appetite, thinking to himself at one point that Boylan ought to pay for her favours. He will forgive Molly and the long marriage, deeply peculiar like every long marriage, will continue. The alternative of separation is not an option for Bloom.

Just before beginning *Ulysses*, in the notes for his only play, *Exiles* – which also deals with jealousy and infidelity – Joyce wrote: 'The soul like the body may have a virginity. For the woman to yield it or for the man to take it is the act of love. Love (understood as the desire of good for another) is in fact so unnatural a phenomenon that it can scarcely repeat itself, the soul being unable to become virgin again and not having energy enough to cast itself out again into the ocean of another's soul.' This is not a fashionable view nowadays. Few would accept that only one love is possible in a lifetime. But the moulding together of two complex sets of beliefs, desires, habits and neuroses, through conflict, anger, humiliation, compromise and pain, is a task of such exhausting enormity that it is difficult to undertake wholeheartedly a second time.

Unfortunately, couples committed to the long haul will find few inspiring role models in the arts. The long relationship is a perfect example of the same that is never the same but either growing or dying. Work at the relationship and it may grow, neglect to work and it will certainly die. But such subtle change does not provide sufficient action or drama. Happiness and commitment are notoriously difficult to make interesting.

Again, the films of Mike Leigh are among the notable exceptions. Many – for instance *High Hopes*, *Life is Sweet* and *Vera Drake* – have long, loving and happy relationships at their heart. As with *Ulysses*, the lesson is that what sustains such relationships is not so much romance and passion as forbearance and endurance. The long relationship encourages, indeed demands, what Hannah Arendt defined as the most important human attributes – the ability to control the past by forgiveness and the future by promises. In *Another Year*, released in 2010, Leigh manages to make compelling just such a relationship, between an apparently unprepossessing and uninteresting couple in late middle age who grow vegetables on an allotment, cook meals and drink wine. However, one aspect of long relationships that Leigh does not show is mature sex – totally taboo in mainstream cinema. In the movie world, no one middle-aged, much less, old, can be seen doing the wild thing.

Joyce had no such inhibitions. Bloom, energised by his eventful day, shocks Molly by assertively asking her to bring *him* breakfast in bed in the morning, and then shocks her even more by a renewal of desire. They have not made love for over ten years, since the death of their son, and a conventional novel would end with tearful reconciliation and passionate intercourse. Instead, Bloom gets into bed with his head facing Molly's feet and, before dropping off to sleep: 'He kissed the plump yellow smellow melons of her rump, on each plump melonous hemisphere, in their melon yellow furrow, with obscure prolonged provocative melonsmellonous osculation.'

Sex is even more peculiar than the love it serves, as Joyce and Proust both understood. Sex is everywhere in their enormous oeuvres but there is never a scene of conventional penetrative intercourse. Where this is mentioned it happens offstage, as with Molly's adultery, or in memory (as when Molly at the end of *Ulysses* recalls her first surrender to Bloom). Instead of passionate lovemaking, Joyce and Proust offer real, everyday sex, often a combination of fetishism, sado-masochism, voyeurism and masturbation. In *À la recherche* Marcel, after several hundred pages of love longing, finally succeeds in luring Albertine to his apartment – but gets most pleasure from spying on her while she is asleep and doing some surreptitious frotting. When the two eventually lie down together the unromantic consummation is that Albertine administers a quick little toss off. In fact, after solitary masturbation, this kind of service may well be the most common sex act. At any given moment, all over the world good-hearted women are ruefully, patiently and skilfully tossing off desperate men. The earth probably fails to move but everyone involved enjoys significant relief.

Alice Munro is also good on realistic sex. In *Lives of Girls and Women* there is a memorable scene where a middle-aged man, Mr Chamberlain, a suave and sophisticated radio newsreader, takes the young girl narrator out into the country. The girl is both curious and willing so the expectation is of a Lady Chatterley-style romp in the woods. Instead, Mr Chamberlain whips out his penis and smilingly masturbates to orgasm in front of her. 'Quite a sight, eh?' he remarks afterwards.

And the sexual tastes of Joyce and Proust themselves were even more specialised than anything in their books. Proust was a sadist who had rats delivered from an abattoir in order to torture them to death with a hatpin. Joyce was a masochist who fantasised about beatings ('I would love to be whipped by you, Nora love!'). Proust was a butcher fetishist and also stimulated himself by insulting his dead mother's memory. Joyce was a knickers fetishist (always referring to them reverently as 'drawers' and carrying in his pocket a miniature pair which he used to divert his drinking companions) and a coprophiliac (a typical endearment to Nora was 'O my sweet little brownarsed fuckbird'), two tastes that could often be happily combined ('I loved to look at the brown stain that comes behind on your girlish white drawers').[176] As they say frequently in Ireland, 'We all have our own wee ways'. But Joyce's preoccupation has been surprisingly common among Irish writers and there is a monograph to be written on their abiding fascination with faeces. I offer to scholars the surely intriguing title: *Forty Shades of Brown: Excrement in Irish Literature from Swift to Roddy Doyle.*

Joyce and Proust were familiar with the madness of male sexuality that not only creates and attempts to implement specific fantasies but is driven by a general urge to more and more extreme excess. In sex women are largely guided by their sensible bodies but men are driven crazy by their feverish minds. Men love to think and talk about sex; women enjoy it while it lasts, if they can, and have little interest in pre-match build-up or post-match analysis. Joyce and Proust also understood this. Proust has a female character say, on the subject of love, 'I make it often but I never talk about it'. Joyce has Molly Bloom think to herself, on the same subject, 'sure there's nothing for a woman in that all invention made up', and 'do it and think no more about it'.

Even now, almost a century after it was written, Molly's monologue is startling in the unapologetic exuberance of its coarseness. Imagine having the nerve to give a female character thoughts like this: 'if he wants to kiss my bottom Ill drag open my drawers and bulge it right out in his face as large as life he can stick his tongue 7 miles up my hole as hes there my brown part'. This is a rare example of Joyce giving Molly his own fetish. At other times she is impatient with the Joycean fetish of Poldy: 'drawers drawers the whole blessed time till I promised to give him the pair off my doll to carry about in his waistcoat pocket *O Maria Santissima*'. And Molly is equally impatient with sadomasochism: 'sure theres nothing for a woman in that'. This is all psychologically accurate – and while a man writing about female sexuality is always suspect, the evidence from female writers like Munro and Ernaux suggests that Joyce got much of it right. Molly seeks her own sexual satisfaction and is frustrated by the selfishness of men ('they want to do everything too quick take all the pleasure out of it'), masturbates ('he had me always at myself 4 or 5 times a day sometimes'), and enjoys cunnilingus but is scornful of Poldy's technique ('he does it all wrong too thinking of his own pleasure his tongue is too flat or I don't know what he forgets'). Like the heroines of Munro and Ernaux, she sees love as the most effective way of re-enchanting the world ('it fills up your whole day and life always something to think about every moment and see it all around you like a new world').

Men have always suspected that women get more pleasure from sex – but are still unable to resist fantasising, even though the fantasies are essentially absurd and always mocked by that merciless demystifier, reality. The problem with golden showers is that they always smell of piss.

So, attempts to implement fantasies are great material for comedy. Proust is at his most droll and deadpan in the long brothel scene near the end of *À la recherche*. This is based on the homosexual brothel Proust owned, but in the novel Marcel claims to mistake it for a hotel when he is seeking sanctuary in a First World War blackout during a bombing raid on Paris. So we are required to believe that he witnesses all the shenanigans by accident.

The clientele includes army officers, writers, artists, politicians, aristocrats and even a priest who, when teased by his soldier companion about the discrepancy between behaviour and calling, says with clerical sententiousness, 'What do you expect? I am not (I expected him to say "a saint") a good girl.' Here again Proust gets the detail right. If a priest puts his hand in his pocket it is only to play with himself. So the good Father tries to slip off without paying, only to be pursued by the *patron*, Jupien, a man with a 'ready wit' who rattles a box of coins, crying, 'For the expenses of the church, Monsieur l'Abbé!'

As Jupien points out, running this establishment is not as easy as it might seem. The requests are as various as the customers and he is required to supply Canadians, Scotsmen in kilts, footmen, choirboys, negro chauffeurs and, for one insistent old gentleman 'in whom curiosity of every kind had no doubt been satisfied', disabled young soldiers.

But the most demanding client is Baron de Charlus. Jupien complains bitterly that none of his lazy staff will help him lug the heavy chains upstairs to Room 43. Then the Baron insists that the wooden bed in the room is replaced by one with an iron frame, more appropriate for the chains. The next problem is that he wishes to be beaten by the most authentically brutal instruments, namely those employed for punishing sailors in the navy in the nineteenth century – but these are all obsolete and almost impossible to find. Finally, he wants the punishment to be administered by a murderer – but Jupien has difficulty getting hold of a genuine killer and asks a young man to pretend to have 'knifed an old hag of a concierge in Belleville'. Unfortunately this young man is entirely good-natured and is not only unconvincing at insulting the Baron as a 'filthy brute' but actually reveals that he is doing this work to earn money for his family. The revelation of kindness by his chastiser is a genuine insult and the Baron expresses his outrage to Jupien who offers what evidence of viciousness he can muster: 'Still, he's on bad terms with his father. It's true they live together, but they work in different bars.'

The equivalent in Joyce is the long Nighttown brothel scene where Bloom the masochist is humiliated in various ways. This has its moments, especially in the contributions of a great double act, Biddy the Clap and Cunty Kate, but the comedy is too exaggerated and farcical and the scene goes on too long. The finest comic sex in *Ulysses* is the encounter of Bloom and Gerty MacDowell, when Gerty exposes her drawers and Bloom masturbates into his trousers, his orgasm coinciding with the effusions of a Roman candle in a firework display. This passage is not only funny but erotic, tender and lyrical, ending: 'And then a rocket sprang and bang shot blind and O! then the Roman candle burst and it was like a sigh of O! and everyone cried O! O! in raptures and it gushed out of it a stream of rain gold hair threads and they shed and ah! they were all greeny dewy stars falling with golden, O so lively! O so soft, sweet, soft!'

But Joyce does not neglect the bathetic detail. Afterwards Bloom thinks to himself, 'This wet is very unpleasant. Stuck. Well the foreskin is not back. Better detach.' I don't know of any other writer who has mentioned this consequence of male excitement – the retracted foreskin leaving the penis head exposed and chafed.

There is even an extra joke in that this scene is a parody of Stephen Dedalus's epiphany in *A Portrait of the Artist as a Young Man* when he has a spiritual experience on seeing a young girl in the sea. Where Stephen's statuesque young girl wades majestically in the ocean, lame Gerty MacDowell limps away across the sand. Where Stephen utters an exalted paean to life and art, down-to-earth Poldy shoots off in his pants.

Proust has two masturbation scenes – when Marcel has a fizz in his trousers while wrestling with Gilberte in the Champs-Élysées gardens and when he jerks off out of his bedroom window in Combray and smears the leaves of a flowering currant with 'a natural trail like that left by a snail'.

Both writers do equal justice to fetishism. Proust describes an old gentleman, known as 'the hairdresser', who visits a heterosexual brothel only in order to pour oil on the girls' loosened hair and then comb it. Swann and Odette's term for making love is 'doing a cattleya', which means that Odette wears on her dress a cattleya, a type of orchid, and Swann pretends to inhale its fragrance while looking down her front. Later, Marcel's love-making is also all peeping and sniffing.

The combination of fetishism and voyeurism inspired Joyce to some of his most lyrical flights. In the *Sirens* chapter of *Ulysses* Lenehan begs a barmaid in the Ormond Hotel to '*sonnez la cloche*', which means marking the hour, four o'clock, by snapping her garter four times.

> Bending, she nipped a peak of skirt above her knee. Delayed. Taunted them still, bending, suspending, with wilful eyes.
> – *Sonnez*!
> Smack. She let free sudden in rebound her nipped elastic garter smackwarm against her smackable woman's warmhosed thigh.

There is even a touch of S&M in there, with the 'smackwarm' and 'smackable', which makes it a 3-in-1 experience. No wonder Joyce was so lyrical. The barmaid of course regards it all as idiot male nonsense. 'She smilesmirked supercilious (wept! aren't men?).'

Joyce and Proust were themselves avid voyeurs. Joyce's most intense voyeuristic experience, almost causing him to faint with excitement, was seeing a woman in a nearby apartment pull down a toilet chain; Proust was similarly aroused by the sight of a butcher boy chopping meat.

In *À la recherche* Marcel does a good deal of peeping, not always plausibly. Early in the book he wanders out into the country, falls asleep and wakes up to witness, through a lighted window, a lesbian seduction scene that features sadism for foreplay. Now, if I bought a house in the country, lived to be a thousand and walked out every evening in a different direction then fell asleep, would I ever wake up to see 'a few feet away' a perfectly lit S&M intro to girl-on-girl action?

Bloom's voyeurism is less dramatic but more plausible and frequent. As soon as he goes out to buy food for breakfast he is following the girl next door to enjoy her moving hams and the strong arms that whack so vigorously carpets on the clothesline. Then when he brings Molly breakfast in bed he looks calmly into her nightdress at 'her large soft bubs'. No sooner out and about for the day than he is transfixed by an attractive woman getting into her carriage. 'Watch! Watch! Silk flash rich stockings white. Watch!' Even when he has his religious moment and goes into church he watches the women in the congregation, a greater reward ('seventh heaven') than the paradise of the after-life. And when he thinks of Molly with erotic tenderness, what he recalls is not lovemaking but the pleasure of watching her dress and undress.

'Aren't men frightful idiots?' is the rhetorical question put by one barmaid to another in the Ormond Hotel. But deploring the idiocy and attempting to suppress the details is not going to do any good. It is surely better, and possibly more effective as a deterrent, to see it as comically absurd.

All men do not have the full range of idiocies – but voyeurism is surely universal in the male sex. Every heterosexual man since Adam has looked at women with sexual pleasure and will continue to do so regardless of who disapproves. Bloom is a habitual voyeur, as is his American counterpart, Harry Angstrom. There is a wonderful scene in John Updike's *Rabbit Is Rich* where Harry sneaks into the bedroom of a married couple and discovers photographs of them having kinky sex. Here, Updike creates three levels of voyeurism – the reader is spying on Harry who is spying on the couple who are spying on themselves.[177] In the final volume of the tetralogy, *Rabbit at Rest*, Harry, now fifty-five, is still at it, greedily eyeing the spandex crotch of his daughter-in-law's swimsuit. Though what stirs him most is not the woman's youth but her flaws – the ridges of fat at the edges of the tight suit, a vaccination mark on the top of a thigh and, above all, the cracked and chipped nail polish on her toes. Only the imperfections can be heartbreakingly real.

Voyeurism may even be common among women. I conducted an informal survey of female friends, beginning with the question, Do you look at men with sexual pleasure? In each case the response was the same – a long, wary, almost resentful silence followed by a deeply reluctant 'Yes'. To the second question, What specifically do you look at?, initial reactions were similar, though there was an even longer, even more resentful silence, but the answers were various – 'shoulders', 'jaw', 'hands', 'buttocks' (at this stage one respondent became surprisingly animated, cried 'black men's buttocks' and actually sculpted her ideal in the air). The good news for modestly endowed men is that apparently women do not measure the package.

So the only difference between the sexes on voyeurism may be that women are more discreet. As one woman commented dryly, 'We don't do that swivel-head gawping like men.'

And why should the sexes not look at each other in wonder and gratitude? I freely admit to being an inveterate voyeur. Looking at women is one of the great pleasures of my everyday urban life and the pleasure is especially keen in spring when the newly exposed white limbs and shoulders are the blooms of the city. Every year I exult in this miraculous blossoming. Never mind the white hawthorn blossoms of Proust. Give me always the living breathing white flesh of women.

PART V

The Everyday Environment

11

The City

When I informed Irish friends and relatives that I was moving to London the reaction was horror at the very mention of this hell of depravity and desolation, where you would not only lose your immortal soul but, even worse, be overcharged outrageously for every cup of tea on the road to perdition. In fact, London was paradise. From the moment I arrived it felt like home. This was the astounding revelation – the city was homely and it was home that was alien. Soon there came another revelation – many Londoners had almost as little regard for their city as the Irish, and the most effective way to impress them was to explain your plans for getting out of London. I had a job teaching maths in a comprehensive school and at the first half-term holiday most of the maths department went walking together in Snowdonia. When I said that I wanted to go walking in London they looked at me as though I was soft in the head.

This anti-urban prejudice is common in England, which was first to industrialise and go urban and has had longer to develop nostalgia for the pastoral. The influence of the Romantic Movement, with its horror of 'dark satanic mills' and love of skylarks and daffodils, remains strong, especially in the middle and upper classes. And wherever there is inchoate yearning for a lost age of simplicity and innocence the city is likely to be held responsible for the loss. It is easy to see a street of fried-chicken outlets, littered pavements and graffitied walls as a symbol of man's fallen state.

The city is also feared because it is process at its most large-scale, tumultuous and overwhelming – an unrelenting change that denies any possibility of stability and permanence. The music of the city is a clamorous duet for wrecking ball and concrete mixer.

And nationalists and fundamentalists hate the city because it weakens the grip of tradition. Some immigrant groups resist such weakening with a willed petrifaction that locks them in time. So the Irish in English cities are often more Irish than the Irish in Ireland – and the Chilean writer Roberto Bolaño once remarked that the only place where the Chilean Spanish of 1973 is still spoken is Stockholm because this was the final destination of many fleeing the military coup in Chile. But this kind of fanatical resistance only demonstrates the power of the city to loosen bonds. Urban pluralism undermines most forms of traditional group superiority and reassurance, replacing community with isolation, security with vulnerability, importance with insignificance, recognition with anonymity, tradition with change, simplicity with complexity and certainty with doubt. The city raises questions as the country raises cows.

But many of these existential terrors may be reinterpreted as advantages. Allegiance to city is more benign than allegiance to country because it is based on a welcome for difference rather than similarity and for mixing rather than separation. Indeed city allegiance is so unassuming that it has never been given a name – there are many nationalisms but no cityism. Maybe cityists should become more vociferous (so I'll admit that I feel more allegiance to London than to England).

And the city as the concrete representation of process (pun intended), a continuous creation of the unpredictably new, demands an acknowledgement of the individual as a similarly creative process, and stimulates curiosity, empathy, engagement, learning, the examined life. Socrates: 'I'm a lover of learning, and trees and open country won't teach me anything whereas men and the city do.'[178]

If the city dweller belongs to a group it is often the group of those who do not wish to belong to a group (one reason why cityism has never developed is that no true cityist could sit through meetings). The rise of the city and the individual are inextricably linked. And a community of strangers confers many benefits. Anonymity, for instance, supposedly one of the most grievous deprivations of the city, can be exhilarating. Alice Munro's narrator on her first urban experience: 'I felt my anonymity like a decoration, like a peacock's train.'[179] In small towns and rural communities personal knowledge is used as a form of superiority, to degrade and humiliate. Someone, usually a woman, will look you over contemptuously and say, in a vicious tone, 'I know who *you* are,' pausing to allow you to attempt to deny this and then continuing as though you have, '*You* think *I* don't know you,' further pause before concluding in venomous triumph, 'but I know who *you are*.'

Anonymity is actually a great gift. The less visible the observer the more visible the world. So be unseen to see and be unknown to know. Roam like one of Shakespeare's dukes in disguise through your realm. As Baudelaire put it, 'The observer is a prince enjoying his incognito whenever he goes'.[180]

And Baudelaire invented flânerie, the ruse of walking in the city just for the hell of it and embracing aspects of the urban experience usually dismissed as repugnant. Urban theorists tend to see, and be suspicious of, the top-down, planned city; urban walkers see and love the randomly evolved, bottom-up (in every sense), emergent city. Such walking is an act of personal appropriation (De Certeau compared the walker in the city to a reader appropriating a text), a non-utilitarian progress of non-utilitarian attention that has no direction or destination and no distracting companions.[181] The flâneur is a monad nomad, unaccompanied and unburdened, either physically or mentally, the arms free to drive back and forth, each in time with the opposite leg, and the mind free to attend and associate, running the memory/perception loop on turbo power and full speed.[182] In fact the entire unified organism of mind and body is running on turbo, and meshing harmoniously with the superorganism of the city, which, combined with the freedom of wandering and the guile of perpetrating a ruse, is what gives such walking its tingle and zest.

Following Baudelaire ('Commerce is, in its very essence, *satanic*'[183]), French flâneurs have traditionally been detached, ironic and elitist, scornful of the manifestations of capitalism and the popular culture of the alienated masses, though this changed in the second half of the twentieth century with the likes of Georges Perec, a dedicated champion of the urban everyday: 'What I miss above all is the neighbourhood cinema, with its ghastly advertisements for the dry cleaner's on the corner.'[184]

Following Walt Whitman ('Let objects gross and the unseen soul be one'[185]), American flâneurs have been more involved, accepting and enthusiastic about all aspects of the urban scene. Frank O'Hara, New York's Flâneur Laureate in the 1950s, even outdid Whitman in excitability. 'What is the poet for,' Frank exclaimed, 'if not to scream / himself into a hernia of admiration?'[186]

But Walt was a more subtle writer than many of his followers and could temper his desire 'to exalt the present and the real' with a measure of detachment:

> Apart from the pulling and hauling stands what I am,
> Stands amused, complacent, compassionating, idle, unitary,
> Looks down with side-curved head curious what will come next,
> Both in and out of the game and watching and wondering at it.[187]

This catches perfectly the harmonious balance of inner and outer, involvement and detachment, amusement and compassion, the necessity of being 'both in and out of the game'. And Leopold Bloom demonstrates this difficult balance throughout *Ulysses.* It is as easy to lose the self in the world as it is to lose the world in the self. Too close an involvement with the world causes the inner self to atrophy, and too much introspection loses sight of the world. In *Ulysses* the worldly Dubliners have the first problem and the egotistical Stephen Dedalus the second. Only Bloom has the maturity to maintain a balance as he walks around Dublin simultaneously observing and ruminating.

Like everyone else, Bloom occasionally fantasises about going back and living his life over. 'Can't bring back time. Like holding water in your hand. Would you go back to then? Just beginning then. Would you?' But almost immediately he is seduced by the sights and sounds of the city and especially its women and their apparel displayed in the stores.

> Gleaming silks, petticoats on slim brass rails, rays of flat silk stockings.
>
> Useless to go back. Had to be. Tell me all.
>
> High voices. Sunwarm silk. Jingling harnesses. All for a woman, home and houses, silk webs, silver, rich fruits, spicy from Jaffa. Agendath Netaim. Wealth of the world.
>
> A warm human plumpness settled down on his brain.

Bloom has his moments of regret but they are rare and short lived. He is too aware that life is soon over and even more quickly forgotten. As he reminds himself at the funeral of Paddy Dignam, 'Pray for the repose of the soul of. Does anybody really? Plant him and have done with him. Like down a coal-shoot.' As Dignam is buried, Bloom consoles himself with the thought, 'Plenty to see and hear and feel yet'. And the plenty that feeds his spirit is the life of the city, its streets and crowds, noises and smells, bars and shops, businesses and advertisements. Bloom sells advertising for a living and studies ads not in disgust but with professional interest. So he disapproves of a horseshoe-shaped poster of a cyclist, which he thinks would have been better as a wheel, 'Damn bad ad' – but is impressed by the use of a boat on the Liffey to display an ad for Kino's trousers, 'Good idea that'. As John Updike has pointed out, Joyce was the first novelist to show and accept that 'the texture of daily life has become predominantly commercial'.[188] There is no hatred of commerce or advertising in Joyce, who would probably be more amused than horrified to learn that Dublin is now as full of fake French cafés as Paris of fake Irish pubs.

In *Ulysses* the city is rendered not just visually but through all the senses via its noises, smells and even tastes. Like traffic in the city today, horses are a constant background presence, bringing 'the sweet oaken reek of horsepiss' and the 'jingle of harnesses, hoofthuds lowringing' – and the very *feel* of horse riding is conveyed: 'A cavalcade in easy trot along Pembroke quay passed, outriders leaping, leaping in their, in their saddles.' This is such an effective mimetic sentence that reading it too often could cause saddle sores.

Like the human consciousness that attempts to come to terms with it, the protean multitudinousness of the city defies definition by thinkers or writers but, as also with consciousness, *Ulysses* succeeds better than most works in conveying a sense of the city as ongoing process, a huge living superorganism whose cells are its citizens, themselves complex organisms, the city woven together and animated by the paths of these citizens, a multiplicity of singularities, each with its own peculiar burgeoning life.

As many and various as the paths are the ways of seeing. In the end every city dweller has to create a personal city, some unique combination of concept, geography, movement and perception. I probably learned my own form of selective attention from Walker Evans, whose favourite writers were Baudelaire and Flaubert, and who combined cool French irony with warm American inclusiveness in his photographs of ramshackle shops and businesses, peeling posters, garish advertisements and homemade signs. 'A connoisseur of the commonplace', was how the critic Andy Grundberg aptly summarised Evans.[189] So, with the discrimination and avidity of the collector, I walk in the urban wilderness, the unfashionable districts that combine the exuberance of disorder, the comedy of the incongruous, the innocence of bad taste, the pathos of naïvety, the poetry of dilapidation and the beauty of decay.

But when the affluent move into, and gentrify, these areas the price of enhanced safety and order is loss of vitality.[190] In John Updike's novel *Roger's Version*,[191] there is a marvellous ten-page description of the narrator, Roger Lambert, simply walking down the street – a broad city avenue that begins in a salubrious university area and gradually becomes more impoverished, its degree of liveliness increasing as property values go down. Like Bloom, Roger muses erotically on his wife, 'her underparts in the sunlight . . . fed to my eyes like tidbits of rosy marzipan', while paying close attention to his surroundings – dog-torn bags of garbage, stacks of flattened cartons, old rusting cars, a gas station forecourt with a puddle stained by leaking antifreeze to an astonishingly pure green colour, a dog turd of equally astonishing blackness, burned-out and abandoned buildings with doors and windows plywooded over, graffiti ('TEX GIVES BEST HEAD'), advertisements ('MEGABUCKS *You Could Be Our Next Millionaire!*'), wildly unlikely businesses ('ADULT PASTRIES *Erotic Cakes and Droll Candies*'), gaunt drunks and bums, eccentric old women, Vietnamese immigrants and a young black man carrying on his shaved head, like a fantastic turban, a bright peach-coloured padded semi-chair, with a back and arms but no legs, and wrapped in crackling, transparent plastic. 'The irrepressible combinations of the real!'

Walker Evans would have loved this walk – and that filling station is surely the one described by Elizabeth Bishop:

> Oh, but it is dirty!
> this little filling station,
> oil-soaked, oil-permeated
> to a disturbing, over-all
> black translucency.
> Be careful with that match!

This is a family filling station, Elizabeth goes on to tell us, run by a father and 'several quick and saucy and greasy sons' who live behind the pumps in a house whose cement porch has a few comic books, a doily-draped taboret, a begonia and a sofa with greasy wickerwork bearing a dirty dog.

> Somebody embroidered the doily.
> Somebody waters the plant,
> or oils it, maybe. Somebody
> arranges the rows of cans
> so that they softly say:
> ESSO – SO – SO – SO
> to high-strung automobiles.
> Somebody loves us all.[192]

But if Updike were to walk down that street again he would probably find it completely changed by urban 'regeneration' (a cunning new word for redevelopment that suggests internal organic rebirth rather than external top-down planning). And if Bishop were to revisit the filling station she would find it had been taken over and homogenised by one of the big oil corporations.

My local London high street used to be spectacularly extravagant, full of peculiar little businesses that rejected all constraints of category – UNEEK ENTERPRISES, which announced itself as not just a 'Video Hi Fi Television and Radio Dealer' but also a 'Personal Export Insurance and Travel Consultant', though the shop itself was full of second-hand cookers and gas fires. Or MASTER SPARKLE DRY CLEANING Keys Cut Discs Engraved Shoe Repairs While U Wait. Or BOBY'S HOUSE OF SAREES Stainless Steelware & Books. Or BRIGHT LAUNDERETTE Alterations Watch Batteries Accessories. Or BRAZILIAN BEAUTY PARLOUR Thai and Swedish Massage. Even the businesses that stuck to their specialisms were extravagant – Fotofare for instance, with its montage wedding photographs of couples cavorting inside champagne glasses or laughing through the sheet music of *Love is a Many-Splendoured Thing.* Or The Catholic Repository whose windows displayed holy-water fonts and bottles, miraculous medals, statues of Blessed Martin de Porres and the Child of Prague, framed prayers to St Joseph (patron saint of things lost) and to St Jude (patron saint of lost causes), The Irish Penal Rosary (as used in the periods of religious oppression) and lots of those little pictures that, when turned in the light, showed St Christopher in two different scenes, first carrying a child across a river in spate and then converting to Christianity the two beautiful pagan women sent to tempt him.

All these uneek enterprises are gone, replaced by homogenous estate agents, mobile-phone shops, chain supermarkets and chain cafés (the stages in an area's gentrification can be marked by the number of coffee shops, and the final stage is a knick-knack shop selling, at outrageous prices, ylang-ylang-and-patchouli-scented candles, silver jewellery based on the ancient designs of the Incas, and handmade greeting cards with embroidered flowers and tiny hearts attached to red ribbons). This transformation seems to be underway in many areas. As with butterflies, songbirds and wild flowers, there are fewer outrageous puns, bizarre advertisements and gauche handwritten notices, and much less carefree substitution of K for C and Z for S. Is there a creeping uniformity, a loss of exuberance? Maybe cities, like people, grow old and tired and petrify. For energy and extravagance, crazy collisions and juxtapositions, go to Lagos, Mumbai or Mexico City.

There are still collectors' items, but no longer in profusion – a hairdresser's, Kurl Up and Dye; a shoe shop, R. Soles; a fireplace vendor, Alexander the Grate; a fish and chip shop, Oh My Cod (also The Codfather and Fishcotheque); a Thai restaurant, The Thaitanic; a pizza restaurant, Eataly; a used car dealer, Karz 2 Go; a beauty salon, XcentriK; a bar with a huge sign proclaiming it The One Stop Jerk Centre; and the establishment advertised on a flyer, Sister Mary's 'Psychic House of Heeling' ('Sister Mary will bring back loved ones, end loneliness, stop jealousy, help with family, bring a better career – you owe it to yourself to see these God gifted woman'). But none of these uneek establishments seem destined for long life. Miracle Fashions and the Charisma Café are already defunct and boarded up.

It could be argued that it is a mistake to seek only the singular and, worse, to patronise lack of sophistication by treating it as a source of amusement. Georges Perec was always scolding himself: 'You're noting only the untoward, the peculiar, the wretched exceptions; the opposite is what you should be doing.'[193] And he attempted the opposite with a detailed description of the run-down Rue Vilin in the Belleville district of Paris and an even more detailed, fifty-page account of three days observing the Place Saint-Sulpice. This exercise in attending to the commonplace ('the things people don't usually note down, that are unremarkable, unimportant: what happens when there is nothing happening, and nothing going by except time, people, cars and clouds')[194] revealed the difficulty of sustaining attention and the complex nature of attention itself. Despite the desire to suppress his own personality in order to register the ever-changing totality of the unremarkable (what he described as 'emergence' decades before the term was adopted by the scientific community), Perec found himself noticing the exceptions – nuns, a man parking badly, pigeons rising up when there had been no obvious disturbance. The experiment revealed once again that, while attention may be improved by exercise, it is always intermittent, selective and personal. There is no objective city, only the many subjective versions.

The solution is to extend limited awareness by appropriating the selective attention of others, for instance the transfiguring of the unremarkable in the work of another George – George Shaw, the English painter who began as a conceptual artist but soon abandoned this as 'rubbish' and took to painting scenes from the Tile Hill estate in Coventry where he grew up – to be precise, only scenes within a half-mile radius of his childhood home. So Shaw is an authentic obsessive with a personal vision.

These scenes have no people because Shaw rejects narrative with its 'ends which always disappoint'.[195] Instead they feature the drably anonymous fabric of contemporary Britain – graffitied walls, shuttered shops, broken fences and gates, poorly lit subways and underpasses, pitted and puddled roads, littered ditches, forlorn play areas with rusting swings and patchy playing fields with sagging goalposts, dilapidated bus stops, phone boxes and dog-shit bins, padlocked outhouses and garages, rows of uniform estate houses and concrete institutional buildings (usually viewed from the back or the side – a frontal view might be too dramatic). And, as though to emphasise the terminal dreariness, Shaw often envelops these scenes in a nuclear-winter-grey pall. Yet the images are compelling, uncanny in the Freudian sense of suggesting something more than what is present, something usually concealed or repressed. The details are scrupulously mundane but the overall effect is disturbingly numinous, frequently menacing in some indefinable way, like a crime scene just after the police tape has been removed, or the site of some troubling but inchoate dream. These paintings are contemporary epiphanies in the Joycean urban tradition – and this was the express intention of the artist.

In an essay on his favourite colour, Payne's Grey (an introduction for an exhibition of watercolours using only shades of grey), Shaw quotes Joyce on epiphanies.[196] But the autobiographical content, the connection to childhood, also imbues the paintings with a Proustian sense of past merging with present, of time not as a linear progression but a dreamlike and puzzling swirl of interpenetrating images and sensations. Shaw: 'As my own work unfolds in front of me I sense familiar time – that within reach – dissolve into the endless days beyond.'

In terms of painting, the obvious influence on Shaw is Edward Hopper, in particular the Hopper of people-free works like *Early Sunday Morning*, which shows a deserted street of terraced houses, and *Approaching a City* – the entrance to a railway underpass, both of these commonplace sights unsettling and mesmerising in the same way as Shaw's work. How do they do it? It does not seem to be a matter of technique. Neither painter is a virtuoso and there is no bravura draughtsmanship or brushwork, no Van Gogh-style impasto, no expressionist blobs and drips, no attention drawn to the paint or its manner of application (Shaw even emphasises his own rejection of painterliness and fine art by working with the Humbrol enamel paint used by hobbyist model makers). Everything is subordinated to the image and the image must be drawn from real life. Hopper managed only a few paintings a year because each had to be based on what he called a 'motif', a real-life image that fired his imagination. Shaw returns regularly to the Tile Hill estate and takes several hundred photographs each time – but only a few of these serve as the inspiration for paintings. Why do some mundane images have meaning while most others do not? This is one of the mysteries of personal vision. And rather than trying to fathom this mystery it would be better to try to emulate it, in whatever limited way possible. It is not so much a question of finding a way of seeing paintings as making use of paintings to find a way of seeing.

Seeing a retrospective of Shaw's work (under the wonderful title *The Sly and Unseen Day*) certainly had a galvanising effect. Tile Hill estate seemed to me the new Venice, grey the new yellow, dreariness the new sublime. I wanted to catch a train to Coventry and a cab to Tile Hill – but this would be to miss the point. The lesson is to see the world *via* Tile Hill.

Among many other things, Shaw is the poet of neglect, dilapidation, dereliction and decay – dead shops and pubs locked and boarded up, walls split and crumbled by weeds, window frames rotting, concrete cracking, doors and gates smashed in, fences holed, roads pitted, drain pipes and corrugated iron corroded by rust. It is just this kind of dereliction that people fear and hate in cities, reading it as a symbol of sinister urban degeneracy[197] – but Shaw celebrates it as a natural consequence of process. View the city like this, he exhorts us, in the 3-D of Dilapidation, Dereliction and Decay.

There is something especially poignant about abandoned warehouses and factories. The cliché is that spires dream – but spires are far too self-important and attention-seeking to dream.

On the other hand, working buildings, when deprived of their functionality by abandonment, either temporary or permanent, take on a strange new autonomous life and seem to be saying, 'We were created to serve but no one is only a servant. We are not your creatures. Emancipated from service, we will live on and become ourselves in our own inscrutable dream.' Their years of loyal service give them dignity in dereliction and beauty in decay.

Many have learned to appreciate these qualities.[198] I am content to marvel from the street but there is a cult of urban exploration dedicated to seeking out and exploring abandoned warehouses, factories, hospitals, asylums, theatres, cinemas, swimming baths, churches and underground tunnels. These explorers are addicts of decay, intoxicated by the splendour of ruined façades, the crunching of broken glass underfoot, the drippings and creakings and soughings of wind, the flutterings of pigeons and the scurryings of rodents and the heady aromas of damp and mould. This is an extreme form of ruse, seeking out and enjoying what is usually feared. For these urban worshippers the Mecca is Pripyat, an entire Forbidden City deserted since the nuclear disaster at Chernobyl and developing unimaginable beauties in decades of uninterrupted decay.

It is encouraging to know that this form of urban adventure was also invented by poets, initiated by none other than Walt Whitman himself, when in 1861 he explored an abandoned subway tunnel, the Atlantic Avenue Tunnel in Brooklyn, and wrote up the experience in the *Brooklyn Standard.* For once the French were slow to get in on the ruse. It was not until 1921 that a Dadaist group, including the poets André Breton, Paul Éluard and Tristan Tzara, organised an exploration of an abandoned church in Paris.

And it was not until the 1990s that the activity became generally popular and given the abbreviation 'urbex'. The Marco Polo of the cult was a Canadian, Jeff Chapman, known in the urbex world as Ninjalicious, who died in 2005 just after completing the classic urbex guide book.[199] Chapman was an interestingly complex character who believed in ethical exploration ('take nothing but pictures and leave nothing but footprints'), disapproved strongly of theft, vandalism or any form of anarchistic trouble-making, took an almost religious attitude to his avocation ('Our tourism is not one of exploitation, but rather of reverence') and described it with the lyricism of a poet ('Half castle and half playground, the abandoned factory or hospital or theatre or train station that looms darkly on the edge of the skyline is virtually irresistible to those with a passion for discovering the unknown and forgotten. Abandoned buildings can be incredibly moving and beautiful places; the whole tragic process of decay and entropy is both sad and breathtaking to behold'). Chapman was also a shrewd psychologist, offering sound advice on how to avoid detection (carry credibility props like fake business cards and look important so that people will assume you are indeed important) and how to behave if accosted – let the officials do the talking, never contradict or argue, avoid lies if possible and smile all the time. He even understood the value of facetiousness. If, while exploring a partly occupied building, someone official asks, 'Do you work here?' the most effective response is to offer a twisted grin and grunt, 'Not when I don't have to.'

The urbex cult thrives on its underground, transgressive status and, like many such movements, fears becoming too popular and even, God forbid, fashionable. Decay could become the new growth area by encouraging Decay Tourism (Don't ruin your holiday – let us ruin it for you) and architects might even create pre-decayed buildings in the way that fashion designers produce pre-torn jeans. (This is not as unlikely as it may seem. In the eighteenth century fake classical ruins were all the rage for gardens – shattered pillars and armless statues were the equivalent of decking and water features. And in Ireland in 1740 a Lord Belvedere actually *built* a ruined abbey.)

For those too old or too fearful for urbex, there are retired functionaries that require no transgression to explore – I refer of course to one of the great urban glories, the canal. However strenuous the attempts to restore, clean and beautify, canals seem to be able to retain a redeeming suggestion of seediness. And water that has been stagnant for over a century enhances the dreaminess of lost function, the serenity of decay. Canals offer a unique sense of timelessness, a closeness to eternity that is profoundly restful to the troubled spirit. Walking along a canal is yoga in motion, though the harmony is occasionally disturbed by having to go under a dank, dark old bridge and experience time travel to Dickensian London – you half expect to see Bill Sikes appear at the other end brandishing a cudgel.

The laureate of canals is the Irish poet Patrick Kavanagh who, after an operation for lung cancer, discovered that sitting by the Grand Canal in Dublin created in him a new mood of serene, uncaring acceptance. Here he wrote some of his most beautiful poems:

> Leafy-with-love banks and the green waters of the canal
> Pouring redemption for me, that I do
> The will of God, wallow in the habitual, the banal,
> Grow with nature again as before I grew.[200]

'O commemorate me where there is water,' Kavanagh prayed, 'canal water preferably, so stilly greeny at the heart of summer.' Dublin eventually obliged by placing on the canal bank a bronze statue of Kavanagh sitting on his own bronze seat, with a space next to him. This is one of my own holy places and whenever I am in Dublin I go to sit beside him and contemplate along with him the stilly greeny redemptive waters. Last time, though, there was a young girl on the seat and another in Kavanagh's lap, both drinking cans of Strongbow cider. I seethed with frustration and resentment – but the Master reproached me by displaying an even deeper Nirvana than before.

Why, though, be *commemorated* beside a canal? Better to live by one. My urban pastoral dream is a room looking down on a somnolent canal and a railway bridge sheltering under one of its arches a filthy little garage with several quick and greasy and saucy mechanics wending their way around puddles iridescent with oil. Presiding in occult power over this scene is a huge sign across the railway bridge: FIT FERODO DISC BRAKE PADS.

Waste ground and vacant lots are other sites of dereliction easy to access. The French poet and flâneur Jacques Réda ('Despair does not exist for a man who walks'[201]) has pleaded for Paris to establish a Society for the Preservation of Waste Ground (*l'Union pour la Préservation des Terrains Vagues*). Like Kavanagh with the Grand Canal, Réda finds vacant lots conducive to meditation and serenity – and the equivalent of the stagnant canal water is 'weeds'. I put this word in inverted commas because there is no such thing as a weed. The concept of the weed has been created entirely by snobbery, with 'weed' a term of abuse for any plant considered undesirable. (This is a special case of a rule formulated by Bergson: 'Disorder is simply the order we are not looking for.'[202]) And to compound the insult, 'weedy' is used to describe those who are sickly, feeble, diffident and pusillanimous, when there is nothing on the face of the earth more vigorous, strong, indomitable and exuberant than a weed.

The range of strategies adopted by weeds to spread and multiply and fill the earth is truly inspiring and humbling. These endlessly creative organisms first produce vast quantities of seeds (one Canadian fleabane can release over 400,000), then employ a wide variety of dispersal techniques, first using their own resources, from exploding pods to gliders designed to make use of wind, and then going further by hitching a ride on vehicles, cargo, packaging, bird dung (weed seeds are not fastidious), animal tails and hoofs and human footwear and clothing (Charles Darwin raised 300 plants of over 20 weed species from the dirt in his trouser turn-ups). Attachment techniques are just as varied and ingenious, with all manner of hooks, hairs and glue (the hook-and-loop technique of the burdock burr is so technically ingenious that the Swiss inventor George de Mestral used it as the basis for Velcro).

When seeds arrive at a destination they have as wide a range of germination speeds as they do dispersal techniques, from the lightning opportunism of the criminal (tumbleweed seeds are capable of germinating in 36 minutes) to the unlimited patience of the deep-cover agent or the deep-frozen astronaut (dyer's rocket seeds germinated after 2000 years when a Roman site was excavated). And in growth weeds are masters of disguise, assuming the appearance of desirable plants to avoid detection and making use of human attempts at weeding to spread further, with the ability to regenerate from tiny pieces of severed root left under the ground or the rooted weed left on the surface. Some weeds are capable even of chemical warfare, exuding pheromones that inhibit the germination of rival plants, and many have developed immunity to the human chemical warfare of weed killers.

Weeds are exemplary Stoic philosophers, turning to advantage whatever circumstances they encounter, and also dynamic results-oriented self-starters, always on the lookout for opportunities to expand growth. They should be cherished equally by philosophers and management gurus. Even the names are wonderful, like a roll call of goblins – fuller's teasel, noxious hemlock, bristly oxtongue, hairy bittercress, stinking hellebore, black medick, fleabane, fumitory, toadflax, spear thistle, woad, woundwort, wormwood, nipplework, charlock and devil's guts.

Who could fail to admire the initiative, determination, tenacity, guile and engineering skills of weeds? Many people in fact. Anyone tolerating weeds in a suburban garden is likely to be visited by outraged neighbours – and, if not compliant, to suffer vigilante action. And the USA is fanatical not just about law and order but lawn order. In Houston, Texas, it is illegal to have 'any uncultivated vegetable growth taller than nine inches' which is 'covering or partly covering the surface of any lots or parcels of real estate'.[203] Buffalo, New York, has a similar law and when a Thoreau fan allowed his front lawn to grow wild he was prosecuted, ordered to mow down these 'noxious weeds' or face a fine of $50 a day, and for his persisting civil disobedience ran up fines of $25,000. So in the USA, land of the free and champion of intrepid individualism, you can tote an assault rifle, machine pistol and pump-action shotgun, but if you grow weeds on your front lawn you're in deep shit, buddy.

Not only inspiring and beautiful, urban weeds are also asylum seekers fleeing from the death squads of repressive suburban regimes. We should cherish them on railway lands, canal banks, waste ground and vacant lots.

So many visual glories in the city – naïvely hopeful businesses, weird signs and notices, majestically derelict buildings and waste ground blossoming with weeds, the hardy natives and the illegal immigrants, Japanese knotweed the Genghis Khan of weeds, a rampant, merciless conqueror, and buddleia the Carmen of weeds, a beautiful gypsy queen flaunting purple blossoms up to thirty feet in the air.

What calls out to the champions of the urban everyday is the oddity of the city's individual elements, the even greater oddity of their juxtapositions, and, above all, the poignancy of the transitoriness of it all – once and once only just like this and never again. But most fleeting and therefore most captivating are the 'irrepressible combinations'. The city was the first, and is still the most original and imaginative, collage artist.

Fortunately some of these collages have been preserved. One of the great achievements of the twentieth century was its new practice of street photography – Robert Doisneau and countless other French photographers wandering the streets of Paris daily in search of the decisive combination (Doisneau: 'There are days when the technique of an aimless stroll works like a charm, flushing out pictures from the non-stop urban spectacle'[204]), Walker Evans and countless other Americans pounding the streets of New York (Evans: 'Stare. It is the way to educate your eye and more. Stare, pry, listen, eavesdrop. Die knowing something. You are not here long'[205]).

A good street photograph has the impact of a good joke, but is even more effective because the surprise at incongruity is instantaneous and the incongruity is not contrived but actually out there in the world. If all the elements are harmoniously combined, as in a good photograph they should be, there is the additional surprise that the world can offer such perfect compositions for the taking, and the rueful feeling, unique to photography, that because this art seems to require no special talent or training, anyone can do it and so *I could have taken this shot.* And a street photographer usually combines voyeurism and engagement and so becomes, like Whitman, both in and out of the game. If the photograph includes people, caught unawares, it may capture absorption, the secret self, and show, as did Vermeer, the interaction of inner and outer realities. So the subjects, as well as the photographer, are both in and out of the game. All these factors give street photographs a uniquely compelling immediacy.

This art form has not been greatly blighted by postmodernism and has benefited from technical developments and acceptance by galleries and museums. The famous black-and-white street photographs of the twentieth century were usually taken from a human perspective, at eye level, and published at no more than A4 size in magazines and books. Now wide-angle lenses can take in so much more and the prints have expanded to fill gallery walls. The result is vastness from a God's-eye perspective, as in Andreas Gursky's photographs of entire enormous office and apartment blocks and Thomas Struth's photographs of the South Korean city Ulsan. The street view celebrates, with warmth and humour, the human oddity of cities but the God view is mysterious and unsettling, with the vertiginousness of looking down from heights or the terror of looking down into deep water. Seen from above, the living organism of the city is revealed as insanely excessive, with ever more piled up, crammed in and jammed together, and all of it ceaselessly scurried through by ever more blind, restless ant-like creatures and plastered over by ever more numerous and more garish signs competing for attention like rainforest plants hungering desperately for sunlight.

Another technical development is the light and compact video camera which permits easy filming of the urban scene. The Swiss video-maker Beat Streuli used a small Sony video camera, hidden, to film crowds entering the Pallasades shopping mall in Birmingham, and exhibited the resulting film with no soundtrack and in slow motion, which created two different but equally strange effects. First, the absorbed, secret selves of individuals can be studied in a way that would not be possible in reality. Second, the relentlessly oncoming waves of people, appearing, floating by and abruptly vanishing, gives a sense of mass humanity endlessly repeating itself in the process of birth, momentary flourishing and disappearance into oblivion. So a simple video conveys both the mysterious processes of the individual and of the species in general. Who would have thought that such mystical wonder could be a response to heavy crowds in a shopping mall in Birmingham?

But many photographers are no longer content to be passive recorders. They have often intervened, by asking people to pose again for a missed moment, but now they create entire original tableaux, like Gregory Crewdson's elaborately staged American urban scenes which look like stills from some weird David Lynch movie. Again the intention is to create an atmosphere of menace. Why is menace so sexy? Is it because fearfulness increases with affluence?

Back in London the street artist known as Slinkachu creates micro collages by adding tiny figures to tiny areas of urban space and photographing the results. So a tiny youth skateboards up a piece of orange peel, a tiny couple sit side by side on a Kentucky Fried Chicken bone, tiny children swim gaily in an abandoned tin-foil container of chicken curry and a tiny wondering man points out to his even tinier son a tiny deer lapping the edge of a milk-shake spill. So even the most disgusting form of urban disorder, discarded partly eaten food and spilled drink, has been redeemed, transfigured and enchanted by imagination, humour and mystery.[206]

But for delight in human absurdity there are few to compete with Martin Parr, whose photographs of ordinary people – out having fun in garish leisurewear or at home in ghastly interiors, knocking back booze or stuffing themselves with fast food – provoke the ambivalent and excruciating laughter that is mixed with groans. Parr is the Mike Leigh of still photography.

And, taking all these together, the huge range of personal visions and techniques, it is obvious that urban photography is enjoying a golden age.

I once had an ambition to be a photographer but could never be bothered with the technical side of it, so now I settle for cameraless urban photography. An alleyway with an allegory of modern life – an empty overturned shopping trolley next to an overflowing wheelie bin. Garbage in, garbage out, and both now on wheels.[207] A cluttered builder's yard with dirty, expressionist, cloud-reflecting puddles. A tumultuous little everything-for-a-pound store with garishly coloured household goods packed onto shelves from floor to ceiling, hanging down in stalactites from the low ceiling and spilling out over tables on the street. An electricity junction box serving as a pedestal for a classic still life – newspaper, Coke can, apple core and crisp bag. A wine glass sitting on the WAIT sign of a pedestrian crossing. A ragged stack of multi-coloured plastic crates beside an open mud-spattered van in whose window dust someone has written with a finger, MY WIFE IS EVEN DIRTIER THAN THIS. A National Slimming Convention office above a newsagent advertising 'A MARS A DAY'. An old art deco cinema now hosting a born-again Christian evangelical rally and sporting a banner whose admonition sounds like the rallying cry of atheists, 'JESUS CHRIST discover the truth for yourself'. A charity shop with, just below its official slogan on the window, 'caring when it matters', a handwritten sheet in blue marker, 'To the DKNY bag thief YOU STINK'.

Beholding these glories, I can only repeat Whitman's cry of acceptance: 'I take to your reckless and composite chords.'

Such an irrepressible combination of irrepressible combinations! Here a thriving business combines with advanced dereliction – a minicab office in the last functioning room of a derelict building with, as though carefully aligned by a scrupulous mixed-media sculptor, a horizontal frieze of waving weeds running across the top of the office window (bearing a handwritten notice, 'All base pickups must pay in advance') to meet a garishly illuminated vertical sign, Diamond Cars, that leads down to the pavement and the corner of a densely populated semi-circle of flattened butts.

There must be equally resplendent minicab offices in all the unfashionable run-down districts of all the cities of the world. Some photographer should capture them before it is too late. Martin Parr, minicab offices have need of thee.

Now total dereliction – between a boarded-up window and a pigeon-shit-splattered drainpipe a magnificent clump of buddleia blossoms outrageously from a scabby wall. What hothouse plant could match this trick? Further on, another clump sprouts from a concrete windowsill – a new concept in gardening, the window box without a box. Buddleia, my wild gypsy queen, 'I dare not proceed till I respectfully credit what you have left wafted hither' (Walt again). Even better is a vacant lot with a full expanse of weeds below a gable wall with neat squares of different wallpaper marking the positions of vanished rooms. But even this is only as a trailer for the main feature, an abandoned factory with every window smashed, rearing up into the sky in gaunt majesty, the urban equivalent of a blasted oak. Each pane has been broken in an individually jagged pattern and catches the light in an individual way. It looks as though everyone in the local community has contributed to this masterpiece, or at least everyone capable of throwing a stone. This is an example of a new genre – Site-Specific Found Conceptual Community Art.

Like most ruins, it is even more impressive now at dusk, the broken panes hoarding rich light against the darkening façade. What could equal such splendour? This is my Taj Mahal. I stand still and silently scream myself into a hernia of admiration.

The city is most beautiful and mysterious at this hour of serene dusk, when the lights come on in buildings lifting geometric silhouettes against a lurid, flowing sky. In the brief interlude between the tyranny of the God of Work and the equally tyrannical God of Fun there is a moment of meditative gentleness. Even the harsh neon glows softly, elegiac with its own passing, as well as that of the day. For neon, the brash radiance of the twentieth-century city, its very name meaning newness, once so lurid and sinful, advertising LIQUOR and GIRLS in acid pink and lime green, is already becoming a thing of the past, superseded by LED displays and bound for oblivion.

And the neon also seems to sense a presence in the air. As do all those not consumed by the need to rush home. Barmen languidly wiping counters pause to look up. Ruminant waiters stand in doorways. Cab drivers lay aside the evening paper and sit still like plump Buddhas awaiting enlightenment. In the windows of office blocks late workers log off and gaze out.

What is this presence, this longing, so intense but unlocalised? It's eternity yearning for the splendour of transience, for the fading light of passing day.

And for the equally fleeting splendour of the human. After dark the city's strangest fauna emerge. Like exotic birds descending on a tropical lake at sunset, flocks of young women appear on the streets, their long false eyelashes curling up as extravagantly as their long false and intricately patterned nails curl down, their glossy lips blazing even more effulgently than neon, tattooed dragons rearing up on their shoulder blades, red roses blooming on midriffs, butterflies cavorting around ankles – but with little else covering the naked skin, only tiny tight tube tops and tiny tight skirts, or equally tiny and tight strapless dresses. In a fusillade of clacking stilettos they advance, laughing and shrieking, as, without breaking stride, they hook thumbs under armpits to hike up the tops that will always slip down and bend to tug down the hems that will always ride up.

Where are the photographers and painters to catch this glory on the wing? It is evanescent, fleeting. It flares for a moment and is gone.

Where is the composer to write a percussion work for a

Stiletto Orchestra of forty young women in six-inch steel heels, with different groups setting up cross rhythms and counter rhythms and creating different timbres by walking on stone, concrete, wood and metal, the polyrhythms punctuated by wild laughs and shrieks. No, of course it would have to be a ballet to include the joined arms, the hiking and tugging, the exchanges of loving slaps, the generous sharing out of shocking-pink and lime-green Bacardi Breezers. No, an opera-ballet to include arias:

'That fake tan of Amber's went all streaky on me.'

'Didn't I get me red mist in the water park? Stood up and there was *a red streak* all down the water slide.'

'So *he* goes to me, you have fabulous titties and *I'm* . . . like . . . *excuse me?*'

'Went to Chantelle's wedding and it cost me three hundred quid. Got pissed as a fart, stayed out till all hours and couldn't get back into the hotel. Three hundred quid and I never even *lay* on the bed.'

Along the street and down the station steps they go now, sideways, holding on to each other, laughing, shrieking, the heel-clacking amplified by the old metal stairs which have rarely experienced such extravagant glory, and tremble, vibrate, thrum and ring.

Oh my God, the train is arriving! A frenetic crescendo of clacking and shrieking – but they all get on board.

How do they manage without coats or even shawls? Don't they feel the cold? Where is their money, their travel cards, home keys? How do they manage *anything* with those incredible false nails? Where do they go and how do they get back home? What do their parents think?

No answer from the shabby, deserted station. Shaken, stunned, the old metal steps settle back into silence.

Does it only seem cooler since the flock has departed or is

this the first chill of impending autumn? Certainly it is time for home now. It remains only to give thanks that mine eyes have seen the glory and I have set mine lips to sound forth the trumpets of praise.

12

The Office

Up, up and up again into the sky it soars, so tall that looking up at its height is almost as vertiginous as would be looking down from its roof, an edifice combining the monumental bulk of a Gothic cathedral with the hieratic elegance of a heron, the sheer glass façade gleaming with occult power, and dwarfing into utter insignificance the human figure emerging from its tall doors to scurry off around the side. This is a woman in her early forties, plump, with a little rounded tummy and heavy fleshy arms exposed in a sleeveless dress and clasped together under her breasts, one elbow holding a bag against her side. Once around the building, she takes from the bag a lighter and a pack of cigarettes and, hunching in furtive guilt, lights up and hungrily, desperately, inhales. Then she resumes hugging herself against the chill and perhaps also against the slings and arrows of outrageous fortune. For she is obviously of no importance in the corporate hierarchy – possibly something inglorious in procurement or the mailroom, one of the rarely seen inhabitants of the dimly lit and shabby subterranean levels now known by the curious new word 'undercroft'. Yet there is no resentment in her features, only a melancholy that moves me to love. I never imagined I would want to smoke but now I have an overwhelming desire to buy twenty Silk Cut and join her. To be outcasts, pariahs, ageing, suffering, guessing, unprepossessing nobodies together! I have never believed in love at first sight but now it has happened. My heart aches with tenderness and my genitals with lust. But needless to say I have an appointment to keep, constrained as always by obligation.

Farewell, too little and too lately known! Sensing an approach, the mighty automatic doors open silently and smoothly to admit the visitor to the presence of an omniscient, omnipotent and transcendent God. A majestically silent foyer combines the spiritual power of the cathedral with the secular power of the palace, and inspires awe by means of redundant space – the amount of space a corporation can afford to waste is a measure of its majesty. So, overhead soars empty cathedral height and underfoot shines equally empty palace floor. Every corporation dreams it dwells in marble halls (attended, as the song continues, by 'vassals and serfs') and attempts to realise this dream by covering a vast expanse of floor with gleaming marble-effect tiles. Here the walls too are of gleaming dark tiles, broken only by a single, gigantic, brightly coloured abstract painting – abstract to avoid any connection with vulgar reality and to function as a giant Masonic symbol, imposing and occult, conveying the timeless Mysterium Tremendum of the corporation, but brightly coloured to convey its contemporary vibrancy and dynamism.

Far back in this marbled hall is a huge shining reception area, also unadorned except for one soaringly slim vase with flowers as tall, slender and unnatural as supermodels, as difficult to imagine growing in soil as it would be to imagine models living in a slum. And behind this reception area is a woman in her early thirties, old enough to have acquired authority but young enough to have undiminished sexual power, in a suit and blouse that are fitted but not so tight as to be sluttish, make-up that is all the more effective by seeming not to be there at all (strictly no glossy lips or false eyelashes), and shoes that have high heels but are not stilettos, in a plain dark shade, unembellished by pattern, glossiness, rosettes, buckles, bows or, God forbid, peek-a-boo toes. This woman greets with a smile as cool, remote and enigmatic as that of the Mona Lisa – and the greeting itself is cool, without vulgar cries of 'No problem!' or gauche exhortations to 'Have a nice day!' Everything in her appearance and manner radiates knowledge and authority, though in fact she knows nothing whatever about anything and has no skills beyond producing laminated name cards.

Initiates may pass through the turnstiles but supplicants are sent like dunces to sit in the corner on the giant sofas with backs too far away to offer support and seats so soft and low they give the impression of actually sitting not just *on* but *below* the floor (atrium seating is designed to make the corporation look grand and the visitor feel small). And displayed on the darkly gleaming table in front of the sofa are symmetrically spread fans of annual reports as expensively produced as high-fashion magazines but as glossily unreadable as the sofas are elegantly uncomfortable.

Eventually my contact arrives, the placement student I am here to visit, and, as so often on these occasions, I am shocked and depressed. The young man I knew in the university, long-haired, stylishly dressed, lively, witty and irreverent, has been replaced by a corporate clone with cropped hair and a business suit, attempting to project both the solemn authority of a high priest and the worldly assurance of a top executive, and already mouthing business babble. His manager wants him to 'claim ownership of his targets' and he is firmly convinced that he is doing so. The worst thing is that he obviously believes this is what I want to see and hear. He thinks that I will be impressed and delighted by his transformation, his progress, his maturity, when in fact he is driving me close to despair. Is this what we educate young people to become? I have an overpowering urge to seize his arm and whisper, 'Listen, let's make a run for it. We'll vault the turnstile and make a freedom dash for the door, taking care not to slip on the fake-marble tiles. Outside we'll pick up a lovely renegade woman I know and the three of us will make for the hills like Butch and the Sundance Kid and his girl.'

I imagine that many cultured liberals would react as I did, seeing the corporation as a malign cult that worships Mammon and wants to claim the souls of young people and make them its creatures. Certainly many, if not most, artists share this view. Few writers, painters, photographers or filmmakers venture beyond the turnstiles and when they do they usually treat the workplace merely as a backdrop, necessary to make the characters in the main story convincing but of no interest in itself – or else they mock it with satirical contempt as a ship of fools.

But this is yet another form of snobbery and superiority. How do the young people themselves see it? After the meeting with my student I remembered an Italian movie I had seen maybe thirty or forty years earlier. This was *Il Posto*, The Job (directed by Ermanno Olmi), and it certainly lived up to its title for it was solely concerned with work and the synopsis would give a Hollywood executive a heart attack – boy goes for job interview, boy gets job, boy does job. *What?* Surely this is a major law firm and the boy discovers its involvement in a sinister international conspiracy? At least he is seduced by the boss's glamorous wife, Gina Lollobrigida in a sheath dress and pointy stilettos?

The great thing about the movie is that we see everything from the point of view of the young man, a diffident, naïve youth from a small town going to work for a big corporation in Milan. And so we share his innocent wonder. Everything amazes and intrigues him, the high ceilings, the long corridors, the desks and desk-top accessories, and most of all the impenetrable expressions and eccentricities of his colleagues, too self-absorbed to pay him any attention. No one treats him badly and no one treats him well. At the interview he is attracted to a pretty girl and it looks as though the movie will be a tender tale of first love – but that would be too formulaic. Life always resists the formula. Instead, the girl is assigned to a different building and her lunch hour does not overlap with the boy's. Eventually they meet again and she invites him to the New Year's Eve staff dance – but then fails to turn up. When the music starts a kindly middle-aged woman teaches the boy to dance but does not resemble Gina Lollobrigida or attempt to seduce him. The band perform a comedy number where one of them passes cardboard clouds on a stick across a spotlight and exhorts the dancers to take advantage of the darkness. None of them do so. The young man gets slightly drunk, does the conga at midnight and goes home alone.

It is instructive to compare *Il Posto* with a celebrated Hollywood work movie made at the same time – *The Apartment*. In the Hollywood version the young clerk, played by Jack Lemmon, has a central city apartment which he lends to executives for extramarital sex and in return receives regular promotion, so there is a running visual gag of Jack carrying a cardboard box of belongings to ever bigger offices on ever higher floors, eventually achieving a luxurious corner office on the twenty-seventh floor. But of course at the end, disgusted by all this venality, he throws it up to go with the lift operator Shirley MacLaine. It is a challenge to decide which part of the movie is most inauthentic – the cynicism of the main part or the sentimentality of the ending. Everything in *The Apartment* rings as false as everything in *Il Posto* rings true.

Remembering *Il Posto*, it occurred to me that my placement student, an Asian, could be the son of first-generation immigrants thrilled to see their son get an education and work for a major company, and that the son could be just as thrilled to make his parents proud. And remembering the youth in the movie marvelling at his desk and office equipment brought back a similar experience. I was over thirty before I had a job with my own office space, desk, chair and access to the stupendously teeming treasure house of a stationery cupboard. And all these things were marvels, wonders, gifts from the Gods. I had a desk by a window and, though the view was only of another office block, on certain days of grace in certain weather conditions a tree was reflected in the glass opposite. Just one tree, briefly dancing – but that was enough. Like everyone else I complained constantly about work and believed that it was crushing my spirit but the truth is that I was frequently happy, though the happiness was unconscious, suppressed by a snobbish notion of myself as a cruelly exploited wage slave.

The desk was plain, a utilitarian rectangle with drawers on each side, but it was made of the light-coloured wood that symbolised a new era. In the optimistic sixties the old style of dim interiors in dark colours with sombre ponderous dark furniture was finally rejected in favour of brightness and airiness, big windows, white walls and light-coloured fittings and furnishings. Even the staid old desk went blonde (and when paper clips suddenly appeared in primary colours I knew that a profound change had come upon the Western world[208]). I loved my slightly worn blonde, marked by use but still brightly blithe. Every now and then, when no one was looking, I laid the palms of my hands flat on its surface in communion and homage.

In those days the desk was dominated by the Anglepoise lamp and to seize the lamp head and feel the joints and springs of its three-way adjustability conform immediately to one's wishes was inspirationally symbolic. Illumination was no longer institutional and remote. Everyone could acquire, adjust and direct an entirely personal and private illumination. Quoth the Anglepoise lamp to the solitary worker, I am *your* Way and *your* Truth and *your* Light. (There is a story that in 1949 Michael Standing, the BBC's Head of Variety, forbade his staff to use Anglepoise lamps because they would encourage furtive ideas and degenerate programmes. If this is true it was the greatest tribute paid to the Anglepoise. And even if apocryphal it is still evidence of the lamp's pro-individual and anti-institutional bias. The Anglepoise lamp is not a servant but an accomplice.)

Then computers arrived, monstrous cuckoos which invaded, occupied and dominated every desk and, not even content with this, refashioned the desk to suit their purposes, replacing rectilinear purity with various biomorphic, curvilinear shapes, and even robbing the desk of its traditional name, decreeing that from henceforth it be known as the workstation. It was a shock to discover that even a desk could be subject to process. But much that seems inevitable and permanent is actually the result of fortuitous contingency – Post-it notes, the ubiquitous symbols of everyday commercial busyness, were invented by a chorister seeking reliable bookmarks for his hymnal.[209]

What faces the desk, the office swivel chair with flexible back and easy-glide castors, which now seems as eternal as the stars (which are not eternal either), was in fact a quite recent development, designed in 1976 by a man called Bill Stumpf, a kind of Zen Master who published a paper with the gnomic title 'A chair is a chair is a problem'.[210] Stumpf's original design was known as the Ergon chair and within a few years every office worker had a copy of this adult version of a baby bouncer – no, a combined bouncer, baby car and carousel which facilitated three kinds of thrilling motion. Not only rock and roll but also the twist. *Wheeeeee*! A swift nifty reverse and spin to check for the reflected tree. Yes, it too dances this morning. Ten o'clock and all's well.

An unobtrusive but crucial feature of Stumpf's design was desk-level arm rests. Any chair without arms is like a thalidomide child but firm high arms for one's own arms convey the sensation of sitting on a throne and dispensing the wisdom of Solomon. To which task shall the wise king devote himself – heroically deleting fifty emails, returning that boring call or filing a tranche of the paper mountain? Slay fifty emails with the sword of righteousness, then pat the strong chair arms in gratitude and execute a joyous rocking swivel of victory.

Like the Anglepoise lamp, another invention of the century of the individual, the swivel chair has a responsiveness which makes it feel personal, not so much an item of furniture as a garment, even an extension of the self. In *The Third Policeman* Flann O'Brien claimed that, as a consequence of constant molecular interchange, the bicycles of frequent riders become increasingly human – and something similar may have happened to my swivel chair. It began to turn *itself* to the window to check for the reflection of the dancing tree, and when a certain female colleague came into the office it was suddenly frisky.

Many office workers must have similar close relations with their chairs and be swivel masters without even being aware of it. This skill should be recognised and celebrated in the new sport of swivel-chair racing. Chair racers would be timed over a demanding office circuit – at the starting gun roll the chair to a desk to retrieve a document from an in-tray, then roll to a photocopier to make six double-sided, reduced, stapled copies, then on to a filing cabinet to file one copy in the appropriate drawer and section, on again to a notice board to attach another copy with four drawing pins, then to a stationery cupboard for envelopes to hold the remaining four, on again to a cooler for a much-needed cup of water, and finally back to the original desk to drop the four envelopes in the out-tray. Yes, it's a really fast time, a personal best for British hope Norman Beaglehole, another typically plucky performance by the stock clerk from Basingstoke, taking him to joint fourth behind the Germans. But how will the British boy cope with the next gruelling leg over heavy-duty office carpet – the equivalent of the mountain stages in the Tour de France?

And surely painters have recognised and celebrated the desk and chair where so many have passed so much of their lives? I know only of Patrick Caulfield's *Inner Office*, where a rectangular desk and swivel chair sit in enigmatic shadow before a large bright window. In this painting the desk objects are seen only in silhouette but Caulfield gave them their due in a later painting, *After Work*, a still life of a desk top in front of a window with a typewriter, a rubber stamp, a chunky calculator and an in-tray containing an empty Styrofoam coffee cup on its side. Outside, the city is growing dark and the painting captures that magical moment in an empty office at the end of the day.

Even more poignant is *Office Party*, another desktop still life where the stamp, typewriter and phone are accompanied by bottles, empty glasses and, the really heartrending touch, a bowl of leftover peanuts. Many of us have attended that party on many occasions. I can almost taste the cheap red wine. And feel the disappointment that, yet again, despite the booze, nothing happened. As in *Il Posto*, the yearned-for soul mate did not turn up. There was only a handful of peanuts to wash down with sour wine.

I remember the joy of requesting stationery and, instead of being grudgingly handed one note pad, receiving the key to a back-room cupboard whose rickety metal door opened on wonders fragrant with newness – not just stationery in every form, memo slips, Post-it notes, sheets, pads and ring-bound notebooks, but boxes of pens, pencils, paper clips in several sizes, dark rubber bands of various lengths and widths, fat rolls of Sellotape and an entire range of chunky businesslike implements – hole punches, pencil sharpeners, multiply compartmented pen holders, massive black-handled scissors the size of garden shears and staplers long and heavy enough to beat out a boss's brains.

In fact the heft of such objects is a crucial pleasure in itself, a weight that encourages not just holding but *wielding*, and offers the primitive reassurance of a weapon for self-defence or pre-emptive attack, an immensely satisfying sensation in the threatening environment of an office. The drive to make everything lightweight is depriving us of the deep reassurance of heft. For the benefit of product designers I have carried out a few experiments and I estimate Optimal Heft Weight (OHW) as between 500g and 600g. Anything lighter begins to feel flimsy and anything heavier begins to feel burdensome. However OHW will probably vary with the individual, so it will be necessary to estimate mean OHW.

After the hefting, stapling with a big machine is also a profoundly rewarding experience, not just because the act usually signals completion, the equivalent of a king stamping his seal on a treaty, but also because it is so physically satisfying, with a rich, deep and resonant crump when the staple engages fully on the far side, especially good when there are possibly too many sheets but the big strong arm sends the staple right through all of them to clip and hold. As so often, success depends on confidence – a swift, resolute downthrust that the machine will respect and reward. Conversely, feeble flapping will be treated with the contemptuous refusal it deserves.

In *The Mezzanine* Nicholson Baker divides the stapling action into three stages: '*first*, before the stapler arm makes contact with the paper, the resistance of the spring that keeps the arm held up; then, *second*, the moment when the small independent unit in the stapler arm noses into the paper and begins to force the two points of the staple into and through it; and, *third*, the felt crunch, like the chewing of an ice cube, as the twin tines of the staple emerge from the underside of the paper and are bent by the two troughs of the template in the stapler's base, curving inward in a crab's embrace of your memo, and finally disengaging from the machine completely.'

Even better than the stapler is an accessory I have often coveted but never possessed – a date stamper, an implement combining the intricate mechanical engineering of a modern printing press with the long handle, metal heft and sacerdotal purpose of a medieval hand bell.[211] And both stamper and bell perform the same function of reminding us that it is later than we think. The bell rings out the hour and the stamp, with a deep thump of serious engagement, impresses on paper and user the day, month and year. (Baker of course also celebrates date stampers – but this ecstatic rhapsody is too long to quote.)

These implements provide the multi-stage pleasures of mechanism, the aesthetic satisfaction of the many becoming one as moving parts harmoniously cooperate with resonant enmeshings, clunks and clicks. And they are a reminder that the price for electronic wizardry, whose operations are intangible, invisible and silent, is sensory alienation from process and so from full understanding, the connection of the physical and the intellectual implied by the two meanings of 'grasp'. As hefty mechanical implements yield to lightweight electronics, grasp and heft while you still can.

One of the objects in the stationery cupboard remained mysterious for many years, a set of sinister-looking tongs with a pair of sharp hooked claws. This not only felt like but *looked like* a weapon, and a really vicious one at that – though eventually someone explained that it was the opposite of a stapler, a *de*stapler, a device for *removing* staples. Of course I had to have one, though I never used it – for removing staples by hand is almost as pleasurable as inserting them by machine. The pleasure is in the difficulty of getting a fingernail under a tine and the satisfaction when this is achieved and the tine yields: 'Thought you could hold out on *me*? Not a chance.'

So I had a staple remover for many years without ever using it to remove a staple. And indeed many of my accessories remained unused – the hole punch for instance, as well as a letter opener, clipboard clips, layered file dividers, adhesive labels, elastic bands, ring-bound notebooks and several chunky cuboid erasers.

But, God forgive me, I'm forgetting, as does everyone, the thing I did use constantly, the most common, most familiar and therefore invisible office object – the pencil. Not even Nicholson Baker, champion of the overlooked and unappreciated commonplace, has acknowledged the pencil. It is nearly always the pen that gets mentioned as the quintessential writing instrument, and rarely the humble, self-effacing pencil of the common man.[212]

It is fitting that this most democratic of instruments was used by Abraham Lincoln to write the Gettysburg Address, and that it is still used for the most important act of democracy. When I exercised my citizen's privilege a few months ago, I made my X with a blunt pencil attached to a piece of string.[213]

The pencil is also a symbol of the agonies and ecstasies of process, wearing itself down to a sad old stub but also enjoying constant, astounding renewal. The act of sharpening a pencil has the symbolic pleasure of a preparation rite, the equivalent, for a writer, of a priest donning vestments or a knight donning armour. Hemingway prepared for a day's work by sharpening a dozen or so pencils.

This is another exquisite three-stage pleasure: *first*, the snug fit of the pencil head in the sharpener; *second*, the firm twist and crunchy engagement with the blade that makes shavings spring up (especially satisfying if the pencil is polygonal and the shaving comes off in a single intact cone, its scalloped edge rimmed with colour from the pencil-paint like the flared skirt of a flamenco dancer); and *third*, the withdrawal of the head miraculously reborn, no longer blunt and grey but with fragrant bright fresh skin and a point sharp enough to stab a dull colleague to death. Not the primitive bludgeon of the savage but the sophisticated rapier of the swordsman. Today you will certainly get my point. On guard, you dim oafs!

And during and after the writing, the pencil can participate in an extensive repertoire of eloquent inspirational or celebratory gestures unavailable to the pen (because of the danger of ink leaks or stains) – twisting, twirling, tapping, tossing, finger pricking, performing the drumstick intro to Brubeck's *Unsquare Dance* and wearing behind the ear or along the upper lip as a wooden moustache. Conversely, for terminal despair a pencil may be broken in two with a fine dry decisive snap (though, touch wood, I have never been this desperate or brutal).

But a pencil should never be used for erasing, which requires a substantial, separate, dedicated implement. Fitting erasers on pencil tops (one of the less fortunate American innovations) is as greedily misguided as trying to combine poetry and jazz. The pathetic little rubber cylinder always falls out when robustly applied, leaving behind an empty ferrule as horrible as a vacant eye socket.

In the mid-twentieth century the majority of pencils were fitted with erasers but the unadorned classic version has regained its supremacy. In fact the plain pencil has not only survived all the developments that were predicted to kill it off – the fountain pen, mechanical pencil, typewriter, ballpoint, fibretip, computer and smartphone – but is selling in greater quantities than ever, one of those surprising facts that restores faith in the human race.

By all means buy new pencils – but to experience the miracle of renewal and so understand that obscurity and rejection need not be permanent, and the commonplace familiar need not be dreary and dull, take an old, forlorn, discarded stub from the back of a drawer and thrust its soiled head into a sharpener for the astounding rebirth into surgical sharpness, virgin brightness and enchanting cedar-wood fragrance.

What makes pencil sharpening unique is this unexpected addition of fragrance to the sensory pleasures and to the potency of its renewal symbolism. I would often use a sharpener, not because pencils needed sharpening, but for the physical and symbolical satisfactions of the experience itself.

And with many other office accessories, it was not so much that I never used them as that I used them in ways for which they were never intended.[214] I *played* with them. They were *toys* – but toys disguised as serious implements to prevent any suggestion of childish frivolity. I possessed, and cherished, several enormous, twin-pronged and strong-springed clipboard clips but had no actual clipboard (like a fire marshal's yellow jacket and loudhailer, a clipboard is usually the sign of a self-important asshole). Instead I loved closing the big black jaws of a clip over my index finger and wiggling it so that it looked like some sort of giant insect signalling with its antennae.

Other play pleasures included opening and closing the hole punch, snapping shut the claws of the destapler, fitting rubber bands over extended fingers to stretch and twang, and prising open a paper clip with a fingernail (a bent paper clip is also useful for cleaning fingernails before a review meeting with a boss). The common factor is resistance, whether of rubber or spring. There should always be an element of resistance in the medium, which explains the satisfaction of securing a notice to a board with drawing pins. When the point of the pin engages, the board at first appears to resist penetration successfully but then, under thumb pressure, unexpectedly yields so that the pin suddenly and deliriously shoots all the way in (this particular pleasure may well be a guy thing).

If I was feeling especially exuberant and crazy, really *mental*,

I would use a stretched rubber band as a catapult to shoot a bunch of staples into the metal bin across the office. The clang of a direct hit was terrifically exciting, especially if the bunch disintegrated, showering shrapnel into the bin.

Lord, how I wish I still had these toys. The only disadvantage of retirement is the lack of free stationery and accessories.

At least I still have pencils and a sharpener – and rubber bands. There is something magical about these. I hardly ever use one for a practical purpose but I have never been able to throw one out. Is the symbolism of the rubber band its denial of process and entropy, the suggestion that we can be stretched badly out of shape but always return to our original form? This would explain why it is shocking and tragic when a rubber band suddenly snaps. Needless to say, I would no more dream of cutting one than I would of detaching a butterfly's wings. Only the other day I spent ages laboriously removing a rubber band wound tightly many times round the green shoots of a bunch of organic carrots – and as I write I am rolling it into a ball between my left index finger and thumb.

Or perhaps rubber bands give an unconscious Proustian memory of childhood. I used to love the little skinny multicoloured elastics that came in cellophane packets like wine gums. Making a coloured chain of these for a catapult was an ingenious way of simultaneously expressing my masculine and feminine natures. When my first Zen Master Willie Sharkey saw me with such a catapult, he posed one of his mysterious questions, 'Which is the stretchiest, skin or elastic?' Needless to say, I chose elastic. Sharkey shook his head in infinite weariness at my irredeemable obtuseness. 'Nah, nah, nah, it's skin,' he sighed. 'Didn't Jesus tie his ass to a tree and walk into Jerusalem?'

Now of course I play mostly with thick, dark-brown, *serious* rubber bands. Adults need toys that do not appear to be toys and I would never risk looking a fool by having explicit executive playthings. Nevertheless I always enjoyed receiving a junk-mail catalogue called *Successories*, so much so indeed that I have kept several issues. These catalogues advertised items like the Executive Stress Ball, a battery-operated foam and plastic ball that made 'the glorious sound of breaking glass' when hurled violently at the 'fun target'. For those of a less aggressive temperament there were Chinese Baoding Balls ('as used in the Ming Dynasty 1368 – 1644'), two iron balls, one tuned high and the other low, so that 'as you gently manipulate your balls the harmonious musical effect is mysteriously soothing'. But the *Successories* speciality was inspirational slogans, available in a dazzling variety of formats, including key-ring chains, pocket medallions, lapel pins, floor rugs, mouse mats, greeting cards and of course luxuriously framed posters. I was particularly impressed by the Gallery of Inner Fire, which displayed images of determined sports people, for instance a grimy, sweaty, helmeted American footballer glaring ferociously above the legend: 'You're either part of the steamroller or part of the pavement'. The equivalent for women was a muscle-bound female tennis player leaping off the ground with a frenzied expression to smash a ball: 'Serve like a girl . . . right into their faces at 85 mph'. Or, for subtler Oriental class, a Chinese girl gymnast upside down in mid-air: 'What are little girls made of? Courage, determination and pride, that's what'.

I cherished all these – but my favourite was a coffee mug:

WE CAN'T SPELL
S CCESS WITHOUT
U

The use of office accessories as disguised toys is in fact a disguised ruse, an unconscious ruse that would prefer to remain to unaware of itself. And it may be that employers tolerate or even encourage this practice, though also unconsciously, so that the employer's (unconscious) ruse is pretending to be taken in by the employee's (also unconscious) ruse. This psychology may seem to be implausibly complex but is common in long relationships such as marriage. And there is evidence for the theory in the batch of 1000 business cards employers print for employees, even though most will distribute only a few of these and mainly in the first year to relatives. Nicholson Baker tells us that one of the most difficult decisions on leaving a job is what to do with 958 fresh-smelling business cards. I felt smug reading this because I had resisted a strong desire to order a batch, partly because my wallet was already bulging with coffee-shop loyalty cards and partly because I knew *none* of the 1000 would ever be used.

There is no shortage of conscious workplace ruses. One study claims that, out of a year's 235 working days, employees spend 24 days complaining about the boss, 21 days gossiping about, and flirting with, colleagues, 19 days making personal phone calls, 14 days daydreaming and 8.8 days hiding in the toilets.[215] Assuming that half the UK population works (it may well be more) and that half of these have access to toilets, it is likely that on any working day there are over half a million employees skulking in toilet cubicles.

But no study can capture the range of site-specific and opportunistic ruses. My own favourite was a scam with the canteen coffee machine which provided the full range of Americano, cappuccino, latte and espresso. The espresso option was presumably intended to be a single shot, though there was no notification of this, but the cardboard cups had to be large enough to accommodate the other options so it was possible to get four espressos into a cup and to conceal the giveaway crema with a lid. Hence an unheard-of extravagance, a *quadruple* espresso, a *double* double, or *doppio* doppio. And for the price of a single. Buy one, get three free. Having to press the espresso button four times was a bit risky, especially if there was a queue, but back in the privacy and safety of the office the full cup was as glorious as a pint of champagne.

But the most sophisticated ruse, the ruse of ruses, is to enjoy work that is not supposed to be enjoyable. This is the theme of *The Pale King*, a novel whose subject matter is tax workers' experience of 'routine, repetition, tedium, monotony, ephemeracy, inconsequence, abstraction, disorder, boredom, angst, ennui'. Wallace tackles this with a strange manic realism that revels – no, *exults* – in the details most would find rebarbative and terrifying, the acronyms, jargon and professional euphemisms, the forms, manuals, rules, regulations and procedures, the job titles, pay scales and organisational structure. Most writers would treat such material satirically, if at all, but, although it has much wonderful comedy, *The Pale King* is much deeper and stranger than satire. At its heart is a speech by a Jesuit tax teacher which inspires a student who has wandered by accident into his class to discover a vocation for the Internal Revenue Service. The speech begins by denouncing the seductions of plot.

'The truth is that the heroism of your childhood entertainments was not true valor. It was theater. The grand gesture, the moment of choice, the mortal danger, the external foe, the climactic battle whose outcome resolves all – all designed to appear heroic, to excite and gratify an audience . . . Gentlemen, welcome to the world of reality – there is no audience. No one to applaud, to admire. No one to see you. Do you understand? Here is the truth – actual heroism receives no ovation, entertains no one. No one queues up to see it. No one is interested.'

The Jesuit goes on to explain the alternative: 'True heroism is you, alone, in a designated work space. True heroism is minutes, hours, weeks, year upon year of the quiet, precise, judicious exercise of probity and care – with no one there to see or cheer.

This is the world. Just you and the job, at your desk.' And he suggests that such heroism is capable of producing 'a denomination of joy unequalled by any you men can yet imagine'.

Like *Ulysses* and *À la recherche*, *The Pale King* has no plot (or even structure), makes use of every possible approach, imaginative, comic, spiritual, psychological and philosophical, and has a megalomaniac desire to capture the multitudinousness of everyday life in all its minutely mundane detail. If Wallace had lived to complete the book it would surely have grown to the vastness of *Ulysses* and *À la recherche* (by page 300 the characters have only just *arrived* at the IRS centre and when the manuscript ends on page 538 we are only getting to know them).

Perhaps the most grievous loss is the demonstration of the everyday heroism advocated by the Jesuit. We know from notes published with the manuscript that Wallace intended to attempt this feat. 'Ability to pay attention. It turns out that bliss – a second-by-second joy + gratitude at the gift of being alive, conscious – lies on the other side of crushing, crushing boredom. Pay close attention to the most tedious thing you can find (tax returns, televised golf) and, in waves, a boredom like you've never known will wash over you and just about kill you. Ride these out, and it's like stepping from black and white into color. Like water after days in the desert. Constant bliss in every atom.'

I love that reference to 'televised golf'. Obviously Wallace never saw televised snooker. At least golf is played outdoors and has changes of scenery.

Could he have brought it off and convinced us that on the other side of crushing boredom there is bliss? I have my doubts – but what a lesson that would have been.

If he had lived, Wallace would surely have tidied up the manuscript, cut the weaker episodes and possibly purged the tiresome residues of postmodernism (that old cliché of a character with the author's name, David Foster Wallace) and magic realism (a tax officer who levitates and a boy determined to kiss every part of his own body). The real problem with *The Pale King* is not its many imperfections but that it often feels self-conscious, willed, researched, a professional project. It lacks the unmistakable authenticity of personal experience. Wallace himself was aware of the mysterious authenticity factor. In an episode about the Peoria underclass, an uneducated teenage girl living in a trailer park reads the Stephen Crane Civil War novel *The Red Badge of Courage*, and 'knew by sheer feel that its author had never seen war'. Similarly, readers of *The Pale King* will know by sheer feel that its author has never been a wiggler (the colloquial term for a tax examiner) and probably not even a turdnagel (a temporary seasonal employee).

Instead of complaining we should appreciate what we have. Like Joyce, Wallace had a great ear for authentic speech, especially that of corporate professionals. He catches exactly the mixture of knowingness, worldliness and tough-guy insouciance, the confident insider use of specialist jargon, the absolute understanding of, and deference to, status and rank, and the slangy tone that tries to convey cynical independence of rank. A tax official in *The Pale King*:

'The Deputy DD's a man-of-the-people type. But very much Glendinning's boy. 907313433, a full CPA, Sheehan is, a GS-13, nine years in. He was auditing out of District 10 in Chicago before he got the degree. Came over with Glendinning. Kind of Glendinning's hatchet man, very hail-fellow, let's all be friends, all smiles but the eyes go right through you.'

Baker too is good on workspeak. The narrator of *The Mezzanine* is talking casually to a receptionist when she takes a phone call and abruptly switches into her professional manner. 'In a voice that was suddenly sweet, efficient, platinum-throated, slightly-breathy, she said, "Good morning, Donald Vanci's office? I'm sorry, Don's stepped away from his desk. May I take your number and have him get back to you?"' Isn't that 'stepped away' just exquisite? A collector's item?

Earlier in the conversation the narrator has been explaining that the new maintenance man is not good at replacing the plastic liners in waste-paper bins. Now the liners always have trapped air, 'a pillow effect'. At once the receptionist responds with, 'I'll bet you enjoy the pillow effect'. This woman, a true professional, is as skilled at flirting as she is at phone talk.

Workplace flirting is the sexual equivalent of facetiousness and, as facetiousness has nothing to do with humour, so this kind of flirting has nothing to do with sex. Not surprisingly, it is usually facetious in tone. And like facetiousness, it is a necessary element of workplace relations – but changes in sexual politics have made it increasingly difficult, especially for men. If a man overdoes it, even by just a little, he is likely to be despised as a sexual dinosaur, and if he avoids it he is just as likely to be despised as a different type of unpleasant creature, the cold fish. Getting it right is like singing in tune, a complex combination of words, melody and pitch. I have never had this gift – I can't sing either – so I have always avoided workplace flirting.

The agony of workplace encounters! Another chapter of *The Pale King* is devoted to a fifteen-minute morning break for tax examiners, when three wigglers step outside the building and one, a new recruit, tries unsuccessfully to break into a magnificently banal conversation between the other two about the previous Saturday's barbecue at Hank Bodnar's house ('You know Hank Bodnar, from over in K-team at Capital Exams, with the glasses with the lenses that turn dark by themselves outside, what are they called'). The new man carefully positions himself farther from the pair than they are from each other but still close enough to signal a desire for inclusion. In the brutal way of insiders the two talkers ignore him, so that eventually he 'feels like running out into the fields in the heat and running in circles and flapping his arms'.

Anyone who has worked for a living will immediately recognise both types, having probably been each in turn, first the desperate newcomer and later the callous old hand.

Baker's narrator, Howie, has several agonising encounters, including the toilet ordeal of having to pee next to a boss, Donald Vanci in fact, who arrives at a neighbouring urinal and begins to urinate forcefully before Howie has begun, so that he will surely be aware of Howie finally beginning – and awareness of this inhibits Howie. His solution is an ingenious and useful ruse. 'When someone takes his position next to you, and you hear his nose breathing and you sense his proven ability to urinate time after time in public, and at the same time you feel your own muscles closing on themselves as hermit crabs pull into their shells, imagine yourself turning and dispassionately urinating onto the side of his head.' This would make a great *Successories* image for guys – a young man at a urinal next to a senior man and thinking to himself, as does Howie, 'Imagine your voluminous stream making fleeting parts in his hair'.

But neither Baker nor Wallace describe the most excruciating, universal and frequent of work encounters – the meeting. In fact, although meetings are regular events in most workplaces, I do not know of an authentic meeting scene anywhere in fiction. Is this because the meeting is simply too awful to contemplate? All through my own professional life I dreaded meetings – and would often attempt to make my soul leave my body for the duration (I still believed in Cartesian dualism at the time). When this failed to work I would bring a small office toy to play with under the table – an elastic band, pencil stub, paper clip (which can be violently twisted out of shape to release uncontrollable fury) or an especially strong clipboard clip, which I clamped on a finger as a foreground discomfort to suppress background pain, and imagined clamping on the testicles of the boss determined at all times to impose his will or the mouth of the woman who talked incessantly in a tone that suggested sharp, independent critical analysis but actually delivered a fulsome endorsement of everything proposed by the boss.

Employees hate meetings because they reveal that self-promotion, sycophancy, dissimulation and constantly talking nonsense in a loud confident voice are more impressive than merely being good at the job – and it is depressing to lack these skills but even more depressing to discover one's self using them. In meetings the trick is to sound detached and sceptical even as you kiss senior management ass, to laugh like a wild, carefree gypsy even as you single-mindedly and ruthlessly pursue power, and to sigh with compassion and sorrowful reluctance even as you rapturously twist a knife deep in the intestines of rivals.

Above all, it is necessary to sound keenly attuned to the times by using state-of-the-art clichés (unlike most other forms of innovation, new clichés always reward the early adopter). At the moment this would involve agreeing to do something by saying, 'I'll action that', requesting assistance by asking, 'May I borrow you?', postponing discussion of an issue by snapping, 'We'll take that off-line', proposing to test a plan by 'kicking the tyres', reporting satisfaction with a product or service by acknowledging that 'it does what it says on the tin', describing a difficult project as 'chewy' or noting with relish that 'There's one hell of a lot of heavy lifting to be done', defining a combination of problems as 'a perfect storm', and, to rejoice at potential cooperation but avoid using 'synergy' for the fifth time, falling back on the older but still useful, 'This will create opportunities for cross-pollination'.

No wonder Bergson chose the work meeting as an example of an event that seems unbearably predictable and dreary but can be transformed if seen as creative evolution at its most exuberant.[216] Work meetings generate continuously in new forms all that is characteristic, interesting and comical about everyday life – excruciating facetiousness, flirting and flattery, petrified self-importance, ingenious self-justification, brazen lies to colleagues only outdone in breathtaking audacity by lies to the self, furtive perverted fetishised sado-masochistic sexual attraction (all those power-hungry animals, brutes in suits), hate-filled and murderous clashes of rival superiorities conducted in the polite tones of afternoon tea, and throughout all of this the most bizarrely inventive speech.

Meetings are perfect for the sport of cliché-spotting, which, unlike train spotting and bird watching, does not require giving up free time and wearing an anorak or wellington boots, and which, in contrast to the rarity of new trains or birds, offers ever-new jargon and clichés in profusion. Clichés are like jokes – no one seems to create them and yet glorious new ones spring up endlessly. There ought to be a Society of Cliché-Spotters whose members submit newly spotted clichés and win points if these are recognised by a majority of other members. At the end of the year there would a Cliché-Spotters Award Ceremony giving prizes for Spotter of the Year and Best New Business, Political, Academic, Journalistic and Sporting Cliché. The new clichés of each year would also be published and these collections would be an invaluable archive for sociologists, anthropologists and especially scriptwriters and novelists.

So now . . . I can scarcely believe this . . . I want to go back to my workplace and beg to be allowed to attend a meeting once more. In fact I want to experience all of the office environment again.

I write novels myself, though I never revealed this to

colleagues, and used to come home from my final job to snarl at my wife, 'That place is so fucking boring I can't even get a book out of it.' The usual presumption and blindness. There were glorious novels all around me if only I had had the eyes to see, the ears to listen and the mind to marvel and record.

13

Home

Home is the locus of all that is most congenial in everyday life – cooking, eating, drinking, entertaining friends, rearing a family and making love. In fact there is no ruse more cunning and no subversion more effective than sneaking upstairs with a partner in the torpid afternoon of some ordinary day, some dismal, overcast Tuesday in November, to snatch from the tyranny of the years an hour of companionable adult pleasure.[217]

But all these are pleasures of the social self, and for the social self to function properly it must have, as its impregnable core, a secret self. This secret self has to be strong, and sustaining its strength requires shelter and nurturing. So a less obvious but just as crucial function of the home is to provide a haven for the secret self suppressed to near extinction by the world. Michel de Certeau: 'Only the cave of the home remains believable, still open for a certain time to legends, still full of shadows.'[218] Note that prescient warning, 'for a certain time'. The problem is that the cave is being transformed into a high-tech entertainment and communications complex – not a sanctuary that nurtures and awakens but the hub of a worldwide network that distracts and disperses, and a fantasy palace that induces a persistent vegetative state. The contemporary home is dedicated to the cultivation of couch potatoes.[219]

For those accustomed to clamour a silent home can be frightening. But to switch on the secret self it is necessary to be alone and still and to switch off the communications and entertainment. Then, bit by bit, rooms, furniture and household objects begin to assume a numinous presence and home to realise the twin meanings of dwelling, as both a living in and a lingering on. In fact to live in *is* to linger on and vice versa. Dwell, the home says to us, learn to dwell.

Slowly silence expands space and slows time. Rooms acquire roominess, space becomes breathing space, a space of time. Home is space-time.

Like lovers and close friends, home reveals that the most familiar is really the most strange. For instance, home always has a unique smell – but only those for whom it is not home can smell it.

Mystery, like charity, should begin at home.

So home is where adulthood is attained by returning to childhood. A child is naturally sensitive to the strangeness and secrecy of home and is drawn to cellars and basements, wardrobes, cupboards and drawers, to the indecipherable messages in damp stains and ceiling cracks, and to the dark hints that gleam momentarily in mirrors. But all this sensitivity is lost in growing up and the adult may regain a vestige of it only after great effort. Then the memory of the original home enriches the current home.

As well as establishing a connection with the lost child, home is where you renew three essential human relationships, those with your inner lunatic, idiot and clown – where you fling open the fridge door to cry in a parody French accent, 'Zee cheese and zee eggs in zee omelette, I seenk.'

Also relationships with the three most faithful and self-effacing four-legged friends – the bed, the table and the chair.

And home is four dedicated spaces in one – the sanatorium of a convalescent, the asylum of a lunatic, the temple of a high priest and the lair of a brute.

Home is where you go mental but also physical. The secret self has a body as well as a soul. Home is where the body can be at its most bestial and the soul at its most spiritual and sometimes even both together, as when you simultaneously fart and contemplate the sublime.

So home is for the two extremes of the human spectrum denied by the world – spiritual exercises and bodily indulgences.

A free home day begins with the bodily indulgence of tarrying in the first four-legged friend, the bed, and enjoying the agreeable tension between the womb warmth that encourages indolence and the call of the new day to arise and be reborn. This period just after waking, when the mind is still partly in thrall to the carnival madness of the dream world but also exulting in the promise of the equally mysterious day world, is the glory time of the right brain when, fresh and free, it is at its most frisky and imaginative. All manner of things may be read in the play of light on the ceiling – though a truly inspirational ceiling should have cobwebs, old damp stains and a network of cracks.

Georges Perec described a cracked ceiling as his 'Muse' and lamented that 'people no longer pay any attention to ceilings'.[220] In *The Third Policeman* MacCruiskeen studied for two years the cracks in the ceiling of his bedroom in the barracks and suddenly realised that these formed an accurate and detailed map of the local district, including even the lane from the main road to Gogarty's outhouse. And after scrutinising the map for another five years he discovered a tiny crack that seemed to have no counterpart in reality, but, on investigation, was a path to a hidden world beyond time. So studying a characterful ceiling may reveal the way to eternity.

The right brain is also intensely stimulated by a shower,[221] an invention of the independent-minded Greeks, improved by the practical Romans and rejected by the thought-resisting Christians right up to the Victorian era. The power of the shower is its combination of bodily indulgence and spiritual exercise. A shower stall suspends activity, enforces solitude and stillness and passivity (but passivity *standing up*, rare at home, passivity erect, alert, *active* passivity) and a surrender to external flow that encourages internal flow, the stream of water encouraging the stream of consciousness. Nudity also helps to unify the body and mind of the secret self. So the shower brings forth the inner idiot, lunatic and clown who wiggle tits or dicks, dance, sing, roar, shout, utter wild affirmative cries of the Molly Bloom YES and conclude by using the navel cavity as a sounding board for jubilant belly slaps.

This experience also provides the day's first opportunity for transgression, though peeing in the shower is not as thrillingly transgressive as the pleasure Bloom anticipates of peeing in his morning bath ('Also I think I. Yes I. Do it in the bath.'). On the ultimate transgression of masturbating, Bloom also gives sound advice. After thoroughly enjoying the Gertie experience he congratulates himself on not having tossed off earlier in the bath. Reject short-term gratification, Bloom counsels, and hold out for the splendour of Gertie's drawers.

Besides, losing bodily fluids too early may diminish the natural exhilaration of morning, the joy at being granted an undeserved pardon and given yet another chance. How to make the most of it this time? Like Marcus Aurelius and Martin Heidegger, William James advocated daily spiritual exercises. But it does not matter which spiritual exercises are used – the Catholic rituals of Ignatius Loyola can be just as effective as meditation and yoga. The important thing is to have *some* form of exercise to keep the right brain awake.

For me, meditation has never been quite enough. Stillness and silence are necessary to liberate the right brain but, if the goal is something more than serene emptiness, the right brain also needs stimulation. To sustain the natural morning high, I snort a few lines.

Emily Dickinson provides the purest and most intense hit:

> I cannot dance upon my Toes –
> No Man instructed me –
> But oftentimes, among my mind,
> A Glee possesseth me,
>
> That had I Ballet knowledge –
> Would put itself abroad
> In Pirouette to blanch a Troupe –
> Or lay a Prima, mad,[222]

'Exultation is the going / Of an inland soul to sea', Emily also said – enjoy the intoxication of the sailor without leaving the comfort of your own home. She herself spent the second half of her life entirely at home – but she disproved the stereotype of the recluse as inadequate, depressed and dim. It was not so much that she was incapable of socialising as that the secret self was so much more rewarding than the social self. So, 'to venerate the simple days' and become 'a Millionaire in little Wealths', she wrote some of the most spirited and zestful poetry and became the most exemplary champion of the secret self that flourishes in clandestine joy ('The Soul's Superior instants occur to Her – alone'). Only Whitman can match her for sheer delight – Walt the open-necked shirt on the open road, Emily the buttoned-up blouse in the closed upper room. Him outdoors and her indoors – but equally exuberant. If only these two could have been persuaded to breed!

The next bodily indulgence of morning at home, a great luxury unsung and often underappreciated, is being free to do a bundle at leisure in the security and comfort of the home toilet. A crap is like a poem, but an inspiration of the body rather than an inspiration of the soul, and like a poem it demands to be expressed at the time of its own choosing, no sooner and no later. A premature attempt will be incomplete and unsatisfactory, and if it is made to wait too long the crap will go into a huff and be sullen and refractory. But if expressed just when the urge is most imperious, the flow can be copious, fluent, relaxed and inevitable, coming, as Keats said of poems, as the leaves to the trees.

Joyce, the poet of intimate bodily function, was the first to celebrate the luxury of evacuation by devoting several pages to Bloom reading *Titbits* on the toilet, where, himself like a poet controlling rhythmic effect, he carefully paces his motion to enhance the pleasure: 'Quietly he read, restraining himself, the first column and, yielding but resisting, began the second. Midway, his last resistance yielding, he allowed his bowels to ease themselves quietly as he read, reading still patiently, that slight constipation of yesterday quite gone. Hope it's not too big bring on piles again. No, just right. So. Ah.'

This certainly conveys the voluptuousness of an unhurried crap. And Bloom's deliberate holding back, giving new meaning to the phrase 'slow motion', is a useful lesson for the age of speed. Bloom, an Irish Bodhisattva, teaches us the art of mindful crapping.

However he also displays modern greediness by reading *Titbits* while at stool. Crapping and reading are mindful pleasures but attempting to combine them diminishes both. The two experiences do have in common an encouragement of right brain associativity but each must be enjoyed separately to allow this to flourish. Only when the mind is undistracted will new ideas enter the top of the body as its waste products leave from the bottom. Only last week I had an inspiration on the bowl while gazing idly at bathroom scales and remembering a newspaper piece about new scales that tweet the owner's weight to a social network. Suddenly it struck me that an even better idea would be an intelligent toilet, a device that first murmurs, in the voice of a favourite celebrity, *thank you for your input*, then analyses the morning's achievement with a readout of weight, composition, transit time and delivery rate, compares these figures to averages and personal bests, and finally tweets all this crucial information to friends. If you should suffer an entirely unproductive day, the caring, supportive toilet will inform all your friends of the problem and, as contemporary friends should, they will be 'there for you' with messages of consolation and reassurance.

But if crapping were socially acceptable it would lose its transgressive appeal. The activity is unmentionable (it's fine to say, 'I'm just nipping off for a pee', but never, 'I'm just nipping off for a shite') and so doing a bundle anywhere at any time feels wonderfully subversive, a marvellous ruse. However conditions outside home are rarely propitious. Crapping at work often suffers from being badly timed and hurried (though it does benefit from awareness of stealing time from work to do something disgustingly vile, the joy of, in every sense, shitting on the job).

Crapping in strange places is even more stressful (with the possible horrors of faulty or non-existent locks, or discovering, too late, that the toilet-paper dispenser is empty) and one of the benefits of London's free museums is access to cool, clean, spacious and well-equipped toilets. Hotels usually also provide a happy experience, though I have often wondered how lovers on dirty weekends deal with the other kind of dirt. Sharing a bathroom with someone unfamiliar must be a harrowing experience, especially as the candlelit dinner was probably rich, and preceded by champagne, accompanied by a château-bottled

Bordeaux and followed by Rémy Martin. In fiction, John Updike is the greatest expert on infidelity and somewhere in his vast oeuvre there may well be useful tips on bathroom sharing for adulterers.

Nicholson Baker, on the other hand, has reminded us that one of the rewards of matrimony can be comfortable frankness about number two. In *Room Temperature*,[223] which does for the home what *The Mezzanine* did for the office, Patty, the wife of the narrator, Mike, surprises and pleases him by indicating the bathroom with her thumb and saying, 'Excuse me for a moment, Changlibore. I have to, I need to go *big job*.' This has a tremendously beneficial effect on the marriage. 'From then on we preannounced our *big jobs* more and more; and if Patty rattled the bathroom door and I called warningly out from inside, "Um! I'm in the middle of something very 'big', baby," she would mock-casually ask, "Jobbing, eh?" and I would reply mock-sheepishly, "I'm afraid I am." '

'Big job' is good but I prefer Don DeLillo's terms for number one and number two – 'Tee Tee' and 'Big Business'.[224] If a visitor to your home should ask for the bathroom, you are guaranteed a laugh by responding, 'Tee Tee or Big Business?'

It was Joyce's celebration of bodily functions that caused much of the trouble with *Ulysses*. Intellectuals could take the sex but not the shite. Ezra Pound, one of the most broad-minded and tolerant readers of the age, begged Joyce to cut down on the farting in *Ulysses*. Joyce of course refused. So Leopold Bloom farts all through the day and Molly Bloom continues with equal abandon in bed at night ('piano quietly sweeeee'), adding a defiant justification ('wherever you be let your wind go free'). A full account of the Bloom family's flatulence on 16 June 1904 would require a learned article suitable for the *James Joyce Quarterly* – but my favourite is when Leopold is reading a famous piece of Irish nationalist rhetoric by Robert Emmet and is constantly interrupted by farts which he blames on the glass of burgundy he had with his lunch, and cunningly conceals under the noise of a passing tram:

> *When my country takes her place among.*
> Prrprr.
> Must be the bur.
> Fff. Oo. Rrpr.
> *Nations of the earth.* No-one behind. She's passed. *Then and not till then.* Tram. Kran, kran, kran. Good oppor. Coming. Krandlkkrankran. I'm sure it's the burgund. Yes. One, two. *Let my epitaph be.* Karaaaaaaa. *Written. I have.*
> Pprrpffrrppfff.
> *Done.*

Home is the place for exuberant farts and burps, leisurely ruminative nose picking, serene mowing of nostril hair with an electric trimmer, nail cutting with a surgically efficient clipper and concentrated plucking of ear hair with tweezers, a task combining the fierce scrutiny of the hunter with the delicate precision of the keyhole surgeon ('Gotcha, you pesky little fucker you, *ha*!').

Nicholson Baker has devoted a nine-page essay to the joys of nail clipping (*Clip Art*[225]) and unequivocally favours clipping over paring or cutting with scissors because clippers work 'with a bracing abruptness, a can-do metallic snap, that leaves their user with the illusion that he is progressively, clip by hardened-steel clip, gaining control of his shambling life'. Baker also enjoys the look and feel of good clippers, the way nail clippings shoot off so rapidly that they actually seem to *disappear*, and the surprisingly sharp facets of fingernails cut with clippers. An expert on the history and development of nail clippers (another great twentieth-century invention), Baker salutes, as the Bernini of clipper design, William E. Bassett, founder of the W. E. Bassett Company, whose late masterpiece was the Easy Hold Clipper.

In the same spirit I can wholeheartedly recommend for ear-hair plucking the product of a fruitful collaboration between the designer Laura Mercier and the manufacturer Tweezerman – the Wide-Grip Slant Tweezer. This has the simplicity of genius, with a large round finger-grip two thirds of the way down, exactly where fingers take hold, slanted jaws to allow for the fact that the plucking hand always approaches the ear diagonally, and, last but not least, Tweezerman's 'superior calibrated tension and perfectly aligned hand-filed precision tips' to catch and yank the little bastards. No hair is a match for such technical know-how. The Wide-Grip Slant Tweezer will detach and brandish aloft its prey like the head of a vanquished barbarian chief ('How do you like it *now*, Mr Sneaky Ear Hair?').

Baker also offers reassurance on nose picking: 'In my experience a certain amount of daily maintenance work on the interior of the nose was *necessary*, physically necessary, simply to avoid panicky feelings of claustrophobia, especially in the dry winter months.' And this maintenance work is immensely rewarding: 'even as a grown man I found the inrush of cool air in a well-picked nostril an indisputable joy'. As well as the physical pleasure, there is the symbolism of clearing channels, passageways, conduits, an opening of the blocked brain to the plenitude of the world.

One of the consequences of the open-plan office is that nose picking is now virtually impossible at work. I was fortunate in that I could get out of sight by scrunching up into one corner by a filing cabinet – but it was a perilous and stressful undertaking. Even at home there can be problems. Baker's narrator, Mike, tells Patty about his maintenance work, though only after much apprehensive soul searching – and caution in this matter is certainly advisable. Women seem to find snot more disgusting than shit and men should not be deceived by the sight of mothers happily, even delightedly, removing bogies from the noses of their infants. I have never seen a woman pick her nose, or heard a woman admit to such an act (questioning is met by angry, close-mouthed silence[226]), or found any reference to female nose picking in literature. Not even Joyce, frank also about female body function (including menstruation and vaginal farts), dared to mention a woman picking her nose (in *Ulysses* it is Stephen Dedalus who picks and leaves the extract on a rock on Sandymount Strand). So ignorant men may only speculate. Do women never pick their noses or is there an insurmountable taboo on mentioning the practice? Take your pick.

After all this bodily indulgence the mind deserves a treat – time for the champagne of morning. Coffee has always provided grounds for celebration, from its discovery in Ethiopia a thousand years ago by the goat-herder poet Kaldi, who saw his goats dancing on their hind legs after chewing the leaves and berries of the coffee tree, tried this himself and promptly spilled out 'poetry and song'.[227] And when in the fifteenth century coffee was first taken as an infusion brewed from roasted and ground beans, it was used by Sufi monks to get fired up for the whirling dervish dance. Soon coffee was the favourite stimulus for the more sober celebrations of imagination and thought and therefore often regarded as subversive; it was banned in 1511 by the governor of Mecca, in 1633 by the Grand Vizier of Constantinople (first-time offenders were cudgelled and after a second offence sewn up in bags and thrown into the Bosphorus), and in 1675 by King Charles II of England, who denounced it as 'the great resort of Idle and disaffected persons' but, in a rare royal U-turn, withdrew the ban after two weeks due to the ferocity of the public outcry.[228]

I would certainly storm the palace if deprived of my daily fix, and I would be only one of a mighty host. For caffeine is the most popular drug in the world and coffee is its most popular delivery system. Coffee is the cocaine of the common man, the performance-enhancing drug of the uncompetitive and the Communion wine of the irreligious. Or, rather, it is the Holy Communion of a different religion which believes that, in the course of grinding and brewing, coffee is mystically transubstantiated into a divine exudate, so that, as champagne has been changed into God's urine, coffee has become the rectal fluid of God.

Coffee improves alertness, cognition, memory, spatial awareness and reactivity,[229] all the faculties needed to attend to everyday life. The neural mechanism for this is fascinating. To pay attention the brain sends excitatory neurotransmitters to the areas required by the particular form of attention, and inhibitory neurotransmitters to the other parts of the brain. But where nicotine improves concentration by boosting the exciters, coffee works by inhibiting the inhibitors. Nicotine helps the brain to narrow in but coffee helps it to open out. So coffee is a friend of both brain hemispheres, a facilitator of logical thinking in the left and imagination and wit in the right. The coffee junkie, Balzac: 'This coffee falls into your stomach, and immediately there is a general commotion. Ideas begin to move like the battalions of the Grand Army ... things remembered arrive at full gallop ... the light cavalry of comparisons delivers a magnificent charge ... the artillery of logic hastens in with ammunition and the sharpshooters fire off rounds of wit.'[230]

Proust too was a coffee addict (Joyce preferred the other divine exudate, champagne) and towards the end of his life, when he was working on his novel, lived almost exclusively on this drink. So *À la recherche* is the greatest ad for the mind-expanding properties of coffee. But like all his domestic procedures, Proust's coffee routine was insane. He would drink only Corcellet coffee from one shop in the Rue de Lévis and it had to be freshly roasted and ground in the shop, then packed tightly into a Corcellet filter for maximum strength and filtered slowly, drop by drop, until there was exactly enough for two cups, a process taking half an hour. Then Céleste had to serve it in a silver pot on a silver tray with a monogrammed bowl and a lidded porcelain jug of milk that had to be boiling hot. Proust always took a cup and a half in the bowl and sometimes had the other half cup later, but if so would never use the same milk, even if reheated. Fresh milk had to be boiled up. The trickiest problem was that Proust could order coffee at any time but was not prepared to wait, so it had to be ready just when he ordered it. If the preparation was begun too late and the filtering was rushed, the coffee would not be sufficiently strong, and if the preparation was begun too early the coffee could not be kept warm or reheated, as Proust would detect a burnt taste and send it away with a cry of outrage, 'This coffee is *revolting*!' So, to get the timing right, Céleste had to learn to predict exactly when the coffee would be required. The perfect servant is not the one who attends to all the master's whims – anyone can do that – but the one who *anticipates* the whims.

As a facilitator of mindfulness coffee is most effective if sipped slowly in silence in a chair with the support of a high seat, firm back and arms wide and strong enough for reciprocal gripping. But contemporary easy chairs are too soft and low, frequently armless (the beanbag is an extreme example), designed to encourage sprawling and lolling, surrender and passivity. The intention is to *lower* using a disguised form of the decadence of the American Lay-Z-Boy recliner (Elvis's favourite chair, from which he would shoot out the TV with a handgun if what was showing displeased him, thereby inventing the concept of remote control). Marshmallow-soft low chairs are a crucial feature of the contemporary home's cultivation of couch potatoes, designed to sap strength and will and discourage any decisive thought or action, especially an attempt to *rise.* Why even bother to get up to do a bundle, they murmur, why not just do it in a nappy like Elvis? Remember that the effort of going to the toilet was what killed the King.

A good chair, on the other hand, while content to offer support for as long as necessary, should also encourage a desire to stand up. It should inspire, elevate, ennoble. A philosopher king needs a suitable throne, an unpretentious, practical, homely throne. Where is the Bill Stumpf of the living-room chair?

The coffee exercise (or, rather, sacrament): sit, sip the dark liquid and be one with the many dark silent monastic brotherhoods of the home, the hangers in the wardrobe in the bedroom, the clothes pegs in the bag in the kitchen, the matches in the box in the drawer, the wines in the bottles on the rack, and, in the vase on the top shelf under the stairs, a motley band of outcasts, the rejected, neglected and unfulfilled – a key ring from Princes Gate Motors, two cuff links (not matching), a chestnut, an elasticated ponytail tie in red velvet, what looks like a match book but, on lifting the cardboard flap featuring an alpine scene, is revealed to be a travel sewing kit, never used (with threads of four colours, three different-sized needles and a minute safety pin), an also unused mercury thermometer resting on a little pad of cotton wool in a transparent plastic cylinder, a tiny whorled Wham-O Superball that has never been permitted to bounce and a Christmas-cracker ring puzzle that has never had an opportunity to baffle.

At such moments it is possible to experience space not as an inert medium, a mere background, but, as Heidegger insisted, intimately and deeply involved with its contents, a living presence. Throughout *Room Temperature* the narrator sits in a rocking chair[231] in his silent apartment at 3:15 on a Wednesday afternoon, with his baby daughter in his arms, and experiences 'awe' at the mystery of his home, as manifested in a child's mobile that moves despite shut windows and the absence of draughts: 'My daughter and I were bathed in a roomful of vertical unfurlings that moved within and past each other as slowly as a tai chi devotee practicing his transitions from pose to pose at dawn in an unsafe park. This room was astir – astir with history.'

The nurturing mystery of the home was a major theme of Dutch painting in the seventeenth century, when individual spirituality and independent thought were exciting new freedoms and privacy and silence were treasured as the means of enjoying these. In many cases the domestic interiors are metaphors for the human interiority they encourage, an effect achieved by bathing the scene in a radiant glow, registering resonant silence by including few or no people and suggesting levels of depth and secrecy by long perspectives through several doors. For instance, in *The Slippers* by Samuel van Hoogstraten there are no people and the view is through the open door of a homely kitchen (with a hanging towel and propped broom) across a hallway (where the slippers of the title are lying) and through another door into an illuminated room with an altar-like table bearing a candle and book on a gold cloth. This final door has a key in the lock, which enhances the aura of significant but unfathomable mystery. Beyond the mundane world of towel, broom and slippers is a secret chamber of illumination.

Dutch silence was certainly golden – and the Dutch homes in Golden Age paintings seem uniquely mysterious and alluring. But every age is a golden age for those who learn how to pan for its gold. Walker Evans found similar mystery in American homes, and preserved it in photographs such as *Burroughs' Kitchen, Hale County Alabama*, also *Door, Nova Scotia* and *White Chair and Open Door, Walpole, Maine*, which has a view exactly like Hoogstraten's through half-open doors across three rooms.

How can mere photographs match the artifice of Dutch masters? It is hard to believe that the cool, numinous beauty of Evans's images has been captured on film rather than cunningly painted. While the world has permitted many photographers to film it as it is, the austere scrutiny of Evans seems to have made the world pull itself together and assume a classical formality and reserve. It is not so much that a moment has been taken from the flux as that the flux has been taken from the moment. There is no before or after, no narrative, no process. The homes seem to have been always like this, poised in some profoundly silent mid-afternoon. Somehow Evans captured a sense of eternity that is not endless time but the absence of time and these images are a reminder that the balm of home is this illusion of atemporality and permanence, the consolation of the children of process and time.

The van Hoogstraten/Walker Evans exercise: imagine the ultimate silence, the silence not just outside of time but *before* time, before the Big Bang started off the whole crazy flux and flow. The pure silence before the madly expanding universe, the wild dance of the vibrating strings at the heart of matter and the unresting turbulence of the human heart. The silence before people, love, sex, cities, work and the endlessly desirous, raging discontented self. This thought is like a cool lemon-scented face wipe offered by a solicitous air hostess on a gruelling long-haul flight.

And the beautiful doors in those paintings and photographs! Contemporary culture encourages doorless open-plan living in a single large bright space that rejects darkness, cubby holes, secrecy, age, imperfection, decline and decay.[232] Homes like these grin with the perpetual youth, bland cheerfulness and flawless, regular white teeth of American television presenters. This domestic abolition of secret space is part of a general tendency to regard all forms of secrecy as sinister and reactionary, and to make 'openness' and 'transparency' as self-evidently good as liberty and equality.

So doors, which have seemed an eternal feature of home, are also subject to process and may soon disappear, imposing an obligation to cherish the unique experience of those that remain.

Approaching a closed door stirs the primeval fear of entering a hidden space and so provides a frisson of alerting and attention, a priming of all the sensors, but especially the eyes, for interpreting a new force field. The contact is by a kind of handshake, a firm grip of the knob – but not only are there fewer doors, fewer have knobs. A sliding door destroys completely the rhythm of entering, and a handle is much less satisfactory than a knob, whose roundness fits snugly and warmly into the hand. I was thrilled to discover that Nicholson Baker, Lord of the Things, is equally passionate about knobs and equally dismissive of handles. 'What is this static modernism that architects of the second tier have imposed on us: steel half-U handles ... instead of brass, porcelain, or glass knobs?'[233] Holding any round object seems to fulfil a deep need – think of the pleasure of hefting a *boule* – so the full-handed twisting of a knob is more sensuously satisfying than depressing a handle and provides a greater feeling of control. The knob mechanism is also more richly complex and more likely to enhance the experience with memories of other doors. Baker particularly appreciates the doorknobs of his childhood home. 'The knobs were loosely seated in their latch mechanism, and heavy, and the combination of solidity and laxness made for a multiply staged experience as you turned the knob: a smoothness that held intermediary tumbleral fallings-into-position.'[234]

Smooth inevitability at all stages in opening and closing a door is crucial. The ideal door experience should have an even, uninterrupted, forward rhythm, like the rhythmic arc of a poem, and as with a poem, there should be a revelation followed by a profoundly satisfying sense of closure as the door returns in a clean balanced swing to ineluctable engagement with a resonant click.

Francis Ponge, the French inventor of 'thing' poetry, celebrated the pleasure of doors and noted that kings never enjoy this pleasure, an idea that gave *me* pleasure (though when I mentioned this to an Irish friend he answered with typically Irish scepticism, 'Kings never touch toilet brushes either – but that doesn't mean it's wonderful to clean shite from a bowl').

The allure of a closed door is its aura of secrecy and this enchantment is present, in a more condensed and potent form, in keys (another common feature of Dutch paintings – a key in a door, attached to a dark, hanging bunch, is at the centre of van Hoogstraten's *The Slippers*). It is shocking to think that keys, like so many familiar objects, may also soon be obsolete, when such doors as remain will either open automatically or respond to the plastic cards already common in hotels, bland corporate whores that will accept any program and open any door. Each metal key is unique, its serrations as singular as a DNA spectrogram, and each fits, and is loyal to, only one lock. This is the sexual symbolism of the key and there is also the spiritual symbolism of access to a hidden world. So a bunch of keys is a numinous reminder of the private pleasures of both body and soul, and losing a bunch has the horror of both physical and spiritual castration. A bunch of keys is the assurance of a secret self and should itself be kept secret in a pocket or bag. The contemporary practice of wearing keys on the belt is another attempt to abolish secrecy.

Secrecy is also the allure of other enclosed spaces within the enclosed space of the home – boxes, chests, drawers, wardrobes, bureaux and roll-top desks. Remember how, as children, we cherished all these dark compartments, no doubt because they were symbols of the secret selves that in those days we knew we possessed and needed to hide from the disenchanted adult world. And within these inner spaces, the more tiny, intricate and numerous the inner compartments the better. To wander in the warrens of innerness! Most exciting of all was the hidden compartment that no one even knew existed but that opened magically at the touch of a hidden lever or knob. I longed for something – *anything* – with a hidden compartment.

Best of all would have been a hidden door offering escape from intrusive grown-ups. The secret self, so much more powerful in childhood, always understood that it was too noble for the pettiness of adults and whispered, 'Maybe you were switched with another at birth, maybe you're really a king.'

The genius of the Narnia stories was that access to the kingdom where royalty was conferred was via the back of an ordinary wardrobe. Few remember the details of the royal children's exploits in Narnia – but everyone remembers that wardrobe. However, fantasies of escape into privilege are strictly for children. William James suggested stepping into a wardrobe for a different sort of magic, not that of a mythical world beyond but of the actual world behind: 'One need only shut oneself in a closet and begin to think of the fact of one's being there, of one's queer bodily shape in the darkness . . . of one's fantastical character and all, to have the wonder steal over the detail as much as over the general fact of being, and to see that it is only familiarity that blunts it. Not only that *anything* should be, but that *this* very thing should be, is mysterious!'[235]

The William James exercise: stand in a wardrobe for several minutes facing the back, until the mystery of everyday existence has registered fully, and then, in the ringing tones of the righteous casting out evil spirits, shout, 'Fuck off Narnia' and bury your face in your beloved's clothes.

Secrecy is also the appeal of the chest within the chest within the chest, the box within the box within the box (and in paintings and photographs the doors opening onto doors opening onto more doors), where levels of ever deeper and more cunning secrecy recede to infinity. Flann O'Brien had fun with this in *The Third Policeman*, where MacCruiskeen reveals to the narrator his life's work – a delightful little brass-cornered wooden chest which he opens with a key to extract a chest identical except for size, which he then opens in turn with an even smaller key to reveal an even smaller chest, and so on until there are twenty-nine chests in a row on a table, the last 'like something you would take out of a red eye on a windy day'. Then MacCruiskeen withdraws two more chests too small to be visible to the naked eye – secrecy taken to the point of invisibility. Finally he explains that he is now working on a chest so minute that the first chest would hold 'a million of them at the same time and there would be room for a pair of woman's horse-breeches if they were rolled up'.

Most children do not have access to a magical wardrobe and make do with little boxes of many compartments holding items of no practical use whose only function is to be personal, hidden things – *my* secret things in *my* secret place. In the film *Amélie* the eponymous heroine finds a little tin box of child's things that a boy has hidden behind a skirting board many decades before. Amélie seeks out the boy, now an old man, and leaves the box in a phone booth for him to come across. The moment when the old man finds and opens the box, tearful, trembling, stupefied, is both hilarious and heartrending. The secret self may be absurd but its loss is grievous. If only some Amélie would give us a box and restore to us our own lost secret selves.

The American artist Joseph Cornell did not wait for an Amélie but recovered the childhood secret self by constructing boxes with many compartments containing commonplace objects rendered mysterious by their shadowy juxtaposition. Cornell, another authentic obsessive driven by a personal vision, was a flâneur of New York by day (in the intervals between selling refrigerators door to door) and a dedicated thingophile by night (in the basement of a small house on Utopia Parkway in Queens), fitting the odd objects picked up on his wanderings into his boxes and, long before Pop Art, creating a new, very American, inclusive form that required no artistic training (he had no talent for painting, sculpting or photography) and rejected the traditional separation of high and low culture.[236] As the poet Charles Simic, himself an exemplary flâneur and thingophile,[237] wondered, 'Is there another serious artist who loved both Vermeer and Barbie dolls?'[238] A typical Cornell box (typically titled *L'Égypte de Mlle Cléo de Mérode cours élémentaire d'histoire naturelle*) contains, among many other things, a doll's forearm, a German coin, a threaded needle, mirror fragments, cut-outs of camels and the head of Cléo de Mérode (a nineteenth-century ballerina), pearl beads, seven balls, plastic rose petals and three tiny tin spoons from a doll's house. Simic reminds us that the technique of collage in literature and art, learned from the greatest collage artist, the city, was another innovative twentieth-century way of celebrating the ordinary. 'Found objects, chance creations, ready-mades (mass-produced items promoted into art objects) abolish the separation between art and life. The commonplace is miraculous if rightly seen, if recognised.'[239] In his journal Cornell wrote of 'being plunged into a world of complete happiness in which every triviality becomes imbued with a significance'.[240]

The Joseph Cornell exercise: create a virtual box of objects in your own head. One such box of mine contains a blurry, stained, torn, black-and-white photograph of a teenage girl squinting awkwardly at the camera, a ballpoint pen with a transparent compartment full of fluid in which a small plastic tiger may be made to move by tipping the pen, a brass compass with a blunt Staedtler pencil stub screwed into its drawing arm and a doll's head with a sinister enigmatic smile. Accessing this box has disturbed the head, which rocks slightly, causing its eyes to open abruptly . . . and then close once more.

Georges Perec celebrated the mystery of objects by what he described as 'the ineffable joys of enumeration'.[241] The theory is that a detailed inventory of an environment will bring out the essential strangeness of its contents – and there is something in this, though the exhaustive can easily become the exhausting. As a small-scale example, Perec listed all the objects on his work table,[242] on a larger scale devoted a novel to the things owned by a young couple[243] and on the epic scale devoted a long novel to a minutely detailed description of the contents of all the rooms and communal spaces in a Paris apartment block. This novel, *Life: a User's Manual*, was Perec's *Ulysses*, though where *Ulysses* celebrates the single day of 16 June 1904, *Life* finds enough in a single moment, just before 8 p.m. on 23 June 1975.[244]

The Georges Perec exercise: enumerate the contents of some area of home. On one shelf of my bathroom cabinet I have just found the following tubes and jars – Little Me Organics Hair and Body Wash with Pear, Mallow and Organic Aloe Vera ('I am a very gentle formulation and I contain no allergens'), Carrot Butter Cleanser, Aveda Men pure-formance grooming clay for texture and strong pliable control, NEAL'S YARD REMEDIES Rejuvenating Frankincense Firming Neck Cream, Redken 5th Avenue NYC Extreme Anti-Snap Leave-In Treatment, NEW Garnier Deodorant enriched with MINERALITE (SKIN BREATHES, NO ALCOHOL, NO PARABENS), Avalon TEA TREE Conditioner with BETA GLUCANS & BABASSU OIL (Avalon creates *Consciousness in Cosmetics*, an awareness of intention, responsibility, efficacy and the value of life), EO Peppermint and Citrus Revitalising Lotion for legs and feet, The Body Shop Warming Mineral Mask kaolin clay and C-System finishing paste for medium hold with complete movement and a hint of shine.

'Question your tea spoons,' Perec also exhorted – but it was Francis Ponge who conducted this interrogation of individual common objects. Ponge was particularly engaged by things which reveal themselves to be latent process – a kitchen match for instance, which seems content to lie in a box as a uniform member of a uniform row but when struck crackles, fizzes and explodes in a halo of fire. At first the flame is low and tentative but then, realising its glory, it billows out:

> Mad with joy that a uniform head,
> Dark and dull, could develop
> Such marvels – a pulsing blue core
> And an undulating yellow and gold aureole.
>
> Now at last it's relaxed, getting into the swing,
> Strong, fulfilled, knowing how it should live
> - When all of a sudden it runs out of wood,
> The succulent white fuel entirely consumed.
>
> And the worst not that this exaltation should cease
> But that what's left is such a disgrace
> - Brittle, ravaged and unrecognisable,
> Bent as an old crone and black as a priest.[245]

No nostalgic traditionalist, Ponge also marvelled at the telephone, the radio and electricity itself. But his greatest achievement was to celebrate humble domestic objects such as doors, windows, shutters, soap, a loaf of bread, a potato, a suitcase, a table, a candle, a plate and a jug.

Poets, painters and philosophers have all celebrated the jug.[246] Jugs are everywhere in Dutch painting, and Cézanne and Picasso painted jugs constantly, even obsessively. Picasso several times placed a jug next to a skull in a still life, defining the jug as the symbol of life. In his essay 'The Thing' Heidegger suggested that the modern world's abolition of distance has also abolished nearness so that 'the uniformity in which everything is neither far nor near is, as it were, without distance' and the result is 'the annihilation of the thing'.[247] His solution was 'to learn how to attend to the thing as thing', to rediscover the thingness of things, and he used as an example a jug which he described in detail to bring out its thingness.

Why this reverence for the jug? There are several possible reasons. The reassurance of things is their illusion of permanence, their symbolic denial of process and time, and the jug is the only household object to remain unchanged for thousands of years, preserving, immune to fashion and change, its traditional form of rounded body, handle, narrow neck and flowering aperture with spout. When you are getting drunk on a jug of margaritas next Saturday night a useful exercise would be to remember, before the delirious oblivion, that Homer probably got drunk from a receptacle essentially the same. The key to this survival was remaining anonymous. The jug avoided attracting attention by appearing to be only a humble servant. Yet all the time it guarded in the dark interior a secret self. For the glory of cradling its resonant darkness, the jug was prepared to appear a drudge.

So, as Heidegger explained, the essence of the jug is not its material, shape or finish but the hidden chamber it creates (which is why transparent jugs, another modern innovation, have no character or presence). Yet the jug is prepared to relinquish this chamber. Unlike the vain and purely ornamental vase, the jug offers a handle to the user and has the graspability and weight to provide satisfying heft, although this heft has no suggestion of wielding. A jug could never be used as a weapon. Handle, spout and heft all suggest not aggression but service, a giving, a pouring forth. Even when empty a held jug tilts its spout in an effort to pour. And it surrenders its inner sanctum not only without resentment but gladly. The jug sings as it fills.

So the lesson of the jug is its difficult combination of humility, inwardness and service.

A jug on a table is the subject of so many still lifes because it is the perfect symbol of home. The table is the home's secret heart of oak and the jug is the home's secret heart of gold. The table is the father, foursquare, solid, reliable, unglamorous, like Van Heflin in *Shane.* The jug is the mother, warm, rounded, reserved, giving – Jean Arthur in *Shane.*

The Heidegger/Francis Ponge exercise: lift a jug from a table, heft it reverently for a moment, then fill it, listening carefully as it fills, then heft the full jug once again and finally pour with the rapt concentration of Vermeer's milkmaid.

Though at this time of evening the liquid in the jug will not be milk but wine. Once again the day has gone by with no momentous achievement. But twilight is merciful, compassionate, forgiving.

Day offers two equally necessary sacraments – the benediction of morning and the absolution of dusk. In the morning coffee blesses and in the evening wine absolves.

Now the mystery of home deepens. Floors and stairs creak, the fridge shudders and groans, the boiler sings like Maria Callas in a rapture of yearning and loss.

The Charles Simic exercise: 'Child of the night, hold a mirror in your hand like an open book and call out the names of your father and mother, first name, last name, as they were called out long ago on their first day of school. When your neighbor bangs on the wall, shout even louder, shriek!'[248]

It is the time to seek understanding and solace in a library. Morning is the time of poetry and evening the time of prose. Henry Green: 'Prose is not to be read aloud but to oneself alone at night, and it is not quick as poetry but rather a gathering web of insinuations ... It should slowly appeal to feelings unexpressed, it should in the end draw tears out of the stone.'[249]

Morning is the time of the body and brain, evening the time of the soul. In the legendary library of Alexandria, the greatest library of the classical age, the inscription over the shelves read: 'The place of the cure of the soul'. Often in the evening I am content just to be in the presence of books, to commune with the great exemplars who have paid attention, looked and listened, marvelled greatly and pondered deeply, and concentrated their personal vision into permanent form – the Gods who do not denounce, hector and threaten but charm and seduce us into living more richly. And it thrills me to think of a secret network of champions. Proust, Joyce and Updike adored Vermeer. George Shaw is a fan of Patrick Caulfield (and of Joyce). In philosophy William James and Henri Bergson admired each other's work and corresponded. In fiction John Updike revered, and was influenced by, both Joyce and Proust, and praised Alice Munro, J. F. Powers and John McGahern (who also praised Alice Munro). Nicholson Baker was so devoted to Updike that he wrote an entire book about the obsession (*U and I*). Charles Simic wrote a book in homage to Joseph Cornell (*Dime-Store Alchemy*). In one of the most long-distance connections, extending over thousands of miles and a thousand years, Georges Perec paid homage to his fellow enumerator and thingophile Sei Shonagon. Always hungry for meaning, desperate for the reassurance of not being alone in this need and tireless in seeking out like-minded truth tellers, the champions of the everyday have recognised and saluted each other across the continents and the years.

Of course by library I do not mean a dedicated building or room, only the books themselves, carefully hand-picked. Like the books that comprise it, a library is a creation of personal vision, a living organism that adapts and changes. And the best library is a living room where the books are always available for taking down and opening at random to read. If the passage is not surprisingly good then the book should be considered for culling because, as Conrad said, 'A work that aspires, however humbly, to the condition of art should carry its justification in every line'.[250] The only books worth reading are those that are worth rereading.

But reading should never be regarded as worthily self-improving, like eating cabbage. Instead, reading should be perceived as a ruse, and one of the most cunning and effective. Ruse Master Michel de Certeau defined reading as poaching: 'readers are travellers; they move across lands belonging to someone else, like nomads poaching their way across fields they did not write, despoiling the wealth of Egypt to enjoy it themselves'.[251] My only problem with 'poaching' is that the term is not strong enough. Reading is pillaging, plundering, looting. The true reader is not a sedate scholar but a desperate barbarian hungry for meaning.

But de Certeau's term made me realise why I became a reader, a development that has often puzzled me because my childhood environment was entirely philistine. No one read for pleasure or had any respect for reading, least of all teachers. My parents, also teachers, believed in education only as a form of social advancement and never read anything except the death notices in the local paper. John McGahern, whose mother was a schoolteacher, has remarked on this aspect of Catholic Ireland: 'There were few books in our house, and reading for pleasure was not approved of. It was thought to be dangerous, like pure laughter.'[252] So, as a form of rebellion, a way of transgressing without breaking the rules, in fact by appearing to *love and obey* the rules, the most sublime ruse of all, I went to the local library every week and triumphantly hauled back the maximum six books.[253]

This kind of early reading is a strange phenomenon – voracious but unguided, random, indiscriminate, making no distinction between genres or even between fiction and non-fiction and conducted with no critical faculty whatever. Adult reading is different. McGahern: 'We find that we are no longer reading books for the story and that all stories are more or less the same story; and we begin to come on certain books that act like mirrors. What they reflect is something dangerously close to our own life and the society in which we live.'[254]

Adult reading should seek out these books that act as mirrors – and this secret quest can retain the thrill of transgression. I remember first reading Proust on the train to work and thinking, 'I'm a Scale-One maths teacher, I'm not supposed to be doing this'. With books that have become the preserve of a scholarly elite there is the additional pleasure of reclamation on behalf of the barbarians. Snatch religion back from the clerics and literature from the critics.

The Michel de Certeau exercise: under cover of twilight approach your bookshelves stealthily and quickly slip out a volume as though it contains secret knowledge forbidden to the laity on pain of death. Yes! Perpetrated the theft of sacred fire once again.

As well as the psychological pleasure of the ruse, there is also the physical pleasure of sensuous contact, first with the book itself and then with its author. There is the heft of the book in the hand, its enveloping fragrance when opened, the texture and compliance of the pages when riffled and the upright austere black of print. Then there is the even more rich and complex contact with the author. This is most intimate at night when the home is dark and the only illumination is from the accomplice of the solitary truth seeker, an Anglepoise lamp. Grasp the lamp and direct its cone of light until it fits, lying softly on the shoulders like a golden prayer shawl.

This begins with a wary circling that eventually leads to a tentative grapple, that, if it goes well, becomes in turn an urgent wrestle, that, if it goes very well, develops first into a dance, then a dance that the reader is leading and, finally, on rare occasions of sublime felicity, a dance that the reader is dancing alone. The writer who has initiated the dance has fallen away because the reader is dancing with superior fluency, spirit and grace. The secret self has become the only self and reigns alone.

PART VI

The Centre for the Appreciation of Everyday Life

14

The Centre for the Appreciation of Everyday Life

The lessons of the champions of the ordinary are crucial – but difficult to apply. We get worn down, exhausted, dispirited. The sense of dreariness and futility returns. It is so easy to resent and complain and dismiss and so hard to appreciate that the miracle of consciousness has only a limited time to wander in the gallery of marvels. It is difficult even to remember the champions themselves.

The solution is a Centre for the Appreciation of Everyday Life (open 9:00 – 18:00 daily but with a special late opening to 22:00 on Tuesdays), a combined arts complex, educational institute, café and shop. It may take a while to establish this in reality so in the meantime it will have to be a virtual Centre.

On the ground floor there is a cinema showing the movies of Mike Leigh, a gallery exhibiting the paintings of George Shaw and the photographs of Walker Evans, a book/gift shop selling books of Dutch art and *New Yorker* cartoons, the works of Joyce and Proust and the Jousters who followed them, and T-shirts, coffee mugs and fridge magnets bearing inspirational maxims:

Nothing is less known than what seems familiar.
The ordinary is always the exceptional in disguise.

The same is never the same.
Anonymity is divinity.
Everything happens when nothing is happening.
Silence is the eloquent voice of God.
Immerse to transcend.
Detach to engage.
Awaken to dream.
Be odd to get even.
Be secret to be open.
SUBVERT THE QUOTIDIAN BY SLYLY EMBRACING IT.

The complete 'Everyday Paradox Set' is of course available in special gift boxes with an extra bonus maxim, 'Paradox resigns and rules'.

Next to the shop is a café selling Fairtrade coffee and cranberry and hazelnut bars, with a cutting-edge baker equally adept at moist lemon-drizzle cake and crunchy oat flapjacks, and an award-winning barista who can make espresso with a crema as rich as the head on a pint of Guinness. The importance of the café is signalled by another key maxim displayed prominently above the barista, 'Coffee is the Champagne of Everyday'.

This café looks out on The Garden of Sublime Dereliction, where exuberant weeds sprout around and through a disembowelled mattress, a leatherette sofa with a broken arm, an overturned supermarket shopping trolley with a missing wheel and a television set with a smashed screen. A sign board identifies each weed – but the Centre will also launch a campaign to have common weeds renamed to permit them to exult in their pariah status: for instance as rat's prick, cute huer, blue murder, brazen hussy, fly-by-night, lowlife, gyppo, untouchable, riff raff and scum of the earth.

On the ground floor there is also The Temple of Thingness where visitors may read about the evolution of everyday things, study poems and prose in praise of them, and finally learn to reconnect with thingness by handling and using, in silence and with appropriate reverence, a variety of objects such as a swivel chair, stapler, date stamper, pencil sharpener, box of matches, bunch of keys, Anglepoise lamp, door knob and jug.

The teaching facilities are on the upper floors and offer talks, short courses and full degrees in Everyday Life Studies, which as well as conventional teaching takes students on field trips to motorway service areas, multiplex cinema foyers, council-flat tower blocks and car boot sales, and requires them to spend a placement year working either as a cashier in Poundstretcher and living with a dysfunctional family dependent on benefits, or selling patio doors and living with an outer-suburban family thrilled to possess three cars and an apartment in Marbella with a balcony and a sea view (if you lean out over the edge of the balcony to the left).

On the top floor is the Director's office, where I sit, or, rather, rock, roll and twist, in a top-of-the-range Herman Miller Aeron chair, the Rolls-Royce of swivel chairs (I'm the *Director*, for Christ's sake), designed to provide thermal comfort, optimal pressure distribution and pelvic stabilisation, with adjustability not just for seat height but arm height and angle, tilt tension and tilt limit, lumbar depth and posture fit, and with a woven-mesh material that moulds to the body shape much more efficiently than foam (in the contemporary office even chairs are now open plan). This chair is state-of-the-art but it sits at a traditional roll-top desk with many cunning little compartments, pigeon holes and drawers, from one of which I take a blank pad and a heavy date stamper. At last I have my own stamper, which I lift by the handle, wield to relish the heft, and shake like a bell. Finally I adjust it to 18 May 1922 – and imprint this momentous date firmly at the top of the first page of the pad. Then I ceremoniously sharpen ten pencils, choose the sharpest and begin an account of this especially lustrous day in the early twentieth-century golden age of the arts, when the high priests of low life met for the first and only time.

On this date the wealthy English dilettante Sydney Schiff brought together the leaders in each of the arts, the shocking and thrilling artistic Bolsheviks who had overthrown the traditional order – Picasso who had rejected verisimilitude, Stravinsky who had rejected tonality and Joyce who had rejected plot. But, not content with the merely difficult, Schiff went on to achieve the impossible by also bringing together the foremost novelists of the age, Joyce and Proust.[255]

Schiff shrewdly decided that the best lure for the great ones would be the excitement and terror of a first night, and that the ideal first night would be a *Ballets Russes* premiere, always certain to provoke controversy, possibly outrage, and perhaps even, as with Stravinsky's *Rite of Spring*, a riot requiring police intervention. Diaghilev, the impresario of the *Ballets Russes*, by all accounts almost bankrupt after a disastrous London season, would surely be tempted by the offer of a celebratory supper for the company after the first performance of Stravinsky's *Le Renard*, especially if the guests were to include wealthy potential backers. Choosing *Le Renard* would also ensure the attendance of the composer, Stravinsky, and Diaghilev would bring in Picasso, who had worked closely with the impresario on many stage designs and was not in a position to offend a potential employer since he had recently wed a young wife who lived like a wealthy aristocrat, with couture by Chanel, jewels by Fabergé, fragrances by Guerlain and a household including a maid, a chef and a butler with white gloves.

As for Joyce, the prospect of free drink would attract any Irishman, though for this exceptional Irishman the free drink would have to be champagne. The only real challenge was tempting Proust out of his apartment. But Schiff had been assiduously courting Proust for some time and knew a good deal about his tyrannical habits and tastes. So the party would have to commence late in the evening, the venue would have to be Proust's beloved Ritz and the company would have to include many of Proust's aristocratic friends. The first problem, entirely unexpected, was that the Ritz would not permit music after 12:30 a.m. *But this party is in honour of M. Proust, surely one of the Ritz's most illustrious and certainly most lavish clients*? The Ritz was sympathetic and would dearly love to oblige but explained that it had other illustrious clients who, unlike M. Proust, were fond of sleeping at night. Schiff had to seek an alternative venue and, after much wearisome searching, found the Hôtel Majestic in Avenue Kléber, just around the corner from Proust's apartment in Rue Hamelin and decorated in the *Belle Époque* style congenial to Proust.

So on the warm, sunny evening of May 18th, after the premiere of *Le Renard*, the *Ballets Russes* company arrived at the Majestic, along with Picasso, Stravinsky and the *beau monde*, including Comte Étienne de Beaumont, famous for his masked balls on contemporary themes such as the automobile and jazz (for which he hired a band of black American soldiers and the beautiful exotic dancer Djemil Anik), the Duchesse de Clermont-Tonnerre, author of the *Almanach des Bonnes Choses de France*, who was currently enjoying a scandalous affair with the courtesan Liane de Pougy, and the prognathous-jawed Princesse Edmond de Polignac (née Winnaretta Singer, American heiress to the sewing-machine fortune), who looked like a cross between Dante and Sitting Bull, enjoyed whipping young girls and took a keen interest in the dancers, especially the spirited Lubov Tchernicheva, who had driven King Alfonso XIII to distraction and was said to have been the only woman to excite lust in Ravel.

Schiff delayed supper as long as possible but when midnight passed had to sit his guests down without either great novelist.

When the coffee was being served, Joyce at last blundered in – drunk, confused and not only not in evening clothes but shabbily dressed. Schiff rushed to bring his illustrious guest to the table, where he sat down heavily on the right of his host, refusing coffee in favour of champagne, and soon falling asleep.

It was two-thirty in the morning before the other great novelist finally arrived, a compelling spectacle indeed, the vivid black of his hair and moustache contrasting with the dank pallor of his skin (one wit compared him to a Persian prince released from a decade of imprisonment in a damp cellar), wearing, despite the warm evening, his heavy fur-lined and fur-collared coat and white gloves.

The first encounter between great ones did not go well.

'Doubtless you admire Beethoven?' Proust suggested to Stravinsky.

Stravinsky, always inclined to be peevish and doubtless annoyed at not being admired himself: 'I've always detested Beethoven.'

Proust, doubtless taken aback: 'But, *cher maître*, surely those late sonatas and quartets . . .?'

'The worst of the lot.'

It is entirely appropriate that when Joyce and Proust finally met the exchange was banal, muddled, comical and absurd – and reports of the conversation are even more muddled (it took place in the early hours after a great deal of champagne had been consumed). According to one observer, the conversation was about truffles. Proust asked Joyce if he liked truffles and Joyce said: 'Yes I do.' According to another observer the exchange was entirely negative. Proust asked Joyce if he knew so-and-so and Joyce said no. Joyce asked Proust if he had read such-and-such and Proust said no. A third claimed that the negativity was more specific and personal: 'I have never read your works, monsieur Joyce' elicited the instant response, 'And I have never read yours, monsieur Proust'. There were at least seven different accounts – but the most delightful version claimed that they discussed only health problems.

Joyce: I've headaches every day. My eyes are terrible.
Proust: My poor stomach. It's killing me. I must leave at once.
Joyce: I'm in the same situation. Goodbye.
Proust: *Charmé.* Oh my stomach, my stomach.

But, in whatever version is accepted, the conversation was just *too* exquisitely banal and mean, altogether *too ordinary.* What if it was a charade, a performance arranged by the two men to divert attention from the real meeting later in Proust's apartment around the corner? The evidence for this is that Proust gave Joyce a lift in Odilon Albaret's taxi, which had been waiting outside. Why would he seek more of Joyce's company if the encounter had been as absurd as it seemed?

But Schiff, desperate to hear the two men engage, spoiled the plan by inviting himself and his wife along in the taxi and even accompanying Proust into his apartment.

After this all is speculation. Joyce probably gave up and went home. But wouldn't it be wonderful to imagine that he waited for the Schiffs to leave and then made a secret visit that allowed the writers to talk freely in private away from vulgar scrutiny?

'Monsieur Joyce!' Proust cries in greeting. 'Sovereign of the Transitory.' Joyce inclines slightly in acknowledgement. 'And hence of the Eternal.' Joyce bows deeply.

They exchange a respectful look and then suddenly and simultaneously burst into *fou rire.*

'My eyes!' Joyce shrieks, shading them with an exaggerated gesture.

'My poor stomach,' Proust groans, rubbing it in mock agony.

When the laughter subsides Joyce assumes a grave look. 'But how are you . . . seriously?'

At once Proust turns away to hide the strength of his emotion. 'Every day I descend more rapidly a rigid iron staircase that leads to the abyss.'

'But you're looking well,' Joyce suggests.

Proust exclaims, in pique. 'I have been at the point of death on three occasions today. I have coughed more than three thousand times. My back and stomach are done for. *Everything* is done for. It's madness . . . *madness*. And as if this were not enough I am being systematically poisoned by carbon monoxide fumes from a crack in the chimney. I who crave heat deprived of fires!' He sways slightly and reaches out to lean on Joyce's arm. 'And your poor eyes?'

Joyce looks away. 'Nothing can mend the broken windows of my soul.'

'Have you tried the Coué system?'

'What's that?'

'Keep telling yourself how wonderful you feel.'

'You have done this?'

'Oh yes.'

'And . . .?'

'I was laid up in bed for four months.'

The silence is long and forlorn – but at length Proust recalls his duties as host. 'May we offer you a little port?'

Joyce grimaces. 'Beefsteak . . . *ugh!*'

Proust rings for attention and addresses, with suppressed impatience, the tall severely dressed young woman who immediately appears, 'Champagne for monsieur Joyce.'

'My Céleste,' Proust explains then. 'Beacon to errant sadness, protectress of the sick, haven of the noble banished into a vile world.'

'She's a good-looking girl right enough,' Joyce agrees.

And when Céleste has brought bottles and glasses, Proust resumes his praise. 'A child of many extraordinary gifts. *To think what her soft little hands will soon do.*'

Joyce's casual manner fails to conceal a keen interest. '*What's that?*'

Gripping the champagne bottle cork, Proust twists and averts his clenched face. At the violent report he cries out and staggers back.

'Close my poor eyes for ever,' he sighs, directing the foaming liquid into a glass. Only now, presenting the drink, does he register the interest and emotion of his guest, adding hastily, 'But of course she's just an ignorant country girl. Only today I had to explain that Napoleon and Bonaparte were the same man.'

Far from being disillusioned, Joyce turns towards the kitchen with even more intense yearning. 'I hate a woman that knows anything.'

This revelation of solidarity with common women, perhaps reinforced by an awareness of the Irish talent for imaginative vituperation, kindles in Proust's cavernous eyes, hollowed and ringed with black, a spark of speculation and hope. '*Perhaps . . .* no . . .' He appears to reconsider, taking a swift drink of port. Then he sets down the glass and, crossing the room to a Chinese cabinet, takes out a packet which he weighs with a pondering look, casting swift glances at the Irishman.

'These are photographs of women,' he begins carefully. Joyce does not respond – but his features regain shrewd reserve. 'Women who have meant *a great deal to me* . . . Women I respect and admire . . .' Lowering a countenance furrowed by wisdom and empathy, Joyce applies himself with scrupulous attention to his champagne. 'Women I *love*,' Proust concludes at last.

Raising his glass to the light, Joyce turns it about and studies the effect with grave concentration. 'I understand,' he murmurs softly.

With trembling fingers Proust withdraws the first photograph.

'Comtesse Jean de Castellane, half-sister of Boson de Talleyrand-Périgord, Prince de Sagan.'

Joyce accepts the picture solemnly and bursts into violent, incredulous laughter.

'Jaysus ... *Rosalie the Coal Quay Whore.*'

'You think it's *like* her?' Proust stares wildly at the photograph.

'*Like* her? This *is* her.' Joyce regards the portrait with fond amusement. 'God, we had some nights of it too. Talk about involuntary memory – *Jaysus.*' He shakes his head in wonder. 'They used to have a line about her – *she was only a coal quay girl because her fanny was slack.* But, like, that was only a joke. She was a great favourite really. Very popular at weddings.' About to produce another photograph, Proust halts in sudden dark mistrust. 'They used to get her to sit in a corner ... with her legs apart.' Proust's frown does not relax. Calmly Joyce returns his gaze. 'To keep the flies off the cake, like ... You know?'

For a long moment they regard each other in silence. Then, shivering slightly, Marcel withdraws another photograph. 'Comtesse Adhéaume de Chevigné, née Laure de Sade.'

'Jemima from Monto, you mean.' Joyce sings softly:

> Oh Italy's maids are fair to see
> And France's maids are willing
> But less expensive 'tis to me
> Jemima's for a shilling.

'Jemima was a right sort – heart o' the corn, you know, one of Bella Cohen's girls – but Bella had to let her go in the end.'

Proust can scarcely breathe the syllable: '*Why?*'

'Ach, you don't like to spread these things.' Joyce's expression is clouded by responsibility and scruple. Marcel reaches out to give his knee an imploring squeeze. 'Jemima would give you *anything* – but she couldn't help getting excited and then she always wet herself.' He sighs heavily. 'Quite liked it myself – but I think a lot of the English officers complained.'

Proust falls back in his chair with a whimper of delight. By and by he withdraws the last photograph, throwing it a quick glance before pressing it face down against his heart. Vast and nameless emotions contend on his ravaged features. Lustrous tears illuminate the caverns of his eyes. Slowly, and with the utmost reluctance, he proffers the photograph.

'*Mamma*,' he whispers brokenly.

Joyce reaches out for the photograph – only to draw back in shock and revulsion. 'Aw ... Jaysus ... *Jaysus* ... this is the *pits*. Ah mean ... *Half-Gate* ... *Jaysus*. You'd want to be *really desperate*.' He seizes his champagne glass. 'Ah mean, only ...' Shuddering with disgust, he takes a long bracing gulp.

Whimpering in ecstasy, Marcel once again attempts to give him the picture. Joyce pulls back at once.

'Jaysus, you'd even get a dose from just touching her photograph.'

Issuing from those profound depths where pain and ecstasy fuse, a strange equivocal cry escapes Marcel's lips. He curls up in the foetal position, the photograph once again clasped to his heart.

'Ah mean, ye know what they said about Half-Gate.' Joyce leans to administer the coup de grâce. '*Even the dogs wouldn't eat the green meat that hung from the fork of her drawers*.'

Like a young girl after her first orgasm, Marcel bursts into tears of inchoate fulfilment and wonder. Sitting back with an air of achievement, Joyce rewards himself by finishing his glass of champagne.

Bit by bit Proust recovers, still snuffling a little.

'No one has ever done it better ... *no one*.' With an impulsive movement he seizes the bottle and fills Joyce's glass to the brim. Then he pulls out a wallet and extracts several notes. 'It's just . . . here's a little . . .'

'What do you take me for?' Joyce cries. 'A *Proustitute*?'

'Forgive me the insult. Of course it's not near enough.'

Proust extracts more notes. Joyce declines – but less vehemently than before. Again the process is repeated, with Joyce's resistance visibly weakening. In the end he accepts ten thousand francs and a season ticket for the *Ballets Russes.*

And Proust, fortunate indeed tonight, is about to receive another unique gift.

Odilon knocks softly on the door of the little salon. 'The man from the abattoir has just arrived. With a *beauty,* monsieur Proust. Absolutely magnificent.'

Proust, glancing swiftly at Joyce, 'Well, perhaps just a quick look.'

Odilon enters and sets down on the sideboard a cage containing an enormous rat, its tail thick as an electric cable hanging out between the bars. Joyce shrieks. Instantly captivated, Proust rushes forward to kneel in rapturous veneration, his hand extended to the cage in an impulsive gesture of homage. Standing up on its hind legs, the creature snaps viciously at his fingers.

'A true prince of the sewers,' marvels Proust, gently lifting the tail and voluptuously passing it through his hands.

'Ah Jesus,' Joyce protests. 'Hold on a minute.'

'Fetch the instruments,' whispers Proust.

'All is prepared.'

Assuming a grave and purposeful demeanour, Odilon opens the door and wheels in a silver hostess trolley, from which he offers his master a pair of immaculate white gloves. Proust reaches out impatiently – but, as soon as the gloves are placed in his hand, jumps to his feet with a violent cry of revulsion.

'These have been *cleaned.* They smell of *benzine.*' He flings the gloves wildly across the room. 'This is the kind of initiative *I do not appreciate.*'

When Odilon fetches fresh gloves, Proust tries them on with a wary, mistrustful air, flexing his fingers like a surgeon preparing for theatre. From the trolley he carefully selects a long hatpin.

'Hold him,' he commands Odilon. And then, bending close, in a tender croon, 'Ah my beauty, why resist? Who would want eyes to gaze on such a vile world?' He leans forward with the hatpin.

Utterly rejecting Proust's argument, the animal struggles wildly and utters a shriek of terror and pain.

'And now the other . . .' Again he leans close, only to be disturbed by a sudden loud noise.

Joyce has collapsed to the floor in a dead faint.

'Oh for *God's sake,*' Proust cries in annoyance.

Odilon drags the semi-conscious writer to a chair in the kitchen and leaves him to the ministrations of Céleste, who pours a glass of brandy and waves it beneath the nose of the stricken man. Joyce, reviving, glances wildly about him and remembers suddenly with a cry of fear.

'It's all right,' Céleste soothes.

'It's *not* all right. Seeing a rat is such bad luck. Yet another evil omen.'

'Nothing bad is going to happen.'

'I feel so *helpless,*' Joyce suddenly sobs. 'Helpless, helpless, *helpless.*'

Céleste sits next to him and lays a compassionate hand on his shoulder.

He gazes ardently upon her. 'Believe me when I say that something in you spoke to my soul this evening. Something frank and noble in your bearing. Something tender and gentle in your dark Jewish eyes.' She exclaims and turns away. 'Wait,

Céleste! We have so much in common, the Jews and the Irish. Dispossessed, passive, impulsive, irrational ...'

'I'm *not Jewish.*'

'It is no shame, Céleste. Christ himself was born from the womb of a Jewess.'

'I am *not* Jewish!' she repeats. 'I'm from Auxillac in Auvergne and I go to the altar every week ... Or I did until monsieur asked me not to leave him any more. And my brother married a niece of Monseigneur Negre, the *Archbishop of Tours.*'

'Forgive me,' Joyce murmurs, and, after a moment of remorseful silence, commences to sing, with surpassing tenderness, that most beautiful melody of Faetenhauer's, *Love, could I only tell thee.*

Céleste, overcome: '*Monsieur*!'

Joyce gazes into her eyes. 'Such compassion ... such *nobility.*'

'I am only a poor uneducated country girl.'

'I could surround you with everything fine and beautiful.'

Céleste sighs and casts a sceptical glance over Joyce's worn suit.

'*Is there one who understands me?*' Joyce cries, pulling notes from his pocket and throwing them contemptuously on the table.

Céleste stares in amazement. 'But you carry almost as much as monsieur Proust.'

'A gentleman never knows who will need money.' Joyce thrusts a handful of notes at her. 'Buy a fine evening gown. Buy magnificent furs lined with violet satin. Buy stockings and garters and drawers with frills and crimson bows.' He proffers money with furious abandon. She allows her hand to close over it and he exclaims in gratitude. 'Buy beautiful drawers, Céleste ... and be sure to sprinkle them with some nice scent.' He pauses but is unable to restrain his enthusiasm. 'And also discolour them just a little behind.'

With a cry of disgust Céleste releases the money. 'Men are all the same.'

Joyce buries his face in his hands. 'I have killed your love. I have filled you with disgust and scorn. You believe I am not a gentleman.' He raises a disconsolate face. 'You must be severe with me, Céleste. Punish me as much as you like.' As he rises she lifts a threatening arm. 'Yes! I long to feel my flesh tingling under your hand. Smack me as hard as you wish. Flog me, even. *I would love to be flogged by you, Céleste.*'

'You'll be flogged by my husband if you come any closer,' Céleste warns, getting warily to her feet and backing out of the room. 'Then we'll see who discolours their drawers.'

Joyce, at the kitchen table, sighs and takes a consoling sip of brandy. Then he carries the glass back to the little salon where Proust is once again alone, and apparently disillusioned.

'We are drowning in an ocean of *merde*!' he cries. 'Not to blush at breathing is the act of a *cad*.'

'Ah it's desperate,' Joyce agrees. 'Desperate altogether.'

Proust's breast heaves with emotion. 'It is less absurd to simulate life than to live it.'

'Ah yes,' sighs Joyce, 'where would we be without our books? Put it all in a couple of books.'

'No need for a couple. *One* book.'

Joyce raises his glass in sincere salute. 'Heroic capitalist of the quotidian.'

Proust, considerably moved, returns the compliment. 'Epicurean of ordinariness.'

At peace now, they talk of life and art and the arduous but necessary sacred task of restoring one by means of the other, a task whose benefits are not available to the high priests themselves, remote and solitary in their calling. There is no question of the two men becoming friends, or even meeting again.

'Life is for our readers,' Proust murmurs at last.

Joyce nods. 'We who have nothing will give them the beautiful world.'

'We shall teach them to see once more everyday life ... to break over and over again the crust of habit that renders them blind.'

As though in response, the light of day, not to be excluded even by Proust's heavy curtains, gradually infiltrates the room.

Proust, despite obvious exhaustion, insists on seeing his guest out. 'With the memory of these hours of exquisite pleasure I shall build, deep in my heart, a chapel dedicated to Ireland.'

Joyce is not pleased. 'What has *Ireland* got to do with it? Dedicate it to *me*.'

Proust bows in courtly submission. 'And of course ... If there's anything ...?'

'Just one favour. Let Céleste go to Mass.'

Proust is sorrowfully silent for a time. 'To confer the gift of empathy upon those I serve, my readers, I am obliged to withhold it from those who serve me.'

Joyce nods in immediate understanding. 'A noble sacrifice.'

Together they leave the apartment, descend in the lift to the hallway and make their way towards the bright morning of sovereign, sublime, common day.

Joyce pauses, overcome by a sudden tremulous wonder and reverence. 'Is it Tuesday?'

A similarly sacred awe illuminates the features of Proust – but almost immediately there are darkenings of doubt. 'I'd have to ask Céleste.' Soon, though, the awe returns. Proust takes Joyce's arm in his own and, linked together, they proceed bravely into the light, where Proust cries out in rapture, 'The virginal, vivid, resplendent today.'

But the sudden radiance is so powerful that both are driven back in shock and pain.

Joyce lifts an arm to shield his weak eyes. 'God, that's *brutal*.'

Proust claps a handkerchief on his mouth and nose. 'The spring, the spring. Dust, pollen, horse hair, horse dung.'

Partly protected, they advance defiantly once again, separating to observe the morning activity of Rue Hamelin – the shops opening, awnings going up, Leon Quinot's delivery boys setting baskets of groceries on tricycles, a few sleepy residents coming out onto balconies, others briskly going to work, others still bearing home from the *Boulangerie des États-Unis* bags of fragrant warm croissants and armfuls of baguettes.

'What is the greatest sin?' Proust suddenly cries, turning and experiencing the disillusion of the Redeemer in Gethsemane. For the only one who could watch with him properly has fallen asleep against the door.

Proust is faced with the ineluctable destiny of the race – every man must answer his own question himself.

Directly in front of No. 44 a placid cart horse pauses in the centre of the street and deposits on the cobbles a steaming symmetrical pyramid like a ceremonial mound of cannon balls. Even now Proust does not withdraw. Instead his waxen features tremble with emotion; tears of exaltation make his dark eyes gleam like Japanese lacquer. In a near-suicidal gesture of heroism he removes the handkerchief from his face.

'*To be incurious before the spectacle of the world.*'

Acknowledgements

I would like to thank Jennifer Christie, Kerri Sharp, Frank Carney and Rona Johnson for many considered and insightful suggestions, tactfully offered – and, for invaluable assistance with research that must often have seemed eccentric, thanks to Campbell McIlroy, my daughter Jane and my wife Martina.

Notes

The quotations from Joyce and Proust are from their fiction and essays, collected correspondence and the biographies *James Joyce* by Richard Ellman (Oxford University Press 1983) and *Marcel Proust: a Life* by Jean-Yves Tadié, translated by Euan Cameron (Penguin 2001).

The *À la recherche du temps perdu* quotations are from the translation by C. K. Scott Moncrieff and Terence Kilmartin, revised by D. J. Enright, published by Chatto & Windus in 1992 as *In Search Of Lost Time.*

1 Georges Perec, *Species of Spaces and Other Pieces*, Penguin 1997
2 Iain McGilchrist, *The Master and his Emissary*, Yale University Press 2009. This magisterial work provides a detailed explanation of the functions of the left and right brain hemispheres and the ways in which these functions have influenced and been influenced by cultural developments. It is a heady mixture of neuroscience, anthropology, philosophy, religion, literature and art.
3 N. Mashal & M. Faust, *Right hemisphere sensitivity to novel metametaphoric relations: application of the signal detection theory*, Brain and Language 104, 2008
4 M. Kinsbourne, *Cerebral Hemisphere Function in Depression*, American Psychiatric Press 1988
5 Seneca, *Letters to Lucilius*, Clarendon Press 1932
6 Marcus Aurelius, *Meditations*, Penguin 1964
7 Seneca, *The Epistles of Lucius Annae Seneca,* Ecco 2010
8 *Meditations*
9 Nietszche was another.
10 Henri Bergson, *Creative Evolution*, Dover 1998
11 Ibid.
12 Henri Bergson, *Time and Free Will: An essay on the immediate data of consciousness*, Dover 2001

13 William James, 'The Problem of Novelty', in the anthology *Philosophers of Process*, edited by Douglas Browning and William T. Myers, Fordham University Press 1998
14 William James, 'The Energies of Men', in the anthology, *The Heart of William James*, edited by Robert Richardson, Harvard University Press 2010
15 William James, *Psychology*, MacMillan 1892
16 Ibid.
17 Michael Sheringham's *Everyday Life* (Oxford University Press 2006) is a comprehensive critical study of French theorists and writers on the everyday. But, unusually for an academic, Sheringham is enthusiastic both about his writers and his subject so that his book is an original contribution to the literature of the everyday, with many aphoristic insights ('the everyday is the site of a struggle between alienation and appropriation') and an interesting conclusion ('one should associate the quotidian, above all perhaps, with the act and process of attention').
18 Henri Lefebvre, *Critique of Everyday Life*, Verso 1991
19 Michel de Certeau, *The Practice of Everyday Life*, University of California Press 1984
20 Henri Bergson, 'Laughter: an Essay on the Meaning of the Comic' in *Comedy*, edited by Wylie Sypher, Doubleday Anchor 1956
21 I hate using the word 'art', which always sounds horribly pretentious and pompous, but I can't think of a suitable alternative.
22 Rainer Maria Rilke, *Letters to a Young Poet*, Norton 1954
23 McGilchrist, *The Master and his Emissary*
24 *Chinese Poems*, translated by Arthur Waley, Unwin 1946. Po Chü-I's delightful personality comes through in most translations but Waley's are the best. Also excellent, and with more poems, is David Hinton's *The Selected Poems of Po Chü-I*, Anvil Press 2006
25 Sei Shonagon, *The Pillow Book of Sei Shonagon*, translated by Ivan Morris, Penguin Classics 1971
26 Marten Jan Bok, 'The Painter and his World: the Socioeconomic Approach to Seventeenth-Century Dutch Art', in *The Golden Age of Dutch Painting in Historical Perspective*, Cambridge University Press 1999
27 For a full account of this inspiration see Ruth Bernard Yeazell's fine study, *Art of the Everyday: Dutch Painting and the Realist Novel*, Princeton University Press 2008
28 George Eliot, *Adam Bede*, Penguin Classics 1985. The paintings mentioned have been identified as *Old Woman at the Window*

Watering Her Flowers and *The Spinner's Grace*, both by Gerrit Dou.

29 John Dewey, *Art as Experience*, Perigee 1980

30 Virginia Woolf, *A Writer's Diary*, Hogwarth Press 1953

31 Barrett H. Clark, 'George Moore', in *Intimate Portraits*, Kennikat Press 1970

32 The full story is that, while the fiend is sighing in rapture at the *adagio* of the twenty-first piano concerto, his latest victim, an innocent young girl suffering from a medical condition that urgently needs attention, is trussed up down a disused well, with only a few hours to live. Fortunately she is being sought by the maverick cop who is fiercely dedicated to frustrating evil genius fiends and prepared to break all the rules in order to do so. In fact, as a consequence of this flagrant disregard for authority and procedure, he has been suspended by the careerist superior and warned not to interfere any further in the case. Of course this only makes the outraged maverick even more determined. And finally, inspired by one of the dazzling intuitions that are as much a feature of his life as the boozing and the marital problems, he gets to the disused well just in time. Needless to say, this seriously annoys the arch fiend who in revenge targets the maverick cop's beloved young daughter. A few more intuitions later and the daughter is rescued, again just in time, and the fiend apparently consumed in the flames of his underground torture chamber. But there are still over forty pages left so experienced thriller readers will strongly suspect that the fiend is about to pop up again, now thoroughly enraged and even more fiendishly cunning than before.

33 For a full account of this phenomenon see Christian Salmon's *Storytelling: Bewitching the Modern Mind*, Verso 2010

34 Julian Barnes, *Nothing To Be Frightened Of*, Vintage 2009

35 McGilchrist, *The Master and his Emissary*

36 Samuel Taylor Coleridge, *Biographia Literaria*, Standard Publications 2008

37 *Art as Experience*

38 Coleridge, *Biographia Literaria*

39 T. S. Eliot, 'The Metaphysical Poets', in *Selected Essays*, Faber and Faber 1951

40 Jean-François Revel, *On Proust*, Hamish Hamilton 1972

41 Simon Baron-Cohen, *Zero Degrees of Empathy: a new theory of human cruelty*, Allen Lane 2011

42 Frans de Waal, *The Age of Empathy: Nature's Lessons for a Kinder Society*, Souvenir Press 2010
43 G. E. Rice & P. Gainer, *'Altruism' in the Albino Rat*, Journal of Comparative and Physiological Psychology 55, 1962
44 Sue Gerhardt for instance, in *Why Love Matters: how affection shapes a baby's brain*, Routledge 2004
45 The evidence for this includes an experiment on patients with damage to the right brain hemisphere, in particular to the right somatosensory cortices, the area of the brain that simulates other body states. These patients were shown photographs of people with various emotional expressions and asked to identify the emotions and explain what the people were feeling. Anyone with a normal right hemisphere can do this easily but the patients with damaged right hemispheres found it impossible. Ralph Adolphs et al, *A role for somatosensory cortices in the visual recognition of emotion as revealed by 3-D lesion mapping*, The Journal of Neuroscience 20, 2000
46 Quoted in *Monsieur Proust* by Céleste Albaret, Harvill Press 1976
47 John Updike, 'An Introduction to Three Novels by Henry Green', in *Hugging the Shore*, Andre Deutsch 1984
48 John Updike, Introduction to *The Early Stories*, Penguin 2003
49 There are of course many such books. Three other serious conternders for the shortlist: *The Book of Disquiet* by Fernando Pessoa, the musings of underpaid assistant bookkeeper Bernardo Soares; *The Garden of the Finzi-Continis* by Giorgio Bassani, which features much playing tennis and drinking lemonade; and *Stoner* by John Williams, about a dedicated English teacher, hated by his boss, dismissed as a crank by his colleagues, unappreciated by his students and despised and rejected by his snobbish wife.
50 John Keats, *The Letters of John Keats*, Adamant 2001
51 *The 100 Worst Ideas of the Century*, *Time* magazine 14 June 1999
52 Recent contenders include the English literary critic James Wood, the French novelist Claude Schnerb, the Slovenian cultural theorist Alenka Zupancic, the American behavioural neuroscientist Robert R. Provine, the American cognitive scientist Matthew M. Hurley and, returning once more to England, the English philosopher Simon Critchley.
53 For a comprehensive account of comedy theories see Matthew M. Hurley, Daniel C. Dennett & Reginald B. Adams Jr, *Inside Jokes: using humour to reverse-engineer the mind*, MIT Press 2011
54 Thomas Hobbes, *Human Nature*, Oxford 2008

55 Arthur Schopenhauer, *The World as Will and Representation,* Dover 1967
56 *Inside Jokes*
57 Roger Fouts, *Next of Kin*, William Morrow 1997
58 Simon Critchley, *On Humour*, Routledge 2002
59 Henri Bergson, 'Laughter: an Essay on the Meaning of the Comic ', in *Comedy* edited by Wylie Sypher, Doubleday Anchor 1956
60 Critchley, *On Humour*
61 Bergson, *Laughter*
62 Ibid.
63 George Meredith, 'An Essay on Comedy', in *Comedy*, edited by Wylie Sypher, Doubleday Anchor 1956
64 Alice Munro, *Lives of Girls and Women*, Plume 1971
65 David Foster Wallace, 'Some Remarks on Kafka's Funniness', in *Consider the Lobster*, Abacus 2005
66 Robin Dunbar, *How Many Friends Does One Person Need?*, Faber and Faber 2010
67 O'Brien's *At Swim-Two-Birds* has a direct steal from *Ulysses*:

> Ah, Lesbia, said Brinsley. The finest thing I ever wrote. How many kisses, Lesbia, you ask, would serve to sate this hungry love of mine? As many as the Libyan sands that bask along Cyrene's shore where pine trees wave, where burning Jupiter's untended shrine lies near to old King Battus' sacred grave:
> Three stouts, called Kelly.

68 Joyce has fun with this obsession in 'Grace' when the characters discuss the debate among cardinals on the doctrine of papal infallibility. Martin Cunningham explains proudly that two cardinals, one German and one Irish, John MacHale, were vehemently opposed to the doctrine but at the very moment it was declared a dogma of the Church, 'John MacHale, who had been arguing and arguing against it, stood up and shouted out with the voice of a lion: "*Credo*!".'
69 Karen Armstrong, *The Case for God,* The Bodley Head 2009
70 William Wordsworth, *William Wordsworth*, Oxford University Press 1984
71 William James, *The Varieties of Religious Experience*, Longmans 1902
72 Hegel, *The Phenomenology of Mind*, London 1931
73 Albert Einstein, 'Strange is Our Situation Here on Earth', in

Modern Religious Thought, edited by Jaroslav Pelican, Boston 1990

74 See *Quantum Questions: Mystical Writings of the World's Great Physicists*, edited by Ken Wilber, Shambhala Publications 2001

75 Ludwig Wittgenstein, *Tractatus Logico-Philosophicus,* Routledge 2001

76 Paul Tillich, *Systematic Theology*, Chicago 1957

77 Rainer Maria Rilke, *Selected Poems of Rainer Maria Rilke*, translated by Robert Bly, Harper & Row 1981

78 Paul Davies, *God and the New Physics*, London 1984

79 Stuart A. Kauffman, *Reinventing the Sacred*, Basic Books 2008

80 David Foster Wallace, quoted in *Although of course you end up becoming yourself: a road trip with David Foster Wallace*, by David Lipsky, Broadway 2010

81 Published as *This is Water: Some Thoughts, Delivered on a Significant Occasion, about Living a Compassionate Life*, Little, Brown and Company 2009

82 André Comte-Sponville, *The Book of Atheist Spirituality*, Viking 2007

83 Nietzsche, *The Antichrist*, Penguin 1968

84 Comte-Sponville, *The Book of Atheist Spirituality*

85 Ibid.

86 John McGahern, *Love of the World*, Faber and Faber 2009

87 Michel Hulin, *La Mystique Sauvage: Aux Antipodes de L'Esprit*, Presses Universitaires de Paris 1993

88 Quoted in *The Book of Atheist Spirituality*

89 Aldous Huxley, *The Doors of Perception*, Vintage 2004

90 Quoted in the introduction to *The Doors of Perception*

91 In *Just Looking* (Andre Deutsch 1989), a collection of art criticism, Updike described Vermeer's paintings as 'perhaps the loveliest objects that exist on canvas'. In *The Centaur* the narrator says, of the Vermeers in the Frick and Metropolitan museums in New York, 'That these paintings, which I had worshipped in reproduction, had a simple physical existence seemed a profound mystery to me: to come within touching distance of their surfaces, to see with my eyes the truth of their color, the tracery of the cracks whereby time had inscribed itself like a mystery within a mystery, would have been for me to enter a Real Presence so ultimate I would not be surprised to die in the encounter.'

92 Quoted in *Walker Evans: Photographer of America*, by Thomas Nau, Roaring Brook 2007

93 Mircea Eliade, *The Sacred and the Profane*, Harcourt 1959
94 George Shaw interviewed by Gordon Burn in *The Sly and Unseen Day*, Baltic 2010
95 William Wordsworth, *The Prelude*, Oxford University Press 1984
96 Huxley, *The Doors of Perception*
97 Robin Dunbar, *Grooming, Gossip and the Evolution of Language*, Faber and Faber 2004
98 John R. Weeks, *Unpopular Culture: The Ritual of Complaint in a British Bank*, University of Chicago Press 2003
99 James Joyce, *Stephen Hero*, New Directions 1944
100 Flann O'Brien writing as Myles na Gopaleen in *Cruiskeen Lawn*, the *Irish Times* 06 June 1957
101 Flann O'Brien, quoted in John Ryan, *Remembering How We Stood*, Taplinger 1975
102 Robert Frost, Letter to John T. Bartlett in *Selected Letters of Robert Frost*, Henry Holt 1964
103 Chimpanzees have never been taught to speak because they lack the necessary respiratory control.
104 D. L. Everett, *Constraints on grammar and cognition in Pirahã: another look at the design features of human language*, Current Anthropology 46(4), 2005
105 S. J. Mithen, *Singing Neanderthals: The Origin of Music, Language, Mind and Body*, London 2005
106 Dean Falk, *Finding our Tongues: Mothers, Infants and the Origin of Language*, Basic Books 2009
107 Leoš Janáček, quoted in *The Rest is Noise: Listening to the Twentieth Century* by Alex Ross, Harper Perennial 2009
108 Terry Southern, 'Twirling at Ole Miss', a non-fiction piece in the collection *Red-Dirt Marijuana*, Jonathan Cape 1971
109 This reminds me of a near-epiphany in Paris. I was eating at a communal table in a restaurant and next to me a young Northern Irishman from Ballymoney was talking enthusiastically to an older American woman across the table. Eventually he asked her what she did for a living and she answered with that rich American confidence untroubled by scruple or fear of pretention: 'I'm an aaawwrdist.' This struck him mute and still – but after a moment he rallied gamely with another affirmative classic: 'That's *brilliant*.'
110 Henry Green, 'The Lull', in *Surviving: the Uncollected Writings of Henry Green*, Chatto & Windus 1992
111 Robin Dunbar, 'Why Gossip is Good for You', in the collection, *How Many Friends Does One Person Need?* Faber and Faber 2010

112 Munro, *Lives of Girls and Women*
113 Ibid.
114 Henry Green, 'A Novelist to his Readers I', in *Surviving: the Uncollected Writings of Henry Green*
115 Ibid.
116 David Bohm, *Wholeness and the Implicate Order*, Routledge 1980
117 William James, 'The Dilemma of Determinism' in *The Heart of William James*, Harvard University Press 2010
118 Alison Gopnik, *Explanation as Orgasm*, Minds and Machines 8, 1998
119 Ibid.
120 The two types of orgasm may even be related. Robin Dunbar cites evidence that the intelligence enhanced by seeking explanations improves, as well as life expectancy and career prospects, the chances of finding willing partners (*Be smart ... live longer*, in *How Many Friends Does One Person Need?*)
121 G. Jean-Aubry, *Joseph Conrad Life and Letters II*, 1927
122 *On Proust*
123 Munro, *Lives of Girls and Women*
124 In *À la recherche* the Baron de Charlus affects what he imagines to be extreme masculinity and believes that no one knows he is a homosexual, when in fact this is common knowledge. 'And so M. de Charlus lived in a state of deception like the fish that thinks the water in which it is swimming extends beyond the glass wall of its aquarium that mirrors it, while it does not see close beside ... the shadow of the human visitor amusing himself by watching its movements, or the all-powerful keeper who, at the unforeseen and fatal moment ... will extract it without compunction.'
125 The psychologist Robert Feldman has carried out experiments which show that new acquaintances lie to each other at least three times within the first ten minutes of meeting (*The Liar in Your Life* by Robert Feldman, Virgin 2009)
126 Green, *Surviving: the Uncollected Writings of Henry Green*
127 For a discussion of the evidence and possible reasons for all this, see my previous book, *The Age of Absurdity*, Simon and Schuster 2010
128 Arthur Schopenhauer, *Essays and Aphorisms*, Penguin 1970
129 The power of the radar remains mysterious but neuroscience claims to have located it – in the right hemisphere, needless to say. 'Subtle unconscious perceptions that govern our reactions are picked up by the right hemisphere. For example, it is the area

around the fusiform gyrus of the right hemisphere that is dominant for *unconscious* reading of facial expressions. Emotional shifts that are expressed in minute facial changes are mirrored and synchronously matched by the observer's right hemisphere within 300-400 milliseconds, at levels beneath awareness', McGilchrist 2009

130 Michel de Montaigne, *Collected Essays*, Penguin 1993

131 René Descartes, *Traité de l'homme*, in *Oeuvres et lettres de Descartes*, Gallimard 1952

132 And it is still common. Many contemporary visionaries await with impatience a mystical moment known as 'The Singularity', when machines become better at everything than humans and the smart move will be to become a machine. For these fervent believers the true Messiah will be a robot, and their John the Baptist is a guru known as Raymond Kurzweil, who, in *The Singularity is Near* (Duckworth 2006), exhorts the faithful to amass wealth so as to be able to afford as many machine parts as possible. Artificial intelligence will do your thinking for you and your insides will be maintained and repaired by an army of nanobots, as silently industrious and efficient as Polish plumbers. Suitably refitted, you will live forever in the posthuman paradise. Even if you die before the Singularity, it is not a problem. Resurrection is an important feature of this new religion. Kurzweil intends to resurrect his own father, based on his memories and his father's papers. If this procedure works it would surely be easy to resurrect Proust from the exhaustive detail in *À la recherche*, though it would also be necessary to resurrect his servants or Marcel would expire again after a few hours.

133 Henri Bergson, *Time and Free Will: An essay on the immediate data of consciousness*, Dover 2001

134 Ibid.

135 Cosmology theory has shown that this was an illusion. The void of deep space is not empty but a force field seething with dark energy and teeming with elementary particles constantly fizzing in and out of existence. The void, once believed to be the ultimate inert medium, may well turn out to be the most hectic process of all.

136 Ibid.

137 Ibid.

138 There is support for this theory in the evidence that awareness of self was a late development in evolution. The higher apes, chimpanzees and orang-utans, can recognise themselves in a mirror but monkeys cannot.

139 There have been attempts to link these two by a theory that consciousness is a quantum phenomenon, a claim made by the physicist Roger Penrose (in *The Emperor's New Mind*), the microbiologist Stuart A. Kaufman (in *Reinventing the Sacred*) and the philosopher David Chalmers (in *The Conscious Mind: In Search of a Fundamental Theory*).

140 W. B. Yeats, *The Collected Poems of W. B. Yeats*, Macmillan 1967

141 For a detailed discussion see Richard W. Byrne, 'Social and Technical Forms of Primate Intelligence', in *Tree of Origin: What Primate Behaviour Can Tell Us About Human Social Evolution*, Harvard University Press 2002

142 For instance Tali Sharot in *The Optimism Bias*, Robinson 2012

143 *Time and Free Will*

144 Maurice Merleau-Ponty, quoted in *How to Live: Or A Life of Montaigne in One Question and Twenty Attempts at an Answer* by Sarah Bakewell, Chatto and Windus 2010

145 Proust's gigantically long sentences often flow without appearing to move at all, as lengthy, meandering and serenely imperturbable as the Amazon and, like a great river, frequently silted up with digressions, subordinate clauses, parentheses, comparisons, amplifications, qualifications, second thoughts and third thoughts on the second thoughts. Sometimes the sensation of motionlessness induces sleep and the seeming lack of progress can provoke a scream of impatience. Joyce once said that the reader finished these sentences before Proust but if this temptation can be resisted the conclusion is usually worth waiting for.

146 One of my favourites is when Bloom almost bumped into his wife's lover and 'his heart quopped softly'.

147 David Foster Wallace, 'Good Old Neon', in the collection *Oblivion*, Abacus 2004

148 *Time and Free Will*

149 'The Will' in *The Heart of William James*

150 James, *Psychology*

151 William James, *Talks to Teachers on Psychology and to Students on Some of Life's Ideals*, Dover 2001

152 Alison Gopnik, *The Philosophical Baby*, Bodley Head 2009

153 Henri Bergson, *Matter and Memory*, Macmillan 1912

154 Henri Bergson, quoted in *Everyday Life* by Michael Sheringham.

155 Christopher Chabris & Daniel Simons, *The Invisible Gorilla*, Harper Collins 2011

156 D. J. Simons and D. T. Levin, *Failure to detect changes to people*

during real-world interaction, Psychonomic Bulletin and Review 5, 1998

157 Mark Twain, *Autobiography of Mark Twain*, Vol 1, University of California Press 2010

158 Ulric Neisser & Eugene Winograd, *Affect and Accuracy in Recall*, Cambridge University Press 1992

159 Interview with William Hirst, in *Being Wrong: Adventures in the Margin of Error* by Kathryn Schulz, Portobello Book 2010

160 Jessica R. Escobedo & Ralph Adolphs, *Becoming a Better Person: Temporal Remoteness Biases in Autobiographical Memories for Moral Events*, Emotion Vol 10, no 4, 2010

161 Alfred North Whitehead, *Process and Reality*, Macmillan 1929. This is a long, dense, technical book. For a shorter, more readable summary see *Process Metaphysics: an Introduction to Process Philosophy* by Nicholas Rescher, State University of New York Press 1996

162 Ibid.

163 Ibid.

164 For a full analysis of this phenomenon see *Chavs: The Demonization of the Working Class* by Owen Jones, Verso 2011

165 Bergson, *Laughter*

166 Pierre Bourdieu, *Distinction: A Social Critique of the Judgement of Taste*, Routledge 1984

167 Personal communication from Nick Long to the author.

168 Paula Niedenthal, *More To A Smile Than Lips And Teeth*, New York Times 24 Jan 2011

169 Hannah Arendt, *The Human Condition*, University of Chicago Press 1958

170 McGilchrist, citing evidence: 'Anger is robustly connected with left frontal activation'.

171 Alice Munro, *The Beggar Maid*, Macmillan 1978

172 This may be true of most rebels. Spartacus, the original rebel, had no objection to slavery – he objected only to being himself a slave. The Roman authorities could have saved themselves a great deal of trouble by making Spartacus an NCO in one of their legions.

173 Alice Munro, 'Differently', in the collection *Hateship, Friendship, Courtship, Loveship, Marriage*, Vintage 2002

174 Sigmund Freud, *On Narcissism*, in *The Complete Psychological Works of Sigmund Freud*, edited by James Strachey, London 1957

175 D. Paulus et al, *The Over-Claiming Technique*, Journal of Personality and Social Psychology 84, 2003

176 In my novel *The Road to Notown* (Blackstaff Press 1996) I described Joyce's attraction to Nora as 'love at first shite'.

177 Nicholson Baker, a fervent admirer of Updike, also understands the importance of voyeurism in contemporary sex. In his novel about a sexual fantasy land, *House of Holes*, hotel guests may wander in the Garden of the Wholesome Delightful Fuckers and watch couples having sex among the palm trees – and each hotel room has filmmaking facitities where guests may film themselves having sex and then secretly watch other guests watching their film.

A suggestion of my own is The Tower of Ogle, a building whose walls, floors and ceilings are made of glass so that couples making love in any of the rooms may see at least six other couples also making love.

178 Plato, *Phaedrus*, Penguin 2005

179 Munro, *Lives of Girls and Women*

180 Charles Baudelaire, 'The Painter of Modern Life', in *Selected Writings on Art and Artists*, Penguin 1972

181 The Situationist Guy Debord redefined flânerie as *dérive* but insisted that the *dérive* requires a group of two or three, although he offered no convincing explanation for this. Debord may have been one of those who always need an audience.

182 The flâneur is usually also male. Annie Ernaux is a rare and welcome flâneuse and her two books of urban everyday reportage (*Journal de Dehors* and *La Vie Extérieure*, translated as *Exteriors*, Seven Stories Press 1997, and *Things Seen*, Bison Books 2010) focus on people rather than the physical environment – commuters, shoppers, stall-holders, beggars, beauticians, hairdressers, pharmacists, supermarket cashiers. As always she is alert to clashing superiorities, for instance in the incident where she discovers that the youth behind her on an escalator has his hand in her bag. First she is outraged by his shameless insouciance – getting caught is a joke, part of the game. Then she is even more outraged by his obvious imperviousness to her elegant, sophisticated Frenchwoman allure. Reversing the usual feminist position, she is furious at *not* being regarded as a sex object.

183 Charles Baudelaire, *Intimate Journals*, Methuen 1949

184 *Species of Spaces and Other Pieces*

185 Walt Whitman, *Leaves of Grass*, Barnes and Noble Books 1993

186 Frank O'Hara, *Selected Poems*, Vintage 1974

187 Whitman, *Leaves of Grass*

188 John Updike, *Odd Jobs: Essays and Criticism*, Knopf 1991

189 Andy Grundberg, *Crisis of the Real: Writings on Photography*, Aperture 1999
190 I have to confess that I myself now live in an upmarket district. I've petrified with the years, I suppose, and have come to prefer tasteful safety to the poetry of squalor. I'm too scared of getting my old grey head kicked in.
191 John Updike, *Roger's Version*, Andre Deutsch 1986
192 Elizabeth Bishop, *The Complete Poems*, Chatto and Windus 1983
193 *Species of Spaces and Other Pieces*
194 Georges Perec, *An Attempt at Exhausting a Place in Paris*, Wakefield Press 2010
195 George Shaw, quoted in the exhibition guide to a Shaw exhibition (*The Sly and Unseen Day*) at the South London Gallery 2011
196 George Shaw, *Payne's Grey*, Baltic 2010
197 This belief was developed into an academic theory by the sociologists James Q. Wilson and George L. Kelling, who argued that broken windows and other signs of dilapidation in an area increase crime rates. Subsequent experts, including law professors and criminologists, have rejected the theory.
198 There is a recent book of photographs of derelict buildings actually titled *Beauty in Decay* (CarpetBombingCulture 2010)
199 Ninjalicious, *Access All Areas*, Ninjalicious 2005
200 Patrick Kavanagh, *Collected Poems*, MacGibbon and Kee 1964
201 Jacques Réda, *Les Ruines de Paris*, Éditions Gallimard 1977
202 Henri Bergson, *The Creative Mind*, Philosophical Library 1946
203 Richard Mabey, *Weeds: How vagabond plants gatecrashed civilisation and changed the way we think about nature*, Profile 2010. This is the source of my weed lore.
204 Robert Doisneau, quoted in *Robert Doisneau Paris*, Flammarion 2010
205 Walker Evans, quoted in *Street Photography Now*, Thames and Hudson 2010
206 Also traversing London on his hands and knees is Ben Wilson, who paints minutely detailed scenes on the dark blobs of chewing gum flattened on pavements. To complete its aesthetic transformation, all that the city needs now is an artist to do something wonderfully imaginative with dog turds and vomit splashes.
207 I realised only afterwards that I should have purchased the trolley and bin and entered the combination for the Turner Prize as a conceptual work making a profound comment on consumer culture.

208 In *The Evolution of Useful Things* (Pavilion 1993) Henry Petroski, an engineering champion of the everyday, provides, among many other things, a detailed history of the complex evolution of the paper clip and explains why coloured clips are less effective than the traditional bare metal variety: 'Their rubbery plastic coating gives them a much higher coefficient of friction than metal and this can make it literally an effort not unlike pushing an eraser to attach them to a group of papers, which can be wrinkled beyond reason in the process.'

209 Ibid.

210 Quoted in James R. Berry, *Herman Miller: Classic Furniture and System Designs for the Working Environment*, Thames and Hudson 2004

211 Alas, the serious metal stamper with a handle for great heft is being replaced by pitiful, flimsy plastic stampers with no handles at all.

212 A notable exception is the full-length study *The Pencil*, by Henry Petroski, Faber and Faber 2003

213 In fact the modern pencil, a round graphite and clay core in a round cedarwood case, was developed by another thoughtful American democrat, Henry David Thoreau of Walden Pond fame. Before communing with nature in his cabin in the woods, Thoreau discovered, after much trial and error, that a graphite and clay mixture worked best and that varying the ratio of clay to graphite produced varying degrees of hardness, for which he created a dual grading system still in use (S and SS for soft and softer, H and HH for hard and harder, more logical than the European B for black and H for hard). Only an American sage could be so practical. Thoreau was not just the research scientist but also production supervisor and sales rep for his father's business, J. Thoreau & Co, which made the best pencils in the USA, a claim endorsed by the philosopher Ralph Waldo Emerson: 'Henry Thoreau has made, as he thinks, great improvements in the manufacture, and believes he makes as good a pencil as the good English drawing pencil ... They are for sale at Miss Peabody's, as I believe, for 75 cents the dozen.'

214 This is probably common. In *The Evolution of Useful Things* Henry Petroski cites a survey claiming that only one in ten paper clips is ever used for fastening papers.

215 *Our favourite ways to waste time*, Personnel Today, July 2000

216 'Let them come, be seated, and talk as I expected, let them say

what I was sure they would say: the whole gives me an impression at once novel and unique, as if it were but now designed at one original stroke by the hand of an artist. Gone is the image I had conceived of it, a mere prearrangeable juxtaposition of things already known!' Henri Bergson, *The Creative Mind*, Philosophical Library 1946

217 Annie Ernaux found an unusual way of celebrating this ultimate domestic pleasure – photographing the clothes haphazardly thrown off in the delirium of sex (any subsequent rearranging for aesthetic effect was forbidden). The photographs, when developed, always surprised Ernaux with their enigmatic configurations and sumptuous colours and ability to turn the familiar home into a mysterious elsewhere. Eventually she published the photographs in a book with commentary (*L'usage de la photo*, Gallimard 2005) and some of these images are indeed haunting and poignant. I was especially moved by the conjunction, on a parquet floor, of an unlaced man's boot and a crumpled red-lace bra. The boot is a brutal Doc Martens type but one of its laces reaches down to the bra on the floor with a secret tentative tenderness, like a root tendril groping towards nurturing soil.

218 De Certeau, *The Practice of Everyday Life*

219 In June 2005 the British Potato Council organised a demonstration in Parliament Square, London, to protest at the term 'couch potato', which the Council claimed was insulting to potatoes. As the reader will know, I am a passionate believer in empathy but, perhaps as a result of growing up in Ireland, I still find it impossible to empathise with potatoes.

220 *Species of Spaces and Other Pieces*

221 To capture fleeting genius moments in the shower, the manufacturer Aquanotes has produced a waterproof pad that adheres to shower tiles.

222 Emily Dickinson, *The Complete Poems*, Faber 1970

223 Nicholson Baker, *Room Temperature*, Granta 1990

224 Don De Lillo, *Ratner's Star*, Vintage 1980

225 Nicholson Baker, 'Clip Art', in *The Size of Thoughts*, Chatto and Windus 1996

226 After relentless questioning one woman dear to me did finally admit to this practice – but only after I swore not to reveal her identity.

227 Mark Pendergrast, *Uncommon Grounds: The History of Coffee and How it Transformed our World*, Basic Books 1999

228 Ibid.

229 M. J. Jarvis, *Does Caffeine Intake Enhance Absolute Levels of Cognitive Performance?*, Psychopharmacology 110, 1993

230 Honoré de Balzac, *Treatise on Modern Stimulants*, 1838

231 The rocking chair, another American invention, could be the basis for a new type of living-room chair, both supportive and responsive, the domestic equivalent of the Ergon chair – but the rocking chair is totally out of fashion now. America, alas, has gone off its rocker.

232 In 2011 Edinburgh Zoo ran a salutary public experiment by constructing a typically bright, white contemporary kitchen with transparent but sealed walls, and allowing the kitchen food to decompose for several months. This was a demonstration of the inevitability, necessity and beauty of decay. The air in every home teems with mould spores and food teems with bacteria. So on the battlefield of an ageing ham sandwich mould and bacteria will commence a struggle for nutrients as weirdly gothic as that in the World of Warcraft between the Alliance and the Horde. Both sides are ingenious. The bacteria communicate and cooperate; mould, a single-cell organism with no partners, improves its performance by rapid learning. Creeping slime mould is especially clever, capable of working out the fastest route to food at the heart of a maze. If food particles are distributed in the form of the nodes of the Tokyo transport network, one of the most efficient in the world, the slime builds an even more efficient network for transporting nutrients. We congratulate ourselves on being smart enough to get out of the slime but in some cases the slime remains smarter than we are. Indeed so smart is slime mould that computer scientists are now studying it for insights on artificial intelligence. Sublime slime!

After the moulds and bacteria come the maggots, machines for consumption. A maggot's front end is entirely dedicated to eating so it breathes through its ass, in fact through twin assholes – a possible clue to the future evolution of the obese human race.

233 Nicholson Baker, *The Mezzanine*, Granta 1989

234 Ibid.

235 William James, *Some Problems of Philosophy*, University of Nebraska Press 1996

236 Another Cornell technique used found copies of rubbishy old movies such as *East of Borneo*, from which he would cut out with scissors everything relating to the plot and then tape together the

remaining reaction shots of actors and actresses (he loved movie actresses and paid homage to Lauren Bacall with a box called *Penny Arcade Portrait of Lauren Bacall*, now in The Art Institute of Chicago). This innovative technique of plotectomy strikes me as a great idea, though if applied to most current movies there would be nothing left.

237 Simic on the city: 'Poetry: three mismatched shoes at the entrance of a dark alley.' On things: 'The common object is the sphinx, whose riddle the contemplative poet must solve.' Simic also compared Cornell and Emily Dickinson as major artists of the secret self: 'If her poems are like his boxes, a place where secrets are kept, his boxes are like her poems, the place of unlikely things coming together.'

238 Charles Simic, 'Stargazing in the Cinema: On Joseph Cornell', in *The Metaphysician in the Dark*, University of Michigan Press 2003

239 Charles Simic, *Dime-Store Alchemy: the Art of Joseph Cornell*, New York Review Books 1992

240 Joseph Cornell, quoted in *Dime-Store Alchemy*

241 'Think/Classify' in *Species of Spaces and Other Pieces*

242 'Notes Concerning the Objects that are on my Work Table', in *Species of Spaces and Other Pieces*. The objects include a white ceramic ashtray with 'a charming view of the roofs of the town of Ingolstadt' and 'a desk lamp, a cigarette box, a bud-vase, a matchbox holder, a cardboard box containing little multi-coloured index cards, a large carton bouilli inkwell incrusted with tortoiseshell, a glass pencil-box, several stones, three hand-turned wooden boxes, an alarm clock, a push-button calendar, a lump of lead, a large cigar box (wth no cigars but full of small objects), a steel spiral into which you can slide letters that are pending, a dagger handle of polished stone, account books, exercise books, loose sheets, multiple writing instruments or accessories, a big hand-blotter, several books, a glass full of pencils, a small gilded wooden box'. Note the number of boxes, especially that cigar box full of small objects. Perec also tells us that there are six pencils in the glass and wonders why he needs so many, apparently unaware that it is for the pleasure of sharpening.

243 Georges Perec, *Things*, Vintage 2011

244 Perec relished in particular domestic items with magnificently redundant painted scenes – a Breton shortbread biscuit tin showing a peasant tilling his fields, a wall plate with a priest giving ashes to a believer, a clock with a naked woman beside a little

waterfall, an ice bucket with a short, fat, seated monk in a long grey robe holding a goblet in his hand, a tea tray with a boy in embroidered trousers leaning over the bank of a river where an out-of-water carp twists on a fisherman's line, imitation Jouy cretonne wallpaper with Portuguese four-master sailing ships making ready to put into harbour, and a cash box with a grinning negro in a tartan cape, white gloves, steel-rimmed spectacles and a top hat decorated with the stars and stripes.

Another Perec speciality was printed ephemera such as notices, catalogues, instruction leaflets, advertising brochures, estate agents' circulars and promotional blotting paper. If he was still alive today he would be collecting takeaway pizza flyers. It was the barely noticed transience of all these things that moved him and, in one uncharacteristically melancholy passage, he foresees the demolition of the apartment block itself, reduced by hammers and bulldozers to rubble and dust.

245 This is my own, very free, translation of Ponge. The full poem, *The Match*, is in *New and Selected Poems*, Blackstaff Press 2011. There is a fuller set of Ponge translations in *Autumn Beguiles the Fatalist*, Blackstaff Press 2006

246 The jug features in Rilke's celebrated list (in the ninth Duino Elegy) of essential things to notice: 'Perhaps we are only *here* to say: house,/bridge, fountain, gate, jug, fruit tree, window'.

247 Martin Heidegger, 'The Thing', in *Poetry, Language, Thought*, Harper 1975

248 Charles Simic, *The Monster Loves His Labyrinth: Notebooks*, Ausable Press 2008

249 Henry Green, *Pack My Bag*, Hogarth Press 1940

250 Joseph Conrad, preface to *The Nigger of the 'Narcissus'*, Penguin 1988

251 De Certeau, *The Practice of Everyday Life*

252 McGahern, 'The Solitary Reader', in *Love of the World*

253 McGahern, growing up in rural Ireland, had no such facility, but was fortunate enough to be given the run of a private library, owned by two eccentric big-house Protestants, from which he too borrowed six books a week in an oilcloth shopping bag – an experience that changed his life and made him a writer.

254 Ibid.

255 For a full account of this remarkable evening see *A Night at the Majestic: Proust and the great modernist dinner party of 1922* by Richard Davenport-Hines, Faber 2006

Index